Theology and Sexuality

SCM CORE TEXT

Theology and Sexuality

Susannah Cornwall

scm press

© Susannah Cornwall 2013

Published in 2013 by SCM Press
Editorial office
3rd Floor
Invicta House
108–114 Golden Lane,
London EC1Y 0TG

SCM Press is an imprint of Hymns Ancient & Modern Ltd
(a registered charity)
13A Hellesdon Park Road
Norwich NR6 5DR, UK

www.scmpress.co.uk

British Library Cataloguing in Publication data

A catalogue record for this book is available
from the British Library

978-0-334-04530-4
Kindle edition 978-0-334-04531-1

Typeset by Regent Typesetting, London
Printed and bound by
CPI Group (UK) Ltd, Croydon

Contents

Preface

Humans are sexual creatures. At the most basic level, almost all of us were born as a result of a sexual encounter between two people of different sexes. From our earliest moments, we begin to be identified and socialized according to our perceived physical sex: friends and relatives are usually very interested to know whether a new baby is a girl or a boy, and this often influences the clothes and toys they give as gifts. Through childhood and adolescence and into adult life, most of us develop a strong sense of our own sexuality, in terms both of the people to whom we're attracted and of our relationships to the sensations of our own bodies.

Christian theologians, who are interested in thinking through what the Christian theological tradition says about being human, therefore can't help but reflect on human sexuality. As humans we're inescapably embodied, and many people would argue that to be embodied means to be inescapably sexual too, even if we don't always express our sexuality physically with other people.

In this book, we'll take a tour through some of the different aspects of human sexuality with which Christian theologians have engaged. In the first chapters, we'll explore some broad questions surrounding human sexuality: What exactly do theologians and others mean when they use the terms sex, gender and sexuality? How does sexual orientation map onto gender and biological sex? How do considerations of sexuality fit into theological questions about the nature of God and the nature of humanity?

In the later chapters, we'll come to think about sex in a range of contexts. How should we understand human sexuality when people are not physically sexually active, such as when they've taken a vow of celibacy? How do Christian theologians understand the relationship between sex and marriage? Why are same-sex relationships such a contentious topic within Christian theology? What does Christian theology have to say about other issues such as sex work, masturbation, and more unusual patterns of sexual behaviour like polyamory?

Most of the theologians whose work is cited are those who have been working in the twentieth and twenty-first centuries, mainly because discussions about sex, gender and sexuality have had particular prominence during this period. However, at times the book also engages with thought from further back in the Christian tradition, right back to the early Christian theologians often known as the Church Fathers, who wrote in the first few centuries after Jesus' lifetime. Where possible, I'll give dates for theologians who were active prior to the late twentieth century.

Throughout the book, you'll notice some words, or their derivatives, highlighted in **bold type**. These words have brief definitions in the glossary at the end of the book. You'll also notice that, from time to time, there are breakout boxes containing questions or suggested activities. You might be using this book as a class text, in which case your tutor may ask you to use these questions and activities as a basis for individual or small group work. Alternatively, you might be reading this book by yourself. In this case, you might simply want to use the questions and activities as prompts for your thoughts, and as a chance to pause and reflect on what you have read.

*   *   *

I began writing this book while I was based at the University of Exeter, and greatly valued the support of colleagues in the Department of Theology and Religion and at the South West Ministry Training Course. During the writing process, I took up a new post at the Lincoln Theological Institute at the University of Manchester, where I've valued stimulating conversations with Peter Scott and other colleagues in the Department of Religions and Theology, and with my students.

I've also been enthused by virtual and face-to-face conversations with other theologians and friends, including Loveday Alexander, Philip Alexander, Richard Bastable, Tom Bohache, John Bradbury, Rebecca Catto, Gemma Burnett, Patrick S. Cheng, Frances Clemson, Jenny Daggers, Megan DeFranza, Annemie Dillen, Sharon Fennema, David F. Ford, Siobhán Garrigan, Tim Gibson, Julie Gittoes, Marion Grau, Brutus Green, Symon Hill, Mike Higton, John Hughes, James Hughesdon, Jay Emerson Johnson, Dawn Llewellyn, Gerard Loughlin, Mae Mouk, Noel Moules, Rachel Muers, Philippa Newis, Ralph Norman, Jo Penberthy, John Plant, Nicola Slee, Katja Stuerzenhofecker, Adrian Thatcher, Samuel Tongue, James Walters, Andrew Warner, Alexandra Wörn and Andrew Worthley. Natalie Watson at SCM Press has continued to be an enthusiastic and encouraging influence, and I'm grateful for her support and loyalty.

I am, as ever, thankful for my family's love and support – especially, and always, that of my husband, Jon Morgan. I can't say enough about all he is to me. During the preparation of this book, my mother, Jenny Cornwall née Stephen, died aged 62. She claimed not to be a theologian, but taught me, nonetheless, that all theology is love and justice. It's dedicated to her memory.

Manchester, 2012

1

Sex and Context

What is sexuality?

Think about the following questions before you read on:

- What do you understand by the words *sex*, *gender* and *sexuality*?
- When did you first become aware of your gender? What influenced you in your gender identity then? What influences you now?
- If you were a different gender, would you still be 'you'?
- What, if anything, does your gender identity have to do with the way you understand your relationships with other people and, if you are a person of faith, with God?

Sex, gender and sexuality: some working definitions

At the outset of this book, it's important to set out some fundamental terms and the ways in which I'll be using them. In some of the work with which I'll engage, and in discussion at large, there's overlap between the ways in which people understand the words sex, gender and sexuality. 'Sex' and 'gender', in particular, are often used almost interchangeably. However, I want to suggest that, for the purposes of our investigation, it will be important to recognize a distinction between them. I'll use these terms in the following ways:

SEX: biological maleness or femaleness (or, occasionally, a biological sex which can't easily be classified as male or female). Sex, in this initial definition, is to do with the biology of someone's body, rather than their sense of being a man or woman.

GENDER: someone's identity as a man, a woman, or a member of some other gender. Gender identity may not always 'match' biological sex: some people whose biological sex is male, for example, have a feminine gender identity and want to live as women. Many scholars assert that gender is a *social* category, rather than a biological one: in other words, it's the way in which people present themselves and are recognized by the other people around them in their society.

SEXUALITY means two things, one very specific and the other more general:

1 Specifically, sexuality means **sexual orientation**: that is, the *sex* of a person to whom someone's sexually attracted. We often hear the terms 'homosexual' (for someone sexually attracted to people of the same sex as themselves), 'heterosexual' (for someone attracted to people of the opposite sex to themselves) and 'bisexual' (for someone attracted both to people of their own sex and of the opposite sex).
2 More broadly, sexuality is everything about someone's personhood and energy: the way they interact with other people and the world. In this second definition, sexuality isn't just about the sex of the people to whom we're attracted – it's about everything that stimulates our excitement, creativity and engagement with the world around us.

In this book, then, although I'll certainly be giving consideration to what Christian theologians have wanted to say about sexual orientation as homo-sexual, heterosexual and bisexual, this is not all I'll mean when I use the term 'sexuality'. Moreover, we'll see that other Christian theologians have understood 'sexuality' in many different ways.

The Christian journalist, Jo Ind, describes the experience of receiving a massage from a professional masseur, whom she was interviewing for the *Birmingham Post*. She notes that she experienced physical arousal despite being uncertain about whether the encounter could properly be called a 'sexual' one:

> How would I describe that experience with Phil [the masseur]? I am certain we did not have intercourse. I know the only parts of my body that he touched were my back and my head. I am sure I did not have an orgasm, but I know my vagina juiced. But which of these are the defining characteristics of a sexual experience? Is it to do with the parts of the body that get touched? Is it to do with the acts that are performed? Is it to do with the imagination, the images and fantasies evoked? ... Was it sensual but not sexual or sexual but not genital? What is sexuality anyway? (Ind 2003, p. 7)

What is sexuality anyway?, asks Ind. What do you think?

Some theological accounts of sexuality

ACTIVITY 1

Some examples taken from the writings of twentieth- and twenty-first-century theologians whose work has been significant in the sexuality debate can be found in the quotations below. What exactly does each author seem to mean by 'sexuality'? Does it chime at all with the definition I've set out above? How persuasive do you find each of these accounts of sexuality? Can you identify particular problems with any of them?

ACTIVITY 2

Using the same extracts, try to think of terms which seem to you to sum up the gist of each author's account of sexuality. Here are some to get you started: RELATIONAL; HOLISTIC; EMBODIED; POLITICAL; CREATIVE; MYSTICAL. Which term do you feel best captures each writer's understanding of sexuality?

The command of God ... is the decisive sanctification of physical sexuality and the sex relationship. It sanctifies man by including his sexuality within his humanity, and challenging him even in his bodily nature and therefore in his sexual life ... to be true man: to be a body but not only a body; to be also the spirit-impelled soul of his body ... Because his being in its totality is at stake, physical sexuality and the sex relationship cannot remain outside the scope of God's command. (Barth 1961, p. 132)[1]

Karl Barth, a Swiss Reformed theologian (1886–1968), believed that humans could come to know God only through God's own self-revelation. Nonetheless, he believed that human sexuality, and humans' gendered roles as men and women, provided a useful metaphor for God's relationship to the Church.

---

[1] It's important to bear in mind that Karl Barth, a Swiss theologian, wrote in German, and that, when we read an English translation, the sense of what he means is sometimes obscured. At the time when Barth's work was translated into English, it was still common to use 'man' as an all-encompassing word to mean 'human beings' or 'humanity'. In this quotation, 'man' should be understood as referring to all human beings, not just to males. We should read 'to be a true man' as 'to be a true human being'.

Man[2] really begins to experience his reality when he becomes aware of his sexual nature. Sexuality ... is the living, flowing energy whose physical aspect is but one mode of its expression ... It is also the medium that puts him in contact with other realities and other incarnate selves. Through it he is related to all creatureliness. This means that ultimately man's awareness of creation and of the beauty of creation is a sexual awareness and cannot exist without the intermediacy of sexuality. (Sherrard 1976, pp. 41–2)

Philip Sherrard, who died in 1995, was an English theologian who lived in Greece for much of his life and converted to Greek Orthodox Christianity. Sherrard was interested in the reasons why sexuality had so often been understood negatively in the Christian tradition, and wanted to affirm that human sexuality was actually rooted in God.

Sexuality expresses the mystery of our creation as those who need to reach out for the physical and spiritual embraces of others. It expresses God's intention that we find our authentic humanness not in isolation but in relationship. It is who we are as bodyselves experiencing the emotional, cognitive, physical, and spiritual need for intimate communion with other, with the natural world, with God. (Nelson 1992, p. 22)

James B. Nelson is a Christian ethicist from the USA who is ordained in the United Church of Christ. His work has focused particularly on 'body theology' and the ways in which humans' bodies, genders and sexualities affect their interactions with and understandings of God and one another.

Sexuality ... is linked not only to the incompleteness each person senses as an embodied, sexual creature but also to the potential for wholeness in relationship to others that parallels this fundamental incompleteness ... Hence, sexuality is the dynamic that forms the basis of the uniquely human drive toward bonding. (Grenz 2001, p. 278)

Stanley J. Grenz, who died in 2005, was a Baptist theologian from the USA. His work focused on gender and sexual ethics in evangelical Christian perspective, and on theological anthropology.

Human sexuality is about how men and women respond to themselves as sexual beings, and how sexually they relate to each other ... In

---

2 Similarly, at the time Sherrard wrote, it was still common to use 'man' as a general term to refer to all human beings, whether male or female. Sherrard isn't talking about males exclusively.

remaking us as sexual beings, God, through the Holy Spirit, gives us the power and the vision to make relationships which resemble those relationships existing eternally within God. They will be mutual, reciprocal, equal, open, intimate and partner-affirming. (Thatcher 1993, p. 2)

Adrian Thatcher is an English Anglican theologian whose work has sought to ground theologies of sex, marriage and family life in assertions about the relational character of God as expressed in the doctrine of the Trinity.

Discussion of the Church and sexuality is a proper concern of the Church with itself as a sexed body. It may seem odd to talk about the Church in this way – as a body that has sex – but it is entirely orthodox and traditional ... The Church has ... understood itself to be the bride of Christ, called to bodily union with him, so that the sexual joining of bodies is also part of the Church's imagination of itself, of herself, in her union with, and difference from, the divine. (Loughlin 2004b, p. 88)

Gerard Loughlin is a British Roman Catholic theologian, whose work explores the ways in which understanding the Church as the Body of Christ is altered or affected by understanding this body as 'queer'.

Why is it important to take a ... sexual stance in doing theology? ... Sexual theologies are concerned with structures such as the structures of love and knowledge which regulate affective and political decisions in our lives, run economic thought and may even have exiled God from churches and theology long ago. (Althaus-Reid 2004, p. 103)

Marcella Althaus-Reid, who died in 2009, was an Argentinian theologian, who worked in Britain. She criticized classic liberation theologies for not taking enough account of the sexuality of marginalized people and called her version of theology 'indecent', because it aimed to recover sexuality, including non-heterosexual sexuality, as central to the way in which humans relate to one another and to God. Althaus-Reid believed that sexual, political and economic exclusion usually went hand in hand.

Of course, other Christian theologians and scholars and thinkers outside the field of Christian theology might mean different things again when they use the word 'sexuality'. It's important to think about where these ideas and definitions come from.

In the twentieth and twenty-first centuries, there have been two main schools of thought about human sexuality and its origins: essentialism and constructivism.

Essentialism and constructivism: nature or nurture?

Since the late nineteenth century, a debate has been going on about sexuality which can be broadly characterized as **essentialism** versus **constructivism**. The central question is this: is our sexual orientation something that already exists within us from the time we are born, as part of our essence (essentialism), or is it something that comes about later, constructed either via conscious choice or because of the influences around us (constructivism)?[3] This is sometimes referred to as the 'nature versus nurture' debate.

Essentialism

The essentialist view suggests that bodies and bodily acts have intrinsic, irreducible meanings, regardless of the time or society in which they occur, and that 'the sexual body is universally the same, possessing certain sexual drives and needs' (Nelson 1992, p. 47). As we'll see in Chapter 6, lesbian, gay and **queer** theologians since the mid-twentieth century have often wanted to say that their sexual orientation is inborn – just part of who they are and part of how God created them – so homosexuality shouldn't be dismissed as a sinful or perverse choice.

However, there are some problems with this essentialist, 'nature' understanding of sexual orientation: for one thing, it seems to imply that the only reason someone would be homosexual is that they can't help being that way (or, that if someone *could* have chosen to be heterosexual, they *would* have done). This means homosexuality can still be dismissed as something imperfect or less than ideal, rather than as something good and worthy of celebration in its own right. It also means that some theologians can argue that homosexuality, even if it's inborn, only exists because the world is 'fallen'. In a perfect world without sin, runs this argument, nobody would be born homosexual. (People have made similar arguments about disabilities such as deafness and blindness.)

Essentialism might also be understood as rather passive, making us victims of our circumstances, in contrast to constructivism's acknowledgement that, although we're certainly influenced by social and cultural norms, there's also an extent to which we have 'an active role as agents, influenced by culture, in structuring our bodily realities' (Nelson 1992, p. 46).

Constructivism

The constructivist view also recognizes that our understandings of certain words and identities don't stay exactly the same over time. We can acknow-

---

3 This question also maps onto similar concerns surrounding gender: to what extent must our identity as gendered (masculine or feminine) 'match' our biological sex?

ledge that being a woman in sixteenth-century China is very different from being a woman in twenty-first century Canada, because of shifts in how the role and status of women is understood across times and cultures. (For example, women in these two contexts have faced differences in access to education, economic status, voting rights, patterns of work inside and outside the home, and the freedom or otherwise to make decisions about sexual activity and whether to have children.) Acknowledging this difference might be a good thing when it comes to how we understand bodily sexuality and sexual orientation, because it allows us to note that, for example, the 'meaning' of sexual intercourse between two men in our own time and culture is probably not identical with the 'meaning' of sexual intercourse between two men in the societies out of which the biblical texts were produced. We can therefore begin to see that, as theologians and biblical interpreters, the way we read Christian texts and the Christian theological tradition will always be coloured by the ways in which we read and respond to our own times.

However, there are also problems with the constructivist, 'nurture' model of sexual orientation. Constructivism asserts that sexual orientation, just like other aspects of our identity, comes about because of what's going on around us and the social knowledge we acquire. However, this doesn't explain why a minority of people seem to experience sexual attraction for people of the same sex even in societies where this is deemed deeply shameful and wrong: it seems unlikely that people in such societies would either consciously choose to be homosexual or somehow be socialized into homosexuality.

Both essentialists and constructivists believe that there's an interaction between the desires and sensations we experience physically and the cultures and societies in which we find ourselves. They might, however, emphasize different aspects as more or less important. Nelson suggests that there might be some kind of fruitful 'third way' between essentialism and constructivism in terms of theological understandings of sexuality:

There is still something 'given' about our sexual orientations, however significant the social meanings that shape their expression ... That I have never menstruated but do have penile erections does mean *something* for my interpretation of the world. Yet, just *what* these orientations and differently sexed bodies mean is never fixed once and for all. That is hopeful, for if sexual meanings are socially constructed, they can also be reconstructed when they are not life-giving. (Nelson 1992, p. 48)

7

QUESTION BOX

1 Are you convinced by Nelson's suggestion that human sexuality should be understood as somehow *both* essential *and* constructed? Why?
2 Nelson refers to 'sexual meanings ... [which] are not life-giving'. What do you think he means by this?

ACTIVITY

Write a journal entry or blog post about the depictions of sexuality you hear and read about in theological texts, in the media and in society at large. You may want to gather examples from magazines, newspapers, television and the internet as well as theological books and articles. Do they tend to draw on essentialist or constructivist understandings of human sexuality? Which do you find more persuasive and why?

Early influences on Christian ideas about sexuality

Christian theologians, then, are people of their time who respond to the theories and models of sexuality they see around them. Many theologians and other Christians today and in the recent past have had their views coloured by contemporary assumptions and cultural norms about sexuality. In a moment, we'll think briefly about work by influential nineteenth- and twentieth-century theorists like Sigmund Freud and Michel Foucault, which have helped to shape Western attitudes to sexuality today.

However, since much earlier on, Christian understandings of sexuality have also been influenced by other cultural factors. These include ancient Jewish understandings of sexuality and personhood which influenced Jewish self-understanding at the time of Jesus and Paul; the Greek and Roman cultural norms which were also influential on the Mediterranean societies in which the first Christians lived; the ideas and beliefs of other philosophical and religious movements and groups contemporaneous with early Christianity, such as the **Gnostics** and the **Stoics**; and their grounding in Platonic dualism – that is, the idea that there's a split between the spirit and body and that the spirit is 'higher'. Christian ideas about sexuality sometimes absorb these other norms and sometimes consciously seek to refute or oppose them. We'll consider them briefly now.

Greek and Roman philosophy

Margaret Farley, a Roman Catholic ethicist, provides a useful summary of the ways in which Greek and Roman understandings of sexuality contributed to early Christian ideas. Farley suggests that the ancient Stoic philosophers' attitude to sex, in which sexual passion, like all passion, was deemed dangerously disruptive and to be avoided, had a particularly strong influence on the Christianity which was beginning to grow up alongside it. She notes,

> Aspects of Greek and Roman philosophical thought about sex that were to have a great influence on subsequent Western speculation included a distrust of sexual desire and a judgment of the inferior status of sexual pleasure among other human pleasures, in line with the inferior status accorded to the body in relation to the soul. Sex was not considered evil in itself, but it was thought to be potentially dangerous. (Farley 2006, p. 31)

This 'danger' arose, in part, from the weakening effect sex was believed to have: men who'd recently had sex were, it was thought, likely to be less clear-minded and less physically strong and poised for action than those who hadn't.

Farley notes that sexuality and sexual behaviour in Greek and Roman culture was deeply tied to notions of status and prestige. Sexual activity wasn't about the pursuit of physical pleasure as such (and men having sex with women in order to bring about the procreation of children was considered a necessary but rather tiresome function of sex), but about reinforcing valued relationships and hierarchies between men. In Greco-Roman society it was therefore expected and accepted that adult men would have sexual intercourse both with women in order to produce children and with other men and boys in order to perpetuate particular social structures. Indeed, it was considered that relationships between men were likely to be somehow 'higher' than those between men and women, since women weren't understood to be rational, intellectual beings in the same way as men were.

All sex, however, was governed by strict notions of power and hierarchy: for example, while it was considered appropriate for an older, more powerful man to sexually penetrate a younger or socially inferior man (or a woman, or a slave), a less powerful person penetrating a more powerful man would have been deemed unnatural and against the order of things. Some scholars have suggested that part of Paul's apparent opposition to male–male sex in the book of Romans is actually grounded in this cultural context, and the assumption that, because male–male sex was taking place between older men and young boys, it was likely to be abusive and exploitative rather than egalitarian (see for example Scroggs 1983). We'll return to this point in Chapter 7.

Gnosticism and Manichaeism

The Gnostic and Manichaean movements were roughly contemporaneous with early Christianity. Gnosticism and **Manichaeism** were highly dualistic – claiming that humans were made up of separate, distinct bodies and souls and that the bodily realm was negative while the spiritual soul-realm was good. Attaining knowledge would help humans to escape and transcend their dirty, sinful bodies. The Gnostics believed that human souls became 'trapped' in base, earthly physical bodies and that the soul's greatest desire was to escape the body. For this reason, they preached **asceticism** and felt that excessive eating, drinking and having sex were indulgences which the 'higher' spiritual soul needed to overcome. Virginity came to represent, for them, wholeness and incorruptibility, an avoidance of both physical contamination and the generation of new life which could only end in death. Since the Gnostics associated spiritual rationality with maleness, and bodily physicality with femaleness, they were especially suspicious of women, who seemed to want to 'entice' men into having sexual relationships. Sexual intercourse, for the Gnostics, was considered negative, because it tended to lead to the conception of more human beings, thereby 'tying' more souls to bodies rather than leaving them to exist freely in the higher spiritual realm. Manichaeism, sometimes referred to as a heresy of Christianity and sometimes understood as a separate religion in its own right, also taught that the body was sinful and fallen.

Augustine of Hippo (354–430), who lived in Northern Africa and became one of the most influential figures in the development of Western Christian theology, was himself a Manichaean before he became a Christian, and, although he later renounced Manichaeism, its influence on his ideas might explain his sometimes hostile attitude toward bodily desires and sexuality. Augustine seems to have been influenced by the Manichaean philosophy which suggested that humans' physical bodies and spiritual souls are in conflict.

We know from the experiences recorded by Augustine in his autobiographical book, the *Confessions*, that he himself felt a lot of guilt about his sexual desires and, in particular, his inability to control them. Augustine seemed to believe, for example, that erections which happened spontaneously, rather than because one had willed them into existence in order to be able to procreate a child, were evidence of the flesh's disobedience to the will. The fact that, after the **Fall**, sexual arousal was necessary in order to achieve an erection, meant that even procreative sex was somehow corrupt. Sexual desire, or libido, believed Augustine, was therefore part of what got in the way of humans' capacity to perfectly reflect and live up to God's dispassionate rationality. Augustine argued that **original sin**, the tendency of all humans to sin because of the initial disobedience of the first humans, was passed on via sexual intercourse, which was itself stimulated by sinful cravings. In the Augustinian account, original sin is caused by, and itself is the cause of, **concupiscence** – the desire for the satisfaction of sensual urges. Jesus, as his conception had occurred miraculously and not via sexual intercourse, had escaped the transmission of original sin.

Augustine is often blamed for the ambivalence toward sexuality in later Christianity: sexuality became associated with chaos rather than with what Augustine termed 'continence' (dispassionate, quiet order). Sex transmitted death, via bondage to sin and an inclination to choose evil rather than good, as well as life. Although Augustine rejected Manichaeism and its dualism, and affirmed the inseparability of physicality and rationality in the human person, he seems to have retained a Manichaean-type suspicion of what we might term 'animal passion' which is evident throughout much Christian writing on sexuality in the following centuries.

Even among those much later **Reformation** theologians who wanted to affirm sexual intercourse within marriage as positive and appropriate, such as Martin Luther (1483–1546) and John Calvin (1509–64), there was a sense that marriage was also a necessity in order to control and curtail excessive sexual desire (Farley 2006, pp. 45–7). However, Elizabeth Clark, a scholar who has worked closely with early Christian texts, suggests that a more positive attitude to bodies and materiality began to be asserted by early Christians precisely because they wanted to distance themselves from the Gnostic and Manichaean suspicion of bodies and sex and assert that these things were actually good:

> Over against [the Gnostic] view, the mainstream orthodox Church appealed to the goodness of the created world and noted that God himself in Genesis 1 had pronounced the various aspects of creation 'good'. However wayward humans might be, our physical bodies were essentially part of the good creation. If the Creator gave humans sex organs and told the first couple to 'reproduce and multiply' ..., sexual intercourse and childbearing ... were not to be pronounced evil. Thus the Fathers' misgivings about sexual relations were guaranteed to run up against their theoretical claim that it was God who had given us bodies and an ordinance for reproduction: that claim was a deterrent to a wholesale advocacy of asceticism for all Christians. (1983, p. 19)

The Jewish tradition

The Jewish heritage was also deeply influential on Christianity. The earliest Christians almost certainly didn't consider themselves members of a new religion; rather, Christianity was understood at first as a sect or movement within Judaism. In some respects, the Jewish heritage was strikingly different from the Greco-Roman philosophical tradition. In contrast to the highly dualistic Platonic understanding of personhood in Greek and Roman philosophy, in which the rational and spiritual realms were considered separate from and 'higher' than the physical realm, ancient Jewish anthropology saw no such distinction between body and rationality. The human person was a holistic being, for whom sex was an appropriate and positive activity. Within Judaism, fertility, sex and marriage were considered holy: sexuality was a gift from God, to be enjoyed, though it also had a pragmatic function in bringing about new human beings (which was especially important for a people who'd often understood their survival as being under threat – Farley 2006, p. 34). Jewish culture shared with Greco-Roman culture an impulse to regulate sex, but in the Jewish case this was in order to secure inheritance rights and promote stable family situations.

All these strands feed into early and subsequent Christian understandings of sexuality, which may go some way toward explaining why the Christian tradition sometimes seems rather ambivalent about sexuality, and why it can simultaneously affirm the good of embodiment and the material world and seem hesitant about endorsing particular manifestations of sexuality. The 'body-suspicious' strand persists uncomfortably in the Christian tradition to the present day, even alongside the stream which actively asserts the goodness of the material, created world including human bodies and sexual activity. In Chapter 2, we'll think in more detail about the importance of incarnation in Christian theologies of sexuality.

ACTIVITY

Think about the images of sexuality you've come across in your theological reading, and, if you attend a church, in the sermons, teaching and liturgy you've encountered there. Do these Christian understandings of sexuality appear to be more grounded in the 'body-positive' anti-Gnostic approach; the 'body-suspicious' Augustinian approach; a mixture of both; or neither? Construct a diagram, mindmap or word cloud showing how they differ and overlap.

Psychology and sexuality

Whether they're essentialists, constructivists or something in between, Christian theologians are influenced both by the Christian tradition specifically and by the other norms and ideas in the contexts in which they work. Christians doing theology in India have a different context from Christians doing theology in China. Christian theologians in the twenty-first century don't have the same worldview as those in the tenth century had. For this reason, it's important to think briefly about some of the influential psychological ideas about human sexuality that have helped to constitute the climate of belief about sexuality in the West today. These have been particularly important in terms of influencing shifting beliefs about the possible causes of homosexuality and whether it should be understood as a moral issue.

Sigmund Freud

Sigmund Freud (1856–1939), the German psychotherapist, has been deeply influential on how sexuality is understood in social terms. Freud suggested that most people moved through a series of stages in their psychological development and that these affected their eventual adult sexuality. Freud suggested that all young children, both boys and girls, identified so deeply and passionately with their mothers that their feelings and desires for them could be described as sexual. As children got older, said Freud, girls continued to identify with their mothers and to desire the love and approval of men (and competed with their mothers for their fathers' love and attention), while boys came to resent their fathers for being a stronger and more powerful male presence than themselves in their mothers' lives.

Freud argued that this dynamic was played out by all children, but that they learned to repress it, because it was so socially unacceptable to think that one might sexually desire one's mother or father. This **repression** led, in turn, to the repression of many kinds of other sexual thoughts and desires. Freud believed that repression was extremely unhealthy, and that humans' true sexual desires were always fighting to get out. He interpreted many of his patients' dreams as being evidence of their secret sexual desires. One of the key elements to Freud's ideas, which is significant when it comes to thinking about theological accounts of sexuality, is his sense that sexuality and sexual behaviour are fundamentally to do with psychology rather than morality. If someone exhibits sexual behaviour which is 'disordered' or somehow inappropriate, suggests Freud, this should be understood as stemming not from simple moral failure on their part, but from some kind of psychological trauma, which has caused their sexuality to be repressed or to develop along unhealthy lines.

Importantly, Freud believed that experiencing homosexual feelings was a stage which all children went through, but that 'healthy' people would grow out of it, and come to be attracted to people of the opposite sex. Homosexuality in adulthood was understood by Freud as arrested development, perhaps the result of a young boy's failure successfully to differentiate himself from his mother.

Freud has been criticized for many reasons, including over-emphasizing the importance of sex (and for asserting that all psychological trauma probably arose from the repression of sexual desires or memories of past sexual events), for the fact that his analysis is so **heteronormative**, and for basing his assertions about sexuality on relatively few case studies drawn from a relatively homogeneous group (mostly middle-class Jewish women). There are few scholars today who would go along with his ideas wholesale. Nonetheless, his ideas remain influential within psychology, psychotherapy and broader social readings of sexuality, and his belief that sexuality is influenced by early childhood experiences and that sexual 'problems' might come about not because of perverse choices but because of the influence of these formative psychological experiences, has been important to theologians who have sought to reframe sexual ethics within a broader social framework.

Other nineteenth-century psychologists whose work has been significant in subsequent debates about human sexuality include Carl Gustav Jung, Richard von Krafft-Ebing and Havelock Ellis.

Carl Gustav Jung

Carl Gustav Jung (1875–1961) was initially a student of Freud, but later moved away from Freud's ideas because he felt they overplayed and misinterpreted human sexuality. Barbara Engler comments,

> For Freud, all higher intellectual processes and emotionally significant experiences are ultimately substitutes for sexuality and can be understood thereby. For Jung, sexuality itself must be seen as symbolic. Sexuality and the creativity it represents have a mysterious quality and cannot be fully analyzed or completely depicted. (2009, p. 70)

Unlike Freud, Jung didn't believe that the human unconscious was full of repressed sexual thoughts trying to get out. Rather, Jung believed that the key was what connected humans together, a web of shared images which he called the 'collective unconscious'. All humans, he suggested, had shared ways of thinking and of understanding themselves, which he called archetypes, and human sexuality was simply one manifestation of these common images, a way of getting in touch with a broader shared life-force. Human sexuality could therefore be understood as having a spiritual, divine element: even if God existed only in the collective unconscious, sexuality was still a way that humans sought to get in touch with this divine power.

Jung himself was suspicious of Christian ethics, which he felt were too obsessed with sexual sin. Nonetheless, Jung's influence can be seen in the ideas of Christian theologians who want to understand human sexuality as holistic, as symbolic of broader truths about personhood, and as being about encountering and respecting true 'otherness' in one's partner or partners.

Richard von Krafft-Ebing

Richard von Krafft-Ebing (1840–1902) was a German psychiatrist who published his work slightly before Freud. In his 1886 book *Psychopathia Sexualis*, Krafft-Ebing grouped homosexual orientation together with other 'perversions' of sexuality including oral sex, voyeurism, **sadism** and **masochism** (see Chapter 7) (Diamant 1995, p. 10). Krafft-Ebing's characterization of homosexuality as a disease may have been influenced by his Roman Catholic background. Krafft-Ebing believed that homosexuality was caused by hereditary mental illness, rather than psychological responses to events solely within one's own lifetime. Some Christian theologians today continue to characterize homosexuality as a disease, as Krafft-Ebing did. However, in later editions of the book and in subsequent work, Krafft-Ebing moved away from understanding homosexuality as degenerate.

Although Krafft-Ebing's work was less influential than that of Freud at the time and immediately thereafter, Harry Oosterhuis argues that Krafft-Ebing's legacy shouldn't be underestimated: it was Krafft-Ebing, says Oosterhuis, who made the shift from categorizing sexuality according to homosexuality versus heterosexuality, rather than simply according to non-procreative versus procreative acts, and who eventually presented heterosexuality and homosexuality as variations rather than a norm and its perversion (2000, pp. 278, 284). It was also Krafft-Ebing who first used the terms sadism, masochism and **paedophilia** (p. 278).

Havelock Ellis

Havelock Ellis (1859–1939), whose work spanned the late nineteenth and early twentieth centuries, also believed that homosexual orientation was inborn, though he noted that some people (including Oscar Wilde) believed they had chosen to be homosexual. Ellis' book *Sexual Inversion* (published in English in 1897) included 'histories', detailed accounts from people describing the development of their sexual desires and activities. Ellis commented on these without moral judgement: he didn't consider homosexuality degenerate (the term 'inversion' referred to someone whose sexuality was 'inside out', but Ellis didn't mean this pejoratively). Ellis was not in favour of masturbation, because he felt that it unhelpfully separated sexual sensation from love. Ellis was also influential in figuring **transgender** as a separate category from homosexuality.

Other psychologists, in the early to mid twentieth century, suggested that homosexual orientation might result from a fear of the opposite sex or a fear of the responsibility that a heterosexual relationship might entail (Diamant 1995, p. 12). Some of these assertions continue to be repeated in contemporary Christian responses to homosexuality in the USA, as Anna Gavanas notes (2004, pp. 148–53).

A philosopher influenced by Freud: Michel Foucault

In the middle of the twentieth century, work on sexuality by the French philosopher and cultural critic Michel Foucault (1926–84) became particularly important. Although he came to reject many of Freud's ideas, Foucault himself was also influenced by Freud's work. A constructivist, Foucault believed that identities such as heterosexual and homosexual did not arise 'naturally', but were affected by the time and culture in which one lived. Identical behaviour (such as a male having sex with another male) might be understood as 'homosexual' in one context but not in another. Foucault noted that ideas of homosexuality and heterosexuality as separate identities had only come into existence in the nineteenth century (Foucault 1990).

Relatedly, Foucault argued that the way in which sexuality and desire are to be interpreted is profoundly linked with the phenomenon of power. Power affects the ways in which humans interact with and relate to one another; the way we understand sexuality should therefore not be understood as 'natural' or somehow 'just the way things are', but as an effect of the dimensions of power that influence every area of our lives. The ways in which we do and don't talk about sexuality are affected by who has power in a given situation and the kinds of ideas about sexuality that are considered more or less legitimate in a particular culture. Societies where most of the people in government and leadership are heterosexual men, for example, may be less open to homosexuality than those whose government and leadership are more diverse in terms of gender and sexual orientation. Margaret Farley explains,

> Power ... creates, produces sexual desire as well as represses it; and in Foucault's view, power produces and constitutes sexual desire much more than it represses it. What this means is that cultural and social forces shape our sexual desires, so that what is sexually charged (whether thin bodies or plump ones, uncovered breast or covered, broad shoulders or great height or whatever) in one era or place may not be in another. (2006, p. 20)

In Foucault's account, the things about our sexualities that we believe to be 'natural' or 'just the way things are' are actually effects of the way in which discourses of power have played out in our culture. Some feminist and queer Christian theologians in particular have drawn on Foucault's ideas to suggest that mainstream Christian beliefs about gender roles and sexual orientations may result from particular groups having imposed their authority on less powerful groups (such as women or homosexual people). We will return to questions of power and control throughout this book.

16

Twentieth-century sexology

In the mid twentieth century, researchers began to study sexuality in a more and more scientific way. Some of the most famous studies published at this time included those by Kinsey, Masters and Johnson, and Hite.

Alfred Kinsey (1894–1956) was an American biologist who carried out a widespread study into sexual practices among American men and women in the 1940s. Kinsey is famous for his argument that hardly anyone is exclusively heterosexual or exclusively homosexual in orientation, but that most people fall in between, somewhere along what's come to be called the 'Kinsey Scale'. For instance, someone who's a 'Kinsey 1' is mostly heterosexual, but has occasional homosexual feelings. A 'Kinsey 3' is fully bisexual, that is, with equal amounts of homosexual and heterosexual desire. Kinsey himself preferred not to label people's sexuality in this way, recognizing that in many people it could and did shift over time. Kinsey's reports (Kinsey, Pomeroy and Martin 1948; Kinsey, Pomeroy, Martin and Gebhard 1953) were very controversial when they were published, since many people were shocked that almost half of the men who'd taken part had had at least one homosexual encounter and that over a third said they'd had homosexual feelings toward other men at some point.

William Masters (1915–2001) and Virginia Johnson (b.1925) were scientists from the USA who researched the details of how physical sexual arousal took place for men and women. They observed over 600 people taking part in over 10,000 sexual acts in total and recorded the physical changes and responses that took place throughout. Their work on the nature of the female orgasm is considered particularly important, because they argued that women could orgasm via stimulation of either their clitorises or their vaginas, but that the physical response was the same either way (Masters and Johnson 1966). Importantly, Masters and Johnson argued that people – especially women – who had grown up in religious contexts, where sex was viewed with suspicion as 'dirty' or sinful, were more likely to have problems in their sexual relationships and suffer from vaginismus[4] or be unable to reach orgasm (pp. 24, 254–6).

Shere Hite (b.1942) is a German sexologist, whose work has built on both Kinsey's and Masters and Johnson's. Her work has mostly involved gathering data from thousands of people about their sexual experiences via questionnaires (Hite 1976; Hite 1981). She claims that seventy per cent of women don't have orgasms just from penetrative vaginal sex, but that almost all of them can orgasm via clitoral stimulation, during solo

---

4 Vaginismus is an involuntary spasm of the vaginal muscles making penetration by a penis, tampon, sex toy or anything else difficult or impossible. The causes of vaginismus are not well understood: many doctors and psychologists believe it results from negative psychological associations with sex, while others believe there's a more direct physical cause.

masturbation or with a partner. Prior to Hite, many doctors, including Masters and Johnson, had followed Freud's idea that clitoral orgasms were somehow 'immature', stemming from young women's penis envy, and that mature women 'should' orgasm vaginally and were repressed or sexually dysfunctional if they couldn't. Hite also notes that what we find sexually arousing is influenced by our cultural context: while men in one society might be sexually aroused by the sight of breasts, in another culture, breasts might not be considered sexual at all. Hite makes clear that what's often considered 'natural' in sexual terms is actually always cultural. Importantly, this means that our ideas about what's *un*natural might also be contingent on the time and culture in which we live.

The work of Kinsey, Masters and Johnson, Hite and other researchers has been significant to subsequent discussion of sexuality, because it makes clear that, at least in statistical terms, homosexual feelings and activities are far from being a rare 'aberration'. It also demonstrates that what is most sexually pleasurable, especially for women, is not necessarily what most directly leads to procreation. This disrupts the link between sex and reproduction which has often been stressed in theological accounts of sexuality, raising questions about what sex and sexual pleasure are really 'for' in the first place.

Summary

We often talk about sexuality just in terms of sexual orientation, and this in itself is often divided rather crudely into heterosexuality and homosexuality with little acknowledgement that things can be more complex than that. However, we've begun to see in this chapter that theologians working in a Christian context understand sexuality in multiple ways, only some of which concern the sex and gender of the people to whom we're attracted. In Chapter 2, I'll go on to consider the later Christian tradition in more detail and will discuss how Christianity's affirmation of the good of embodiment influences Christian theological understandings of sexuality today.

Jo Ind suggests that it's particularly unhelpful to think about sexuality primarily in terms of heterosexuality and homosexuality. She suggests that sexuality is as much about the *situations* and *types* of activity people find arousing as about the sex and gender of the people to whom we are attracted, and notes that people have reported feeling sexually aroused by beautiful architecture and music, particular circumstances, and other phenomena (2003, pp. 24–5). She says, 'The terms "heterosexual" and "homosexual" have a place, but no more than terms like "visualsexual", "audiosexual", "cerebralsexual" or "tits'n'bumssexual"' (p. 33). Ind believes that sexuality should be constructed as acknowledging desire and the capacity to be 'turned on', not solely according to the gender of person to whom one is wholly or mostly attracted. She notes that the psychology of how and why we're attracted to certain people or situations is deeply complex, and will, for some people, be rooted in early childhood experiences. Indeed, some people find that their childhood experiences – be they negative experiences of violence or abuse, or more positive ones – shape and influence their adult sexualities many years down the line.

In this chapter, I began by thinking through definitions of sex, gender and sexuality and then looked at some different understandings of sexuality drawn from inside and outside the Christian theological tradition. I considered essentialist versus constructivist models of how human sexuality is formed. I noted that, as well as broad and recent understandings of sexuality, Christianity was also influenced, particularly during its early history, by beliefs about embodiment and sexual behaviour drawn from Jewish and Greco-Roman culture. I noted, for example, a suspicion of embodiment in Gnostic and Manichaean philosophy, and suggested that this might have caused some Christians to be very positive about sex and bodies in order to distance Christianity from these other traditions, while other Christians, including Augustine, might have carried more negative understandings of sex and bodies forward into their theologies. I touched on some influential understandings of human sexuality from psychology and sexology which continue to influence discourse today.

Before you move on to Chapter 2, think again about the questions with which we began this chapter.

- What do you understand by the words *sex*, *gender* and *sexuality*?
- When did you first become aware of your gender? What influenced you in your gender identity then? What influences you now?
- If you were a different gender, would you still be 'you'?
- What, if anything, does your gender identity have to do with the way you understand your relationships with other people and, if you are a person of faith, with God?

Questions for study and reflection

1 What do you think are the major influences on the messages about human sexuality communicated by contemporary Christianity?

2 To what extent might Christian theology be able to give insights into the nature and significance of human sexuality which are less evident in other disciplines, such as psychology, sociology and anthropology?

3 Does it make any difference to Christian theology if sexual orientation is understood as inborn rather than a result of social conditioning or conscious choice? How and why might this matter to Christian theologians and ethicists?

Further reading

Cahill, Lisa Sowle, 1996, *Sex, Gender and Christian Ethics*, Cambridge: Cambridge University Press.

Ellison, Marvin M. and Kelly Brown Douglas (eds), 2010, *Sexuality and the Sacred: Sources For Theological Reflection*, second edition, Louisville, KY: Westminster John Knox Press.

Farley, Margaret A., 2006, *Just Love: A Framework for Christian Sexual Ethics*, London: Continuum.

Rogers, Eugene F. (ed.), 2002, *Theology and Sexuality: Classic and Contemporary Readings*, Oxford: Blackwell.

Thatcher, Adrian, 2011, *God, Sex, and Gender: An Introduction*, Oxford: Wiley-Blackwell.

2

Sexuality, Incarnation and Erotic Love

In this chapter, we'll consider how sexuality has been understood in the context of theological thought about God, incarnation and personhood. Then, we'll turn to the important concept of **eros** – the Greek word for sexual love from which we take English terms like 'erotic' and 'erogenous'. We'll see that, far from being something alien to theology, *eros* has actually often been central to the ways in which Christian theologians have interpreted human relationships to God, to other people, and even to the rest of the environment.

Sexuality and incarnation

> Christianity is the religion of the Incarnation. Christians' core belief is that God entered the human world of bodies and senses in the person of Jesus of Nazareth ... As the religion of the Incarnation, Christianity is about the construction of Christian bodies and, according to Christian belief, the perfection of Christian bodies in the resurrection of the flesh. (Miles 2005, pp. 1–2)

> At the centre of Christian devotion is not a revealed doctrine, a religious ideal, or even a right way of life, but an embodied human person. Christianity began not with *beliefs* about Jesus, but with people who had *known* Jesus ... 'That which was from the beginning, which we have heard, which we have seen with our eyes, which we have looked upon, and our hands have handled ...' (1 John 1:1). The heartbeat of Christian faith is embodied encounter. (Myers 2011)

Bodies and sexuality have been understood ambivalently across Christian history. However, many Christian theologians in recent times have returned to 'body-positive' theologies, appealing to the centrality of the doctrine of **incarnation** for thinking through responses to human sexuality. Jesus' incarnation on earth, in a human body, is often read as a profound affirmation of the goodness of embodiment – even though there are, obviously, also ways in which bodies are problematic (they sin; they suffer pain; they tire, wear out, and eventually die). Some of the most vehement disagreements between early Christians surrounded the question of incarnation; Margaret Miles summarizes,

> In the religion of the Incarnation, the status of human bodies altered when God entered the sensible world in a human body. The first theological disputes were between second- and third-century Christians, who believed in the real human flesh of the incarnate God, and Gnostic Christians, who claimed that the Incarnation was in appearance only. Christians who believed in Christ's real humanity taught that the goal of Christian life was bodily resurrection in a life after death. (2005, p. 4)

There is no suggestion in the Bible that Jesus was married or engaged in physical sexual intercourse with anyone. Nonetheless, this doesn't mean we should think of Jesus as non-sexual. If sexual desire is understood as part of the goodness of being human, rather than something sinful or problematic, then, like most other human beings, Jesus presumably also experienced sexual desire (even if he remained celibate). Moreover, says Gerard Loughlin, it's significant that Jesus had a body at all, since this demonstrates a clear divine investment in bodies and materiality. It also signifies something profound about the respect Christians should have for the bodies of other people, since 'God only comes to them in the body of the other' (2004a, p. 12).

Nelson: sexual bodies as vehicles of God's embodiment

For James B. Nelson, as for Loughlin, incarnation is central to our relationships to God, not only because God was once made incarnate in Jesus but also because God continues to be made incarnate in each and every one of us in our own bodies. Nelson calls this 'the scandal of God's continuing incarnation' (1992, p. 23) – scandalous, because it implies that we encounter God in and through *every* aspect of our embodied nature, including our sexuality and aspects of our embodiment which we might understand as negative, shameful or embarrassing.

While the Christian tradition has affirmed that God is love, it hasn't often called God a 'lover' in a sexual sense (p. 24). But many theologians believe it's important to consider human sexuality as reflecting a sexual dimension *in God*, particularly if the world is to be understood as God's 'body' (as in the image closely associated with the work of Sallie McFague – see McFague 1987). Our embodied, sexed and sexual selves are the means by which we meet God; 'Creation, far from being a hurdle on the road to God, is that very road' (Nelson 1992, p. 28). Indeed, says Nelson,

> Without denigrating the significance of God's revelation in Jesus, incarnation might yet be understood more inclusively. Then the fleshly experience of each of us becomes vitally important to our experience of God. Then

the fully physical, sweating, lubricating, menstruating, ejaculating, urinating, defecating bodies that we are – in sickness and in health – are the central vehicles of God's embodiment in our experience. (p. 31)

This awareness impacts on how we understand and conduct our sexual lives; having a deep appreciation of and regard for our bodies, and our natures as embodied persons whose bodies are sites for interaction with God, means we'll be less likely to use our bodies and sexualities thoughtlessly. When we appreciate the worth of our own bodies, we also appreciate the worth of other bodies, and our sexual relationships are less likely to become exploitative of ourselves or others (Nelson 1992, p. 35).

Importantly, for Nelson, to be sexual and embodied creatures is not all about the genital aspects of sexuality. Our physical experience is always *sexual*, but not always *genital* (p. 45). Where sexuality becomes over-genitalized, it also becomes reductionist: we fail to acknowledge how our sexualities affect all our interactions, and how our spiritual and intellectual facets should also profoundly inform what, if anything, we do with our genitals. We'll come back to thinking about the distinction between sexuality and genitality later on.

Isherwood, Stuart, Althaus-Reid: feminist body theology

While Nelson is particularly interested in male bodily experience, Lisa Isherwood and Elizabeth Stuart come at body theology from a consciously female angle. Importantly, however, they say that they're not trying to reaffirm older ideas about women as being exclusively or particularly embodied to the exclusion of rational or intellectual capability. While women's bodily experience is a good and valuable site of theological focus, women's bodies include their minds (Isherwood and Stuart 1998, p. 10). Body theology, for Isherwood and Stuart, creates theology *through* the body rather than simply being *about* the body (p. 22).

Marcella Althaus-Reid, too, considers embodiment central to theology. She fears that theology's traditional appeals to transcendence ('rising above' worldly things) have left it too invested in the spiritual realm, to the exclusion of bodies and the material world (2004, p. 99). For Althaus-Reid, body theology needs to be about *all* bodies, not just bodies deemed decent, legitimate or acceptable (p. 104). This has implications for ecclesiology (theological ideas about the Church): changing and expanding what theology can say about bodies will also change and expand what theology can say about itself and God, since human bodies in their diversity are said to make up the Body of Christ, the Church. Importantly, says Althaus-Reid, since human bodies often have sex, in some sense the Church made up of human bodies 'has sex' too, and it's appropriate (and important) to speak about the Church in these terms.

Pope John Paul II: theology of the body

'Body theology' provided the theme for a series of lectures given by Pope John Paul II between 1979 and 1984. Many focus specifically on marriage, celibacy and virginity, but some address broader questions of the significance of human embodiment, especially in light of Ephesians 5. Importantly, however, even where he isn't discussing marriage specifically, John Paul II argues that the human body has a 'nuptial' meaning – that is, tending toward marriage – built into it from the start. This 'nuptial' meaning indicates a capacity for self-giving, specifically expressed in the complementary context of marriage. For John Paul II, therefore, it's written into humans' very bodies that they are created male and female *for* one another: human sexuality is, by definition, heterosexual in nature (though he notes that sexuality can be directed toward the Kingdom of God rather than another person, as in the case of celibates). Human bodies, then, are sexual by definition – but this sexuality can legitimately exist only along heterosexual lines if it's to image God's love for humans (1979–84).

John Paul II's argument is clearly situated both in the Roman Catholic Natural Law tradition, in which humans are believed to be created to fulfil certain goods, and in a broader Christian tradition, in which the human marriage relationship is believed to symbolize a deeper truth about the relationship between God and human beings. We'll return to considering this meaning of marriage in Chapter 5. For now, though, it's important simply to note John Paul II's emphasis on bodies themselves as intrinsically bound-up with how as humans we relate to one another and to God.

Describing the Church as a 'body' is a metaphor, and thinking about it as something which 'has sex' is a reminder of quite what a strange metaphor it is. Metaphors are also important elsewhere in the Christian tradition's accounts of sexuality – for example, some theologians are deeply invested in the metaphor of the Church as the bride of Christ. But how far can metaphors go? How significant are biblical metaphors in theological accounts of sexuality? More specifically, how might Christians' metaphorical images concerning God's sexuality, or lack of it, influence theologies of human sexuality?

Sexuality and the doctrine of the Trinity

Does God have a sexuality?

In his introduction to Christian doctrine, Alister E. McGrath states:

> Neither male nor female sexuality is to be attributed to God, in that this sexuality is an attribute of the created order ... Indeed, the Old Testament

avoids attributing sexual functions to God, on account of the strongly pagan overtones of such associations ... The Old Testament refuses to endorse the idea that the gender or the sexuality of God is a significant matter. (2007, p. 204)

McGrath notes that worship of a lone God, rather than paired male and female deities, rendered the ancient Israelites' religion unusual among Ancient Near Eastern belief systems. How different the Israelites' belief actually was is debatable: some scholars suggest that the Israelites may have worshipped a female deity alongside YHWH, and that traces of this may be found in the Hebrew Bible despite later editors' efforts to erase them and make the Israelites seem emphatically monotheistic (Dever 2005; Smith 2002; Hadley 2000). Nonetheless, McGrath's argument that God is no more male than female – and that maleness is therefore no more inherently godly than femaleness – finds good warrant elsewhere.

However, God's sexuality, even where it's understood as different in kind from human sexuality, is evident symbolically in the Hebrew Scriptures. God is figured as a sexually potent husband jealous that his wife has been unfaithful, and the language of Hosea, Isaiah, Jeremiah and Ezekiel is deeply sexual, even violently so, making it clear that only God has sexual 'rights' over this 'wife', Israel. In later interpretation of the Song of Songs, God is a lover involved in a deeply erotic and far more egalitarian sexual relationship, though the book itself doesn't mention God explicitly. Gerard Loughlin comments, 'It is sometimes said that God's sex is merely metaphorical. But if so, it is far from being a dead metaphor. God's sex still orders human lives' (2007, p. 17). Loughlin hits on an important point: even Christians who accept that the biblical descriptions of God as a husband, father and king are metaphorical often find it difficult to think about God as anything other than 'he'. Only some metaphors – especially gendered and sexed ones – are considered legitimate ways of picturing God.

I was once invited to speak on a radio programme about whether churches should use gender-neutral language for God in their prayers and liturgies. One very irate listener phoned in and said that referring to God as anything other than 'he' was blasphemous. He insisted, '*Everyone knows* that God is a heterosexual male!' Most Christians would not state the case so strongly. Nonetheless, Loughlin argues that ideas about God's sex and sexuality continue to pervade Christian theology, and that the supposed heterosexual maleness of God is dangerous for women and non-heterosexual people in particular, since it means they can be understood as more 'other' from God than heterosexual males are.

Appeals to the sexuality of God, whether understood positively or negatively, then, might be understood as rather ambiguous, particularly when they seem to erode the *difference* of God from humanity: Alister McGrath suggests that understanding God as a 'person' with a 'sexuality' might tend to make humans forget that God is different from us as well as like us (2007, p. 205).

Higton: the relational Trinity

Theologians who are interested in sexuality and the doctrine of God often appeal to the doctrine of the Trinity to begin to explain how God can be understood as relational and 'sexual' even without having a sex as such. Mike Higton's summary of the doctrine is a useful one, making clear why the Trinity matters so profoundly to Christians:

> To know God is to be drawn into that love and justice that has its fount and origin in the Father. It is to be drawn into that love in which one is formed by being conformed to the Son, who plays out that love again in a form that one can take on. And it is to be drawn into that Christlike love that is formed within one by the working of the Spirit, who conforms one to the love that unites the Son and the Father. (2008, p. 90)

Higton's account is powerful, deeply rooted in loving relationship. But this relationship, built on a father–son metaphor, seems much more grounded in *family* love than *sexual* love as such. It's those from *outside* our families of origin with whom we expect to have sexual relationships – so what do Christians feel that the doctrine of the Trinity can tell us about sexual relationships and human sexuality as such?

Thatcher and Moltmann: the non-exploitative Trinity

Adrian Thatcher suggests that to 'remake' Christian sexual theology non-**patriarchally** (without the assumption that women are subordinate to men, or that they need their sexuality to be controlled, protected or overseen by men) requires reflection on how human relationships are to mirror the relationships of God within the Trinity. Particularly important, for Thatcher, are the themes of interdependence, interrelation and communion between the persons of the Trinity, along with their profound equality and mutuality (1993, p. 54). Trinitarian understandings of God, adds Higton, have important differences from the ways in which human relationships are to be understood; reflections on the interrelations of the Father, Son and Spirit are about the Father, Son and Spirit specifically, not about *all* other kinds and *all* forms of relationship (Higton 2008, p. 100). Nonetheless, by analogy, reflection on the Trinitarian God-relationships as non-exploitative, non-violent, mutually loving and so on may provide pointers for patterns of good relationship between human beings.

In Jürgen Moltmann's account, '[t]he Trinity corresponds to a community in which people are defined through their relations with one another and in their significance for one another, not in opposition to one another, in terms of power and possession' (1981, p. 198). As such, both God, and the community of humans who seek to love and reflect God, should be understood as existing 'without privileges and without subjugation' (p. 198). Social theorists of the Trinity, including Moltmann, have been especially keen to explore how the **perichoretic** or 'interpenetrating' aspects of the Trinitarian God might be reflected back into the human community too. Although the relationships between the Persons of the Trinity are most commonly imagined as family ones, then, these theologians suggest that they're also useful for re-thinking sexual and marriage relationships.

Rogers: the welcoming Trinity

Some theologians have more explicitly wanted to read human sexuality through a Trinitarian lens. Eugene F. Rogers argues that human sexuality images the triunity ('three-in-oneness') of God, because in both cases there are more than two persons involved. Rather than being a closed relationship of two, says Rogers, the relationships of the Godhead always have a third person involved, a witness who testifies to the love of the others. Similarly, he suggests, human sexual relationships are never just for or about the partners but are also for and about the whole community, who witness to the relationship of the partners and are welcomed into their love. This might include, but is not limited to, their children.

Relationships of love, therefore, argues Rogers, actually become theophanies, living appearances of God in the world (1999, p. 196). You might have seen a famous icon by Andrei Rublev, a Russian Orthodox artist who died around 1430, which depicts three figures seated around a table. Although one title for the icon is *Angels at Mamre*, a reference to the story in Genesis 18 in which Abraham entertains three mysterious guests, who may be angels, many interpreters have also understood the image as representing the three persons of God: another title for the icon is *The Old Testament Trinity*. On the table is a cup or chalice, a clear reference to the Eucharist. Behind one figure is a mountain, which may represent spiritual 'mountain top' experiences of the Holy Spirit; behind another is a tree, which may represent the cross on which Christ was crucified; behind the third is a building, which may represent a house, temple or church, the dwelling-place of God the Father. Significantly, the fact that there are three figures means that, although they're looking at one another, their gaze isn't an unbroken one. It gives space for others to be drawn in: the empty space at the bottom as one looks at the icon has been interpreted as space for the viewer to join the circle at the table, to be drawn into the circle of God's love.

This love can be understood as sexual, but needn't be stereotypically heteronormative. Importantly, suggests Rogers, since humans are made part of God's love via adoption rather than physical birth, procreation isn't the be-all and end-all of human love relationships either: 'Sex before God is for sanctification, for God's catching us up into God's triune life ... The chief end of sex is not to make children of human beings, but to make children of God' (1999, p. 206). Rogers believes that this means same-sex relationships can echo God's love just as well as different-sex ones can (p. 211). Committed human relationships, whether homosexual or heterosexual, glorify God, because their open, embracing love echoes that of the Trinity. Human love-relationships also echo God in their creativity – sometimes procreatively, but always in the sense that they make love, and the glory of God, manifest (p. 214). Human sexual relationships are therefore an important part of what makes God visible in the world (p. 215).

Even if God doesn't have a sex as such in the way that humans do, then, sexual metaphors are some of the most vivid images through which people have tried to express and understand the relationships in God and with God. For Rogers, drawing on Karl Barth, the image of the Church as a (female) Bride of a (male) Christ is deeply significant (although other scholars have suggested that the stereotypical gender complementarity which seems to be embedded in Barth's theology is problematic, as I'll discuss later). God as a Father also loves and generates. Perhaps even more importantly, the sexual element of these kinds of metaphors is significant because it points to God's *vulnerability*: sexual relationships are intimate ones, and it's in a relationship which is figured as being like a marriage (in which people see the best and the worst of each other, lay themselves open, and trust one another not to abuse the power this gives them) where God's love for humanity also becomes God's vulnerability to being rejected by humanity.

QUESTION BOX

In light of the accounts outlined above, how useful is the doctrine of the Trinity as a way of thinking through human sexuality and sexual relationships? What are the advantages and disadvantages of a Trinitarian approach to sexuality? Is it important or beneficial to think about God as having a sexuality? Why? What theological problems might be raised be understanding God in sexual terms?

Eros/desire

English words stemming from the Greek word *eros*:

EROGENOUS ZONE: an area of the body which is particularly susceptible to sexual arousal or pleasure
EROTIC: adjective for something which arouses sexual desire or excitement
EROTICA: sexually stimulating writing or art
EROTICIZE: to present or explain something in a sexual way

Types of love

In the Greek which was in use at the time the New Testament books were written down, there are several words which are all translated by the single English word 'love'. You may come across some of these different senses of love in your reading: they include *philia* (the 'brotherly' love between friends); *storge* (the kind of affectionate love a parent has for a child); *agape* (a deep, self-giving love); and *eros* (passionate love, often referring to the romantic or sexual feelings of lovers).

We saw in Chapter 1 that Augustine was somewhat suspicious of desire, especially the bodily desire for sex, because of its associations with concupiscence and original sin. This suspicion of erotic desire persists in some recent and contemporary Christian theology. In this section, we'll explore the concept of erotic desire in more detail and ask whether it inherently involves a tendency to sin, or whether it can be understood as something divine and something which actually helps orient human beings toward God.

Eros was described by Plato (c.424–c.348 BCE) as a drive in everyone to find and be joined to another person, who would complete them. *Eros* has often been contrasted negatively with **agape** (the word used in the New Testament for the selfless, non-preferential love extolled by Jesus). Anders Nygren (1890–1978), the Swedish Lutheran theologian, wrote in the middle of the twentieth century that 'Eros and Agape belong originally to two entirely separate spiritual worlds' (1953, p. 31, quoted in Burrus 2006, p. xiv). Virginia Burrus explains that, in Nygren's account, while *agape* represents selfless, Godly love, and the loving activity of God directed toward humans, *eros* in texts contemporary with the New Testament represents the active desire of humans to reach God. *Eros* therefore seems more human-centred and easily corruptible, often turning into something 'vulgar' (p. xvi).

Stuart and Loughlin: *eros* and agape *in unison*

Nonetheless, Elizabeth Stuart and Gerard Loughlin both suggest that it's unhelpful to think of *eros* and *agape* as mutually exclusive opposites, as Nygren seems to. Stuart believes that the way in which lesbian and gay people often describe their sexual and romantic relationships in terms of friendship helps to break down the either-or model of *eros* and *agape* (2003, p. 59). Sexual relationships should *also* be grounded in friendship. In human sexual relationship, suggests Loughlin, *eros* is about a realization that the other person to whom one relates can't be possessed or consumed, or they would cease to be really 'other' at all (2004a, p. 4). Just as humans can't possess or consume God, so we shouldn't attempt to possess or consume one another. Far from being the opposite of Godly love, then, *eros* in this account is itself a kind of Godly love. Sexual desire is part of the way we as humans can understand the desire that exists within the Trinity itself, as well as God's love for humans.

Williams: *eros and 'The Body's Grace'*

This idea occurs even more explicitly in an essay by Rowan Williams en-titled 'The Body's Grace':

> The whole story of creation, incarnation, and our incorporation into the fellowship of Christ's body tells us that God desires us, *as if we were God*, as if we were that unconditional response to God's giving that God's self makes in the life of the Trinity. We are created so that we may be caught up in this, so that we may grow into the wholehearted love of God by learning that God loves us as God loves God. (2002, pp. 311–12)

Williams argues that Godly desire isn't about wanting to possess, own or control someone, or about simply wanting to create pleasure for ourselves, but about wanting our bodies and their activities to bring joy to someone *other* than ourselves. This is deeply mutual: 'To desire my joy is to desire the joy of the one I desire: my search for enjoyment through the bodily pres-ence of another is a longing to be enjoyed in my body' (p. 313). People who conduct their sexual activity without thought for the joy or good of others, says Williams, are exhibiting a distorted sexuality, because they're denying the moral and communal significance of all sex (p. 314). Williams calls the joy created in committed sexual relationships 'the body's grace', since desir-ing and being desired by another person helps us to understand what it is to desire and be desired by God. Causing joy and delight to another person is a kind of grace, making us realize we are joyous and delightful. The whole life of the Christian community, says Williams, should be about teaching humans this important fact about themselves. Sexual relationship isn't, of course, the only context in which this can occur. However, Williams' point is that *eros* and sexual desire needn't be thought about in distinction from humans' relationships with God, or as something alien to God.

Pope Benedict XVI: Deus Caritas Est

In contemporary Roman Catholic theology, there's something of a tension between the suspicion of *eros* as put forward in Nygren's thought and a sense that *eros* is indeed right and good. Some Roman Catholic theologians, following Augustine, have sought to show that love must hold together elements of both *eros* and *agape*. Despite his suspicion of sexual desire, Augustine believed that *eros* couldn't simply be dismissed as tending to evil, since human desire also includes a good desire to be like God. Augustine used the Latin word *caritas* to describe this synthesized love, and the term is picked up and explored by Pope Benedict XVI in a 2005 encyclical entitled *Deus Caritas Est* (God is Love). D. C. Schindler summarizes the argument of this letter:

> Although the terms *eros* and *agape* may set into relief different aspects of love, in the end *they do not represent different kinds of love*. Rather, as the pope states forcefully at the outset of the encyclical, *there is ultimately just one love*, with a variety of dimensions that are all necessary in order to sustain the full meaning of love. If we separate these dimensions from one another, however pure or laudable our motives may be, we will end up distorting love and, at the very least, depriving it of its vitality. (2006, p. 378)

For this reason, the two types of love not only balance each other, but actually complete each other. Benedict XVI claims that *eros* shows how much the divine reality is greater than and other than human existence (*Deus Caritas Est* paragraph 5; cf. Schindler 2006, p. 380). *Eros* is a deep, passionate response to goodness and beauty, so it's an appropriate deep and passionate response to God.

Importantly, sexuality isn't, for Benedict XVI, the only aspect of human life within which *eros* can be experienced; however, in our sexuality we are made *physically* aware of the extent to which *eros* is written into us. The implication, says Schindler, is that with no *eros*, there would be no joy in and for the created world and its goodness. It's only when *eros* is separated from its capacity to channel our awareness of the goodness of God's beauty that it becomes corrupt. In no way is *eros* in itself sinful or fallen. Indeed, Benedict XVI asserts, God is indeed love: God is *eros* (*Deus Caritas Est* paragraph 9). Schindler notes that Benedict is drawing here on affirmations that 'God is *eros*' from much further back in the Christian tradition: he points to examples in early figures including Origen (c.184–c.253), Gregory of Nyssa (c.335–c.395), Augustine (354–430), Pseudo-Dionysius (late fourth/early fifth century) and Maximus the Confessor (c.580–662) (Schindler 2006, p. 376).

Chambers: an integrated account of eros

The novelist Aidan Chambers has shown that *eros* as a felt phenomenon can be simultaneously physically sexual and about a far broader experience of beauty and goodness. In Chambers' novel *Now I Know*, the narrator, Nik, aged 17, describes to his friend Julie an experience he had while on a camping trip in Sweden. As you read his account, try to pick out examples where he identifies specifically sexual feelings, specifically spiritual feelings, and general but not sexual bodily feelings:

> As I came to my senses, everything suddenly seemed clearer. There were some birds, some ducks, dabbling about on the edge of the lake and their calls seemed sharper than I could ever remember hearing any noise before. They were all I could hear. Everywhere else was complete silence which the noise of the ducks seemed to make intense, so that the silence was like a noise itself.
>
> My hands were resting on the oars and I could feel the grain of the wood, though up till then they'd seemed smooth. The sun had set, there wasn't a breath of wind. It was the time when you can almost see the dusk creeping in. But that evening everything stood out sharply as I looked, and the colours, though they weren't bright like in sunlight, seemed to glow with a sort of purity I'd never seen before.
>
> And as I looked a deep sense of peace came over me, a calmness that wasn't at all like feeling relaxed, but made me feel full of energy while being quite still inside. And it was as if time was ... not stopped ... but waiting. Hanging in the air. I felt I was looking into eternity and that nothing mattered anymore because everything was in harmony, like a marvellous tune. Nothing mattered and yet everything mattered, every smallest detail, and all was well at last.
>
> I sat there in the middle of the lake expecting that this strange sensation would pass. But it didn't. I didn't move, just stared in a sort of happiness I didn't want to break. I watched the sky slowly change as dusk turned to night and stars came out, needle-sharp points of light in a darkening, deepening blueblack vastness that made me feel I was shrinking smaller and smaller till a sort of pain came over me, a mixture of joy because of the beauty of it all and sadness because of my insignificance compared with all that unendingness. But I was part of it, however unimportant I was. And I wanted to be totally in it. Absorbed into it, not separate.
>
> And then, when the stars were fully out and it was night, even though there was still light on the horizon because of how far north we were, the strangest thing of all happened.

I started getting a hard-on. Honest! I'm not just being rude. I had an erection! And I wanted it – all that out there, I mean. I wanted all that – I don't know ... nature. Peace. Eternity. Whatever it was. Like wanting a girl. I wanted to be in it ... Wanted to belong to it and wanted it to belong to me. And I wanted to hold it in my hands and feel it with my body. And ... honest ... I wanted to come in it!

I know this must sound mad. But it didn't seem like that at the time. It seemed natural. I wasn't surprised or ashamed or anything like that. I just felt this overpowering desire. Stronger than anything I've ever felt before.

I didn't think about it. I just stood up in the boat, and quite deliberately, as if I was performing a sacred act, a ritual ceremony, I took off my clothes, one thing after another, folded them up neatly, which I never do usually, and laid them in the stern.

Then, when I was completely naked, I stood erect, everything erect!, and looked around, all around, part of me still expecting this strange mood to pass, but it didn't. The air was cold by then, northern cold, the cold that comes off snow. And the cold of the air felt as sharp and alive to my skin as the colours and shapes of everything were to my eyes and the sounds and silence, the silence most of all, were to my ears.

And I loved it. Desired it. Was randy for it. Wanted to be in it. And there was only one way. I put a foot on the gunwale, pushed up, and jumped.

I went in feet first, straight down into the dark water. The air felt cold, but the water was freezing. God, it was cold! Knocked the breath out of me like a punch. And knocked down what was standing up as well. Like a fist of ice grabbing the goolies!

As soon as I surfaced I started laughing. And the air felt warm so I splashed about a bit just for the fun of it. Then hauled myself into the boat, shivering, all passion spent!

And I tell you, I shall never forget that evening. Never. It's as clear to me now as it was then. And I know it will be all my life. (Chambers 1987, pp. 92–3)

Sherrard and Farley: eros and beauty

Sexual love, like all love, gives rise to and is the ground of desire – for fuller union with, and greater affirmation of, the beloved. (Farley 2006, p. 171)

Philip Sherrard, a Greek Orthodox theologian, also emphasizes the link between *eros* and beauty. He suspects that the lack of attention given to *eros* in a lot of Christian sexual theology contributes to a similar lack of attention to the idea of beauty, particularly the beauty of the created world (1976, p. 43). Where matter and bodies are considered 'fallen', he says, *eros* is regarded with suspicion; however, the 'desire' which can be lustful and is condemned in Scripture isn't necessarily identical with every kind of erotic gaze. The very fact that Jesus warns men against looking at women lustfully means that it's possible for men to look at women *not* lustfully – that is, without a desire to possess or control them (pp. 45–6). It isn't sexual love and the appreciation of beauty in itself which are bad, but the distortion of sexual love in which power and control are **fetishized** rather than problematized.

Margaret Farley adds that *eros*-love needn't be understand as inherently to do with wanting to possess something which one lacks, but is 'a combination of lack and fullness, poverty and plenty' (2006, p. 172). The awareness of another person who is not the same as oneself (and whom one considers, in some sense, beautiful) prompts one to look beyond oneself. It's in this way, among others, that desire for the divine can be awakened. Nonetheless, suggests Farley, *eros* shouldn't be understood as just a means to an end, a way of 'training' us to look beyond ourselves to God: it's good in its own right, so 'sexual romantic love and desire, even when they are ultimately incorporated in a great love that affirms more than sexual union, need not discard sex or sexuality along the way' (p. 173).

Julian of Norwich: eros and creativity

Thinking about divine–human relationships in terms of erotic love, and drawing on sexual imagery to describe them, is by no means a recent phenomenon. The medieval **mystic**, Julian of Norwich (1342–1416), understood *eros* as bringing together passions for beauty, peace, harmony, and 'a love that, in reaching outside itself toward another, expresses a relational bond that is part and parcel of the reality created by the God who is Love' (Ahlgren 2005, p. 37). In Julian's thought, suggests Gillian Ahlgren, erotic love is creative love. This shouldn't be understood in an instrumentalist way as mostly concerned with the creation of babies; rather, it's about creating loving and just relationships. Ahlgren goes on, 'Incarnating God's erotic love for humanity is part and parcel of the Christian life: as we learn to stretch ourselves erotically – that is, to pour ourselves out, in love – toward others, we make more manifest the body of Christ in our own time and space' (p. 38). Julian doesn't devalue *agape* love; rather, she shows that to focus only on this one kind of love would be to lack an appreciation of the fullness and multiplicity of love. A forerunner to Loughlin and Williams, Julian shows that 'the revelation of God's love can and must be expressed in both erotic and agapic terms; anything less than the full union of all that both dimensions of love convey is less than God' (p. 39).

Ahlgren shows that, although it's unlikely that Julian knew of his work directly, her profound affirmation of *eros* as part of the good love of God expressed in Christ echoes much earlier themes found in Origen, the third-century Egyptian theologian. For Origen, *eros* is a crucial part of expressing the human soul's deep, yearning desire for God. Origen suggests that *eros* love is so passionate and so deep that we are somehow 'wounded' by it. Referring to Christ as a 'dart', and picturing Christ's love for humanity as erotic, Origen suggests that Christ himself 'pierces' and 'wounds' those who experience this love (Origen, *Commentary on the Song of Songs*, 29–30; quoted in Ahlgren 2005, p. 40). Perhaps part of the reason why images of falling in love as having been shot by Cupid's arrow remain so popular is because people recognize its painful or at least uncomfortable aspect.[1]

Jo Ind writes,

[Eros] was a vision of sexuality that resonated with my sense of sex more profoundly than the much more common conceptualization of it as the attraction between male and female. I found the male/female distinction too flat, too polarized and too dualistic to describe the things that turned me on. It left little space for God as an integral aspect of sexuality. What made much more sense to me was to see the primary sexual energy as that of Christ who is holding all creation together. I thought of the attraction between male and female as part of that erotic yearning, even the dominant motif for many of us, but I saw the erotic tug as coming from a deeper source than that. It was also about the longing for connection, the need for belonging, the desire to be centred in the source of the universe. 'Deep is calling to deep' is how the Psalmist describes prayer (Psalm 43.7). It was indeed and I could feel it in my groin. (2003, p.135)

Summary

In this chapter, we came to consider ideas surrounding incarnation, and noted that Christianity's deep commitment to valuing embodiment means that sexual and bodily experiences can't simply be dismissed as fallen or sinful. We considered human and divine sexuality in light of doctrines of God, particularly Trinitarian perspectives, and asked to what extent understanding the Persons of God as existing in relationship with one another might be helpful in shedding light on questions of human sexuality. We ended the chapter with a consideration of the category of *eros*-desire, exploring whether or not erotic love is a helpful and appropriate metaphor for understanding human desire for God as well as for one another. We suggested, with reference to the work of several classic and contemporary theologians,

---

1 Cupid is the Roman name for the character called Eros in Greek legend – the god of love.

that *eros* encompasses creativity and energy and that this aspect of human sexuality shouldn't be understood as sinful or something to be escaped.

According to most of these theologians, desire isn't inherently sinful or ungodly – but, like any other human emotion, it has the potential to become corrupt and to be misused. When desire becomes lust – especially a lust to possess or control another person – it's distorted. Importantly, as we'll consider further later on, every one of us lives as part of a society, which means that our sexualities and our desires are, in part, shaped by influences from beyond ourselves. Elizabeth Stuart and Adrian Thatcher have suggested that living in a capitalist society which encourages us to want and consume more and more might lead us to have 'capitalist' sexual desires too, and to have our desires shaped by advertising and other social pressures (p. 213). A counter-cultural theological account of sexuality might therefore want to engage critically with these capitalist social norms, and to resist the idea that, in order to be fulfilling, sexuality must be about chasing ever more novelty, more partners and more individualistic pleasure.

Tim Gorringe agrees that living in a society which values profit over relationship profoundly affects the ways in which we understand our sexual and other interactions with people. Gorringe argues that our senses and our physical desires therefore need to be *educated*, by recognizing them as channels by which we encounter and live out God's creativity (2001, p. 91). A culture which stokes the desire to consume more and more commodities more and more immediately is likely to be a culture of greed and alienation (pp. 94–5); the way we treat sexual desire can't be analysed theologically in isolation from the way we treat other desires. If we expect all our desires to be fulfilled immediately, by right, no matter what the cost, we're likely to have a similar attitude to sexual desire: but if we are critical of an 'instant-gratification' culture in other respects, we might ask whether it is similarly dubious in sexual terms. Sexual desire can become as idolatrous as the desire for money or things, if it becomes a focus in its own right rather than something which points us onward to God (p. 89).

Graham Ward makes the same kind of observation when he notes that people who understand orgasm as a mystical revelation of God are only getting part of the story (1998, p. 52). As humans, our sexualities and sexual experiences can certainly help us to understand transcendence and the existence of something greater than ourselves, but God can never be limited to or bound up by them. This is important, says Ward, because if it gets to the point where our desire for God and our sexual desire are considered all part of the same thing, we reduce God to being an element of ourselves, and the question then is what is there to desire about God in the first place (p. 54). He concludes, 'Divine desire and human desire are not the same, though human eros, arightly directed, can participate in the greater movement of God's desire for the salvation of the world' (p. 52).

Some of the apparent suspicion of sexual desire in the Church Fathers and among other early Christians stemmed not from a belief that sexual desire itself was bad, but a fear that it could draw people away from God. The greatest and most appropriate focus of human love and desire was God, so anything (including sexual love for another person) which detracted from this was a potential problem. Augustine is often disparaged as being anti-sex, and mocked for his wish that humans could have sexual intercourse without lustful passion. But Augustine's outlook chimes with something which has remained important to many Christian theologians and ethicists in their discussions of sexuality: that is, how can humans conduct their sexual lives mindfully and thoughtfully, always conscious of how their sexual actions promote love for God, other people and themselves?

In Chapter 3, we'll think more about how our sexuality is part of our make-up as whole persons, and consider the ways in which sexuality interacts with sex and gender in particular.

Questions for Study and Reflection

1 How might the Christian doctrine of the incarnation influence the ways we think theologically about human sexuality?

2 Rowan Williams says, 'The whole story of creation, incarnation, and our incorporation into the fellowship of Christ's body tells us that God desires us, *as if we were God*, as if we were that unconditional response to God's giving that God's self makes in the life of the Trinity' (2002, pp. 311–12). To what extent is the doctrine of the Trinity helpful for thinking through theologies of human sexuality?

3 What place is there in a Christian theology of sexuality for *eros* or desire? Are there ways in which it's problematic to think about human sexuality as a means of encountering God?

Further reading

Gorringe, T. J., 2001, *The Education of Desire: Toward a Theology of the Senses*, London: SCM Press.

Kamitsuka, Margaret D. (ed.), 2010, *The Embrace of Eros: Bodies, Desires, and Sexuality in Christianity*, Minneapolis, MN: Fortress Press.

Miles, Margaret R., 2005, *The Word Made Flesh: A History of Christian Thought*, Oxford: Blackwell.

Shults, F. LeRon and Jan-Olav Henriksen (eds), 2011, *Saving Desire: The Seduction of Christian Theology*, Grand Rapids, MI: Eerdmans.

Stuart, Elizabeth and Adrian Thatcher, 1997, *People of Passion: What the Churches Teach About Sex*, London: Mowbray, chapter 8, 'Desire'.

3

Sexuality, Sex and Gender

At the beginning of Chapter 1, I set out the ways in which I'd be using the terms *sex*, *sexuality* and *gender* within this book. I suggested then that sex, sexuality and gender aren't identical, but represent different aspects of our sexual selves: our biological sex as male, female or other; our cultural gender, that is whether we present and understand ourselves as men, women or another gender; and our sexual orientation, that is the activities or persons to whom we find ourselves sexually attracted.

Sex, gender and sexuality revisited

Christian theologians have often assumed that, in psychologically healthy people, these three aspects of sex, gender and sexuality must fit together in particular configurations. For example, many Christians object to homosexuality, because they believe that God's divine plan is for males to be attracted to females, not to other males. In this account, gender and sexuality must 'fit' with biological sex. Christian theologians have often asserted that sex, gender and sexuality must 'match' in healthy individuals. If we represented their ideal of healthy sex, gender and sexuality in a diagram, it might look like Figure 1.

Figure 1: Heterosexual male and heterosexual female

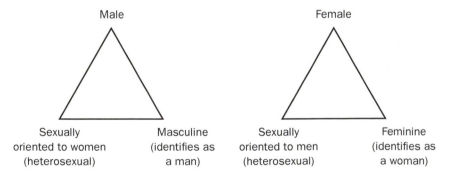

However, these triangles don't in fact represent everyone's experience. It's not the case that all biological males identify as men and are sexually attracted to women. Where any one of these – sex, gender or sexuality – differs from the 'norm', we need to construct an alternative set of triangles to represent the alternative configuration.

Where someone is male and identifies as a man, but is attracted to males rather than females, his sexual orientation varies, and he is termed homosexual or gay. Where someone is female and identifies as a woman, but is attracted to females rather than males, her sexual orientation varies, and she is termed homosexual, gay or lesbian (Figure 2).

Figure. 2: Non-heterosexual male and non-heterosexual female

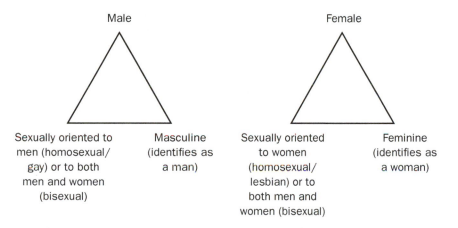

Male		Female	
Sexually oriented to men (homosexual/ gay) or to both men and women (bisexual)	Masculine (identifies as a man)	Sexually oriented to women (homosexual/ lesbian) or to both men and women (bisexual)	Feminine (identifies as a woman)

Where someone is male but identifies as a woman rather than a man, she is termed transgender (and she might identify heterosexually, attracted to men, homosexually, attracted to women, or bisexually, attracted to both). Where someone is female but identifies as a man rather than a woman, he is termed transgender (and he might identify heterosexually, attracted to women, homosexually, attracted to men, or bisexually, attracted to both) (Figure 3).

Where someone has a physical difference which means their body can't be clearly categorized as solely male or female, they are termed intersex (Figure 4). Intersex people might identify as men, women or another gender. They might be heterosexual, homosexual or bisexual.

Figure 3: Transgender male and transgender female

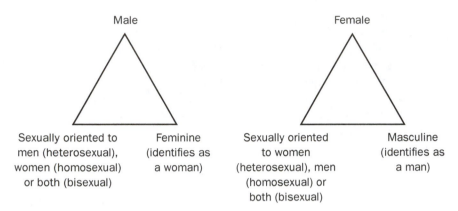

Male

Female

Sexually oriented to men (heterosexual), women (homosexual) or both (bisexual)

Feminine (identifies as a woman)

Sexually oriented to women (heterosexual), men (homosexual) or both (bisexual)

Masculine (identifies as a man)

Figure 4: Intersex person

Intersex (biological characteristics of both male and female, or in between male and female)

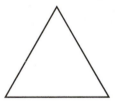

Sexually oriented to men, women or both; may be heterosexual, homosexual or bisexual depending on gender identity

Masculine (identifies as a man), feminine (identifies as a woman) or other (identifies as intersex, 'third', or both masculine and feminine)

Christian theologians have sometimes argued that any variation from the first set of triangles in Fig. 1 represents something which has gone wrong and falls short of the ideal. For example, the Evangelical Alliance's document *Transsexuality* (Evangelical Alliance 2000) insists that transgender is a form of psychological disturbance: since, as they understand it, God intends people's gender to 'match' their sex, if someone believes they were born as the wrong sex, this can't be part of how God intended things to be but is evidence of sin and disruption in the world and God's good order.

Gender relations and the New Testament

Many Christian theologians believe that God created human males and females with distinct roles and responsibilities, which map onto their sexes and gender roles (see for example Piper and Grudem 2006; Köstenburger and Jones 2010). As a result, they believe, human sexual activity should take place only in specific gender combinations: men with women rather than women with women or men with men. This is held to be part of the broader divine plan for the way in which men and women should interact. As evidence, they point particularly to the Genesis creation accounts and to passages in the New Testament which set out the way that men and women should relate to one another in marriage and the family, in church leadership and in the broader community.

The majority of these New Testament teachings are found in the disputed Pauline letters – that is, letters which purport to be written by Paul, but which many scholars believe were probably written by a later member of Paul's community rather than by Paul himself (Horrell 2006, pp. 6–7, 125–32; Dunn 1996, pp. 269–70; MacDonald 2008, pp. 6–8).[1] There seems to be a shift from the extreme equality found in Paul's earlier letters to a more gender-hierarchical, socially conservative pattern in the disputed letters. For example, Galatians 3, which almost all scholars agree was written by Paul himself, says,

> In Christ Jesus you are all children of God through faith. As many of you as were baptized into Christ have clothed yourselves with Christ. There is no longer Jew or Greek, there is no longer slave or free, there is no longer male and female; for all of you are one in Christ Jesus. (Gal. 3.26–8)

This has often been interpreted as a radical passage which seems to suggest that old social divisions have ceased to matter in the same way in light of the new community of equality in Christ. However, by the time of the later letter to the Colossians, the message appears softer and less counter-cultural:

> Wives, be subject to your husbands, as is fitting in the Lord. Husbands, love your wives and never treat them harshly. Children, obey your parents in everything, for this is your acceptable duty in the Lord. Fathers, do not provoke your children, or they may lose heart. Slaves, obey your earthly masters in everything, not only while being watched and in order to please them, but wholeheartedly, fearing the Lord. Whatever your task, put yourselves into it, as done for the Lord and not for your masters. (Col. 3.18–23)

---

1 Horrell, MacDonald and many other scholars have pointed out that, at the time the texts were produced, to write under someone else's name would not have been considered plagiarism or forgery, but rather a way of honouring a respected teacher (Horrell 2006, pp. 130–1; MacDonald 2008, p. 8).

While this is in some respects still a deeply revolutionary teaching – since the idea that women and children deserve as much respect as men would have been a radical one – it no longer carries the sense that gender and social divisions have somehow stopped existing. Colossians implies that there still are slaves and masters, and that it is possible to be a good Christian slave or a good Christian master; Galatians had seemed to imply that Christians should no longer recognize these distinctions at all.

In Ephesians 5—6, these social differences are not only acknowledged as existing, but are given cosmic, theological resonance. Slaves are now told that they should obey their masters 'as you obey Christ', and their masters are reminded that they, too, have a Master in heaven. Wives are told,

> Be subject to your husbands as you are to the Lord. For the husband is the head of the wife just as Christ is the head of the church, the body of which he is the Saviour. Just as the church is subject to Christ, so also wives ought to be, in everything, to their husbands. (Eph. 5.22–4)

Again, the message is more radical than it might sound to modern readers: husbands are to love their wives as Christ loves the Church, a move away from a social-cultural norm in which men have absolute control over the women, children and slaves in their households and can treat them however they please. Nonetheless, the Ephesians teaching still seems less counter-cultural than Galatians' message that, in Christ, distinctions of race, gender and class no longer exist at all.

Other New Testament books give even more detailed teachings about gender roles. The Pastoral Epistles (1 and 2 Timothy and Titus) purport to have been written by Paul, but many scholars believe they were probably written later, partly because their socially conservative message seems at odds with Paul's early letters, and partly because their vocabulary, style of writing and choice of subject-matter seem very different from Paul's earlier writings. (For detailed discussions about the authorship of the Pastoral Epistles, see for example Marshall 1999, pp. 57–80; Towner 2006, pp. 9–26; Montague 2008, pp. 15–26). The Pastoral Letters say,

> Let a woman learn in silence with full submission. I permit no woman to teach or to have authority over a man; she is to keep silent. For Adam was formed first, then Eve; and Adam was not deceived, but the woman was deceived and became a transgressor. Yet she will be saved through childbearing, provided they continue in faith and love and holiness, with modesty. (1 Tim. 2.11–15)

> Tell the older women to be reverent in behaviour, not to be slanderers or slaves to drink; they are to teach what is good, so that they may encourage the young women to love their husbands, to love their children, to be self-controlled, chaste, good managers of the household, kind, being sub-

missive to their husbands, so that the word of God may not be discredited ... Tell slaves to be submissive to their masters and to give satisfaction in every respect; they are not to answer back, not to pilfer, but to show complete and perfect fidelity, so that in everything they may be an ornament to the doctrine of God our Saviour. (Titus 2.3–5, 9–10)

Some Christians believe that the texts were probably not written by Paul but that, since they are in the Bible in any case, they still represent God's word and should be taken seriously. Apparent differences between the earlier and later teaching might be explained by, for example, the suggestion that Paul expected Jesus to return very soon and so did not feel the need to endorse existing social norms, whereas by the time of the later letters, there was less expectation that Jesus would return imminently and so the Christian communities were having to navigate how they should continue to live in the world. Biblical interpreters continue to debate the significance of the women mentioned in Romans 16 who do seem to take active roles in church leadership (such as Phoebe and Prisca) and whom Paul describes as fellow-apostles (such as Junia). Other apparent New Testament mentions of female leaders in the early Church appear in Acts 16.40, Acts 18.26, 1 Corinthians 1.11, and Colossians 4.15.

As with debates surrounding homosexuality, the disagreements surrounding passages about gender relations in the New Testament raise broader questions about the nature of biblical interpretation. Whether or not they were written by Paul, are the teachings in the New Testament representative of God's plan for how men and women should relate to each other across all time, or are they specific to the time and culture in which they were written? Must Christians today still base their lives on these texts, or are they free to look for broader principles about human relationships in the Bible and elsewhere in the Christian tradition?

Feminist theological responses

Some feminist theologians in particular believe that the hierarchical, strongly gendered message of Ephesians, Colossians and the Pastoral Epistles represents a distortion of what they consider the truer teaching of texts like Galatians. For example, Susan Brooks Thistlethwaite notes that Colossians 3.11 seems to present a more limited vision of equality in Christ than Galatians 3.28 does, since women are not mentioned at all in the groups who are now 'in Christ'. She argues that the more hierarchical, conservative vision of Colossians and Ephesians 'developed in response to social criticism of the newfound freedom of Christians' (1985, p. 105).

Rosemary Radford Ruether argues that Jesus' giving-up of male and other privilege, which is endorsed in the early Pauline texts, is a powerful example for Christians, but that its radical quality is lost because of Christianity's subsequent alliance with sexist and hierarchical social norms in the Roman Empire and beyond. Ruether considers that this distortion affects Christian interpretations of both Hebrew Bible and New Testament texts, noting that the hierarchical teaching on gender by theologians like Thomas Aquinas (a thirteenth-century philosopher and theologian) is exacerbated by their integration of beliefs about human biology prevalent at the time. For example, she notes, Aquinas' biology meshed with the dominant worldview of his time, based on the writings of the ancient Greek philosopher Aristotle, namely that there was only one sex and that females were 'lesser' or 'imperfect' versions of males (1983, pp. 96). Aquinas therefore concluded that God had *intended* women to be lesser and inferior, and that this was their divinely ordained place. What Ruether points out is that, although we no longer accept Aristotle's biology, Aquinas' theological anthropology has hung on more stubbornly, and continues to influence Roman Catholic and other teaching on gender to this day.

Evangelical responses

Indeed, many theological beliefs about human sex and gender are grounded in the belief that there is an ontological difference between males and females – a difference in their very being and existence, and one which is cosmically significant. For example, argues the evangelical theologian John Piper, 'The Bible reveals the nature of masculinity and femininity by describing diverse responsibilities for man and women while rooting these differing responsibilities in creation, not convention ... Differentiated roles were corrupted, not created, by the fall. They were created by God' (2006, p. 35). In similar vein, Andreas J. Köstenberger and David W. Jones say,

> The man and the woman are jointly charged with ruling the earth representatively for God, yet they are not to do so androgynously or as 'unisex' creatures, but each as fulfilling their God-ordained, gender-specific roles. Indeed ... it is only when men and women embrace their God-ordained roles that they will be truly fulfilled and that God's creational wisdom will be fully displayed and exalted. (2010, p. 26)

Even more explicitly, Dennis P. Hollinger asserts, 'Being male and female is less a designation of functions, and more a designation of humanity's two-fold ontological way of being' (2009, p. 74). As a second step, such anthropologies assume that it's always possible to know who's male and who's female (which, as we'll discuss below, may not always be the case), and that gender should always 'match' sex. This can be seen in documents like the Evangelical Alliance's report on transsexuality, which says, 'The doctrine of creation with the story of Adam and Eve, and the insistence that "male and female he created them", shows that our sexual identity is part of the "givenness" of how we have been made' (Evangelical Alliance 2000, p. 48). In other words, someone who identifies as a man must always be physically male, and someone who identifies as a woman must always be physically female. In this account, everyone is really, in truth, either male or female, and if there is any ambiguity about this, it's simply because something is obscuring this genuine, basic fact about a given individual.

Gender complementarity

Related to the 'God-givenness' argument is the argument from complementarity. The word 'complementarity' often comes up in theological discussions of human sex and gender. It implies that human maleness and femaleness, masculinity and femininity, complement each other and that human experience would be less rich and less full without both.

In contrast to the egalitarian view, in which people are believed to have been created equal regardless of their sex or gender and to have no particular necessary roles based on sex or gender, the complementarian view states that although males and females are both created in God's image, they have different roles or functions, designated by God. According to complementarians, the different roles for males and females are ordained by God from the beginning of human history.

Some female theologians have embraced the idea of complementarity, since it gives space for femaleness and femininity to be understood as positive and valuable in their own right, not just failed or inferior versions of maleness. Some theologians argue that masculinity and femininity *both* reflect aspects of God, and that to deny the real differences between men and women (as they believe egalitarians do) would be to deny the beauty of the diversity of humanity. In this account, men are not 'better' than women: it's simply that men and women have been created to fulfil different functions. Leadership and governance in families and churches are understood as characteristically masculine qualities; servanthood and submission are characteristically feminine ones.

Complementarian views are particularly common among Roman Catholic and conservative evangelical Christians. However, they also occur elsewhere. Karl Barth (1886–1968), the Swiss Reformed theologian, gave particular theological significance to gender complementarity, since he believed that it reflected God's relationship to humanity. Barth argued that the structure of procession of humans as male and female mirrors the structure of authority from God to Christ to the Church (1961, pp. 116–18, 148–72). More recently, liberal evangelicals have asked whether there might be gender complementarity without hierarchy built in (Pierce and Groothuis 2004).

However, many theologians criticize complementarity on the grounds that it portrays difference and variation in a rather stereotypical way. Is it really true, they ask, that there are things all women have in common which make them different from all men, or does variety happen in a more complex way than that (Farley 2006, pp. 156–7)? Others note that complementarity *appears* to give equal status to men and women but actually reinforces the non-mutual status of the genders: women help, complement and serve men, and respond only to male initiative. Another criticism is that complementarity tends to idealize qualities in each gender which might be considered to perpetuate imperfect human social norms rather than divine ones. For example, gentleness might be considered a particularly 'feminine' quality and courage a particularly 'masculine' one, whereas human individuals and communities might be richer if both gentleness and courage were nurtured in everyone, no matter what their gender. Complementarity risks overwriting permanent theological goods on shifting social norms: Zoë Bennett Moore describes the complementarity idea as 'a pernicious way of thinking' which 'gives religious legitimation' to the social inequalities of men and women (2002, p. 37).

Complementarity also seems to have built into it a sense of lack, an idea that each gender provides for the other something that is missing. Again, this can be interpreted positively: neither gender is self-sufficient, but each brings something valuable and distinct to the picture of what it is to be human. However, the idea of lack can also be understood negatively, particularly if one gender is perceived to be more lacking – or at least more lacking in particular, valued attributes – than the other (Farley 2006, p. 157).

Above Rubies is an evangelical Christian magazine designed to encourage women 'in their high calling as wives, mothers and homemakers'. Its title is taken from Proverbs 31.10, which states that the price of a virtuous woman is above that of rubies. The magazine features articles written by women about their experiences as wives and mothers. The majority of these demonstrate strongly complementarian convictions, to the extent that they border on caricaturing both men and women. For example, addressing other women, one *Above Rubies* author writes,

> Women see the world through the rainbow spectrum of a thousand shades and hues ... a man sees black-and-white. Either a thing is or it isn't. He doesn't analyze how he feels about it. He just knows the facts. For example, when a female friend tells you that she is sick, you do not simply process the fact 'my friend is sick', you feel for her emotionally. You might say something like, 'Poor thing! How are you getting all your house work [*sic*] done?' We instantly relate to another woman's emotional needs, because they are probably very similar to our own. Now just imagine that a male friend told your husband that he was sick (which would be very unlikely, but let's imagine!) Your husband's response would probably be something like, 'Oh. So, who won the foot-ball [*sic*] game last week?' ... When a man attempts to relate to his wife, a highly emotional and

very intimate creature, it is like learning to speak in a foreign language. Things can quickly escalate on a down-ward spiral if the couple has not learned to realize and appreciate their God-given differences. (Howard 2008, pp. 14–15)

Here, women are characterized as inherently empathetic and caring, and men as inherently unemotional. These traits are characterized as 'God-given differences'. All of this is based on an essentialist caricature of what men are and what women are. This does a gross disservice to men and women, let alone all those who don't feel they fit into either binary category. In this account, a man barely has any choice but to be emotionally shallow and unanalytical, for to be otherwise would not be 'manly'. Character traits are pinned on sex. Emotional needs are divided only along gendered lines: the needs of two women will be inherently similar, but a man could not understand them.

This is an extreme form of complementarity, but milder versions underlie much Christian objection to homosexuality, bisexuality and gender transition. But what if the whole idea that humans come in only two kinds, male and female, masculine and feminine, is less certain than we often assume?

Transgender

What is transgender?

Transgender people feel that their gender identity, or sense of being a gendered self, doesn't 'fit' their biological sex according to the usual pattern. While most people who are biologically female identify as women, transgender men are biologically female but identify as men. Some transgender people describe this feeling as having been 'born in the wrong body'. Transgender refers to a whole category of people who have some kind of disjunction between their sex and their gender identity; transsexualism refers more specifically to people who have had surgery or hormone therapy in order to make their bodies 'fit' their gender identities. This might include surgery to remove their breasts, and testosterone treatments to deepen their voices and stimulate the growth of facial and body hair, or surgery to remove their penises, breast enhancement, and hormone therapy to suppress hair growth and raise their voices. Not all people who transition gender also have surgery to alter their bodies, and some people have 'top' surgery (to remove or enlarge their breasts) but never have 'bottom' surgery (to alter their genitals), partly because chest appearance affects many social encounters, whereas genital appearance and function is easier to keep hidden in everyday life.

It's not clear what causes transgender. Some scientists believe that there is an innate biological difference between the brains of transgender and non-transgender (sometimes called **cisgender**) people. Some believe transgender people have a variant gene. Others believe transgender may be caused by foetal exposure to unusual levels of hormones during pregnancy. Still others believe that there's no biological basis for transgender and that it arises for other reasons, such as psychological trauma or particular dynamics within families.

ACTIVITY

Which of the Christian understandings of human sex you have read about so far could be of relevance in constructing a theological account of transgender? Why might some Christians endorse gender transition on theological grounds? Why might some Christians oppose it?

Theological responses to transgender

Some theologians, including the authors of the Evangelical Alliance's documents on transgender, assert that there is no biological basis for transgender and, as a result, that it's not a 'real' phenomenon. These authors believe that transgender represents a psychological disturbance. The Evangelical Alliance therefore calls transgender 'a state of mind ... rather than any concrete set of facts' (Evangelical Alliance 2000, p. 38). The psychological phenomenon of feeling a disjunction between sex and gender is considered less significant or primary than the biological phenomenon of sex itself, which is considered irreducible and inescapable. People who find their gender identity at odds with their bodies are 'fundamentally mistaken given the biblical assertion of the priority of the physical' (Evangelical Alliance 2000, pp. 48–9). Not admitting that gender rests in biological sex is, therefore, alienation from the truth about yourself (Evangelical Alliance 2000, p. 63).

A similar argument arises in the Church of England's teaching on transgender. Transgender people should, it's said, be helped to accept the 'truth' of their biological sex, since this is God-given and should therefore not be changed. The Church of England's *Some Issues in Human Sexuality* (House of Bishops 2003), which dedicates a whole chapter to transgender, draws on work by Oliver O'Donovan, who argues that 'To know oneself as body is to know that there are only certain things that one can do and be, because one's freedom must be responsible to a given form, which is the form of one's own experience in the material world' (1982, p. 15). In other words, our choices about our gender expressions are limited by the sexed bodies in which we find ourselves. Sex and gender must match, but if there's an apparent mismatch, sex must be considered more primary and gender must fit around it. There is a strong emphasis on male and female as being the human types created by God, so that individuals shouldn't seek to change or escape from their sex–gender configuration as given by God: which, it's assumed, will be a cisgender configuration. There are some things about being a human which are too fundamental to change, argues O'Donovan: our sexed bodies are one of them.

However, Fraser Watts counters,

> It is clear that not all aspects of our nature are a given that must simply be accepted. Most Christians would raise no objection to operations that corrected minor physical deformities ... It is also clear that Christians do not accept their personalities as a given that they should simply accept. (2002, p. 75)

In other words, implies Watts, as humans we can and do alter elements of our physical and emotional being. Sex and gender might similarly be aspects of ourselves which we can alter if they present obstacles to our well-being (as many transgender people claim).

Sexual orientation also comes into play here. Some Christian theologians object to gender transition because it leads to 'homosexual' relations. These theologians hold that a transgender woman is still 'really' male, so if she has a sexual relationship with another biological male, this relationship will be homosexual and therefore illegitimate. In fact, argue the Evangelical Alliance writers, not only would a marriage involving a transgender person be 'a deceptive representation of an apparent heterosexual relationship', it would also be 'more subtle and devious than an overt homosexual relationship' (Evangelical Alliance 2000, p. 50), because it may not be evident that it is indeed homosexual.

Other theologians have rejected this kind of analysis, and have argued that transgender represents a non-pathological form of gender variation. A few even argue that the **eunuchs** mentioned in the Bible might be understood as forerunners of today's transgender people. Eunuchs at the time of the Bible often held senior positions as servants or stewards within households, and it's believed that many people in this position had either been born with unusual genitalia or had had surgery to remove parts of their genitalia. Castrated men were considered to make particularly trustworthy servants, since they couldn't impregnate their masters' wives. Victoria Kolakowski, a transgender theologian, argues that, since the Bible doesn't condemn eunuchs, Christians today should also show compassion to transgender people. The Ethiopian eunuch in Acts 8, for instance, is baptized into the Christian community with no special mention made of, or significance attached to, his genitals (1997, p. 24). In Matthew 19, Jesus describes several different categories of people: those who've been born eunuchs, those who've been made eunuchs by others, and those who've made themselves eunuchs for the sake of the Kingdom of Heaven. Some commentators suggest that present-day transgender and intersex people might fall into these categories, and that since Jesus accepts them, Christians should do likewise (Kolakowski 1997; Tanis 2003, p. 79; Hester 2005; DeFranza 2011, pp. 126–7).

Furthermore, Virginia Ramey Mollenkott argues that transgender people have special lessons to teach religious congregations. These include reminding them of the diversity in human beings and in God; helping them make connections between gender, spirituality and justice; and, by occupying an ambiguous space, helping 'to heal religious addictions to certainty' (2009, p. 47). Lewis Reay suggests that much so-called 'inclusive' theology 'fails in [its] task, for just replacing "he" with "she" and "mother" for "father" does not create the radical project that Jesus had in mind with his sayings about eunuchs' (2009, p. 165). Reay believes it is transgender people who can call into question the binary construction of gender, and that the contested middle ground they inhabit is 'God's territory' (p. 165). Justin Tanis believes gender should be understood as a calling, God's call to transgender people to be who they really are, and notes that spiritual callings are ongoing revelations which might last for a period of time or a whole lifetime (2003, p. 168).

Some theological responses to transgender, notably that of the Church of England bishops in *Some Issues in Human Sexuality*, have been criticized. Christina Beardsley argues that the report drew too much on Scripture and tradition to the exclusion of human experience (2005, p. 339), especially the experience of transgender people (p. 342). Beardsley identifies an over-emphasis on passages such as Genesis 1.26–7, and a lack of acknowledgement that what the biblical writers understood by 'male' and 'female' may not be identical with what we mean today (p. 343). Beardsley also suggests the report took too little account of the fact that there is disagreement among scientists about whether transgender has a biological basis (2005, p. 339). The assumption by some theologians that transgender always results from a psychological disturbance is also criticized (Cornwall 2010, pp. 112–4, 125).

Intersex

As we've seen, some theologians and others argue that transgender is fundamentally a psychological phenomenon, some kind of disturbance which means that people can't recognize their sexed bodies as being really themselves. Transgender people are therefore best helped, in this account, by being encouraged to make peace with their bodies and live in the gender which 'matches' their sex as ordained by God.

However, it's much more difficult to explain away the ambiguities of intersex bodies. People with intersex conditions have a difference in their actual biological sex which means they can't easily be categorized as male or female.

What is intersex?

Most foetuses develop along clear male or female lines. We would usually expect XY foetuses to develop testes, a penis and scrotum, and XX foetuses to develop ovaries, a clitoris and vulva. However, people with intersex conditions often have unusual combinations of these features. For example, people with Androgen Insensitivity Syndrome have the XY chromosomes and testes usually associated with males, but the clitorises and vulvas usually associated with females. At puberty, people with AIS grow breasts and hips and look unremarkably feminine, although they don't start to have periods, because they have no ovaries or uteruses. Almost all people with AIS identify as women despite their XY chromosomes and testes.

Some other people with intersex conditions don't simply have a 'mismatch' between their internal and external sexual features, but actually have unusual, liminal features. For instance, many intersex people have 'ambiguous' genitalia which look somewhere in between what we would expect male and female genitalia to look like. It's also possible to have one testis and one ovary or a combined organ called an ovotestis.

Although intersex conditions are much less common than typical maleness and femaleness, they still affect about one in every 2,500 people (Preves 2003, pp. 2–3) – a similar frequency to a condition like cystic fibrosis. You might be surprised by how relatively common intersex conditions are. Until recently, families whose children were born with intersex conditions were encouraged to keep their conditions secret, and many children with unusual genitalia had surgery to alter them and make them look more like typical male or female genitalia. Many people argued that this was the best thing for intersex children, so that they would be able to grow up as 'normal' boys or girls. However, others, including some intersex people themselves, argued that the secrecy and corrective surgery had caused them even more problems, including, for many people, an inability to enjoy sex when they grew up, because their genitals were so scarred, and some had had their penises or clitorises removed altogether. (For more detailed information about how intersex has been treated, see Dreger 1999, Preves 2003, and Karkazis 2008.)

ACTIVITY

Think about the characteristics which define what makes someone male or female. Could you rank them in order of significance? Is there one single characteristic which is more important than all the others? Why or why not? Which do you think is held to be most important by doctors, by theologians and by society at large?

People who are learning about intersex for the first time sometimes ask, 'But what sex is a person with an intersex condition *really*?' This question implies that sex is a real thing, which can always, eventually, be discovered, even if it initially seems unclear. However, the history of the treatment of intersex conditions shows that the definition of what makes someone male or female is less evident than most of us imagine. This is discussed in detail in Dreger 1998 and Reis 2009. At different times, the accepted marker of 'real' sex has been:

- external genital appearance: whether someone's genitals look more male or more female (though some genitals don't look clearly either male or female);
- gonads: whether someone has testes or ovaries (though it's also possible to have one of each, or a combined ovotestis);
- chromosomes: whether someone has XX or XY chromosomes (though it's also possible to have other configurations, such as XXY chromosomes, or some cells with XX and some with XY chromosomes in the same body);
- gametes: whether someone produces eggs or sperm (though some people produce neither);
- gender identity: whether someone feels more like a man or more like a woman (though some people feel 'in between', or feel unlike either gender, or feel more masculine and more feminine at different times);
- hormones: whether someone produces more androgens ('male' hormones) or oestrogens ('female' hormones) (though everyone produces both 'male' and 'female' hormones in differing levels).

Since it's possible to have different combinations of these characteristics, and since it's not clear that any one characteristic 'trumps' the others, doctors who are making decisions about whether it's best for an intersex child to be brought up as a boy or a girl usually try to look at the big picture. Crucially, however, as P.-L. Chau and Jonathan Herring note,

> It is not possible to classify everyone as clearly male or female. It is not that it is hard to find out whether an intersexual person is male or female, but rather that even knowing everything there is to know about them, they do not fall into the accepted description of male or female. (2002, p. 332)

For theologians, questions about what constitutes 'real' sex are even more significant, since if gender assignment for some people is a matter of guesswork and making a best attempt to discern which gender will suit someone best, this raises questions about how clear and unquestionable sex and gender are in the first place, and therefore how legitimate it is to build theological teachings on them.

Theological implications of intersex

Many Christian theologies of sexuality assume and assert that God created and intended all humans to be clearly either male or female, and to have genders and sexualities which 'match' their sexes. However, it might be much more difficult to assert what the 'correct' gender and sexual orientation for an intersex person is. For example, think again about Androgen Insensitivity Syndrome. People with AIS have a combination of features normally associated with males and females. Marriage is understood by many Christians as something which can only take place between a male and a female, but should people with AIS be considered male or female for this purpose? A marriage between a woman with AIS and a man (which is fairly common, given that people with AIS overwhelmingly identify as women) might be considered by some theologians to be illegitimate, since it's a marriage between two people who both have XY chromosomes and are in some sense both male. However, a marriage between a woman with AIS and another woman might also be considered illegitimate, since this would be a marriage between two people who both behave and identify as women. Theologians who object to relationships between couples of the same sex might therefore need to think carefully about what they actually mean by 'the same sex'.

Some Christian theologians (such as Oliver O'Donovan and Rodney Holder) argue that it's appropriate to assign someone a masculine or feminine gender even when their biological sex is unclear, as in the case of intersex people. These theologians believe that God intended everyone to live clearly as a man or a woman, and that this is the case even for people with ambiguous sex. But this in turn raises questions about where the belief that God intended binary gender comes from. If binary gender is grounded in binary sex, what's the rationale for arguing that even people who do *not* have a clear binary sex must also have a clear binary gender? O'Donovan (1982), Holder (1998a, 1998b) and others might argue that this is simply part of the 'order of creation'. However, this suggests that intersex people have failed to live up to the goodness of the rest of creation – that they have, in some way, 'gone wrong'.

Some theologians do, indeed, make exactly this type of argument. Dennis P. Hollinger, the evangelical theologian, says,

> From a theological standpoint we can understand these conditions as results of the fallen condition of our world, including the natural world … We should also understand that such natural sexual conditions and anomalies in no way undermine the creational norms. All distortions in the world are to be judged against the divine creational givens. In a fallen world there will be chaos and confusion that extends even to human sexuality. But the normative structure toward which God calls humanity

is not the fallenness of nature; it is, rather, God's created designs. (2009, p. 84)

However, it might be countered that this stigmatizes intersex bodies, rendering them 'fallen' in a way that other, male and female bodies are not.

Some Christians with intersex conditions have felt excluded from communities of faith because of their conditions. Sally Gross, who used to be a Roman Catholic priest (only taking the name 'Sally' after leaving the priesthood), found that when she tried to be open about her intersex condition, she was denied communion in the Roman Catholic Church. She was also told by other Christians that, because she wasn't clearly male or female, she wasn't fully human, and therefore 'not the kind of thing which could have been baptized validly' (Gross 1999, p. 70). However, Gross counters, 'I am a creature of God, and … I'm created, and intersexed people are created, no less than anyone else, in the image and likeness of God' (speaking in Van Huyssteen 2003).

Indeed, other theologians have contended that intersex is positive and valuable in its own right, and reflects part of the difference and diversity in God. To insist on corrective surgery for all intersex people, or to insist that all intersex people must live as men or women even if they feel that they have another or 'third' gender, is, in this account, to fail to recognize the goodness of intersex. Heather Looy suggests, 'We should at least ask whether intersexuality could be part of God's good creation' (2002, p. 16), and Mollenkott adds, 'God made no mistake by creating intersexuals. Therefore, their condition represents God's perfect will for them' (2007, p. 7). In fact, Mollenkott suggests that if, as some scholars argue, the first Genesis creation story points to human beings who weren't initially distinguished by sex or gender, 'intersexuals are not only part of God's original plan, they are *primarily* so!' (p. 98) and might be 'viewed as reminders of Original Perfection' (p. 99). Patricia Beattie Jung (2006) argues that the fact that Genesis says male and female are made in the image of God doesn't mean that *only* males and females are made in the image of God, or that this is the only legitimate way to be. She says,

> When the church finally recognizes that intersexed, like male and female, persons have been made in the image and likeness of God, then perhaps Christians will come closer to recognizing that God is not male, female, or intersexed but rather truly beyond human sexual differentiation. (p. 307)

Jung's point is important, because theologians have often insisted that sex and gender tell us not only what it means to be human in relation to other humans, but also what it means to be a human in relation to God. For example, famously, the Swiss theologian Karl Barth argued that the way human females were to 'follow' and 'respond to' human males echoed the way that all humans were to follow and respond to God. To deny the order and procession built into human sex and gender, Barth believed, would be to deny the broader divine order. The problem with this, as critics have noted, is that it assumes that a hierarchy of genders simply is natural and indisputable, rather than being a social construction which presents its own problems and might (as Ruether and others have noted) actually prevent women, and people with unusual sex–gender configurations, from developing relationships with God in their own right. (For further discussion of some problems with Barth's theology of gender, see for example Muers 1999; Sonderegger 2000; Blevins 2005.)

QUESTION BOX

1 What difference might it make to theologies of sex, gender and sexuality if more theologians engaged with the existence of intersex conditions?
2 Should theologians take the experiences of intersex and transgender people into account when constructing broader arguments about the theological significance of sex, gender and sexuality? Why or why not?

Summary

In this book, I've been working with the assumption that sex and gender aren't the same thing (see Chapter 1), but that sex refers to biology while gender refers to identity. This definition of sex and gender works to an extent and is helpful for making clear that, for example, not everyone who's biologically male identifies as a man.

Even so, there are ways in which making such a strong distinction between sex and gender causes problems. It might tend to reinforce the idea that biological sex is always clear, obvious, and irreducible – whereas in fact, as we've seen in this chapter, biological sex isn't always clear or obvious at all. Thomas Laqueur, a scholar who's studied the way bodies and sexes have been understood through history, makes the surprising assertion that thinking of human beings as falling into two sexes, male and female, is quite a recent idea. To those of us living here and now in the West, it seems obvious and self-evident that there are two and only two sexes. However, he argues, for a lot of human history, it seemed self-evident and obvious to people that there was only *one* human sex. Males represented a more perfect version of this single sex, and females a less perfect version. Laqueur believes that when we look at human beings now, we see two sexes because that's what we expect to see, what we've been trained to see, and what largely fits into our current scientific and cultural model. Perhaps one of the reasons why it's been so 'obvious' to us for the last 250 years or so that there are two sexes is that we'd *already* developed an idea that there were two distinct genders (Laqueur 1990).

The assumption that sex and gender are clear, binary, fixed and unchanging underlies much theological teaching on human sexuality. However, transgender and intersex show that sex and gender aren't always as straightforward as they seem. Sex and gender don't always 'match' in the typical ways; even at a biological level, maleness and femaleness aren't the only possibilities for human bodies. Theologians interested in human sexuality must therefore think carefully about what transgender and intersex imply. Should transgender and intersex be understood as anomalies, which don't fundamentally disrupt the model of two distinct and separate human genders which map onto two distinct and separate human sexes as intended by God as part of the orders of creation? Or, alternatively, should the existence of transgender and intersex prompt theologians to re-examine their theological anthropologies, and ask whether theologies which assume a fixed, binary model of maleness and femaleness or masculinity and femininity continue to make sense in light of what we now know about human sex and gender? Theologies which assume everyone's clearly male or female can't easily accommodate hard cases. Some theologians argue that intersex and transgender aren't just exceptions to the rule, but actually mean that Christians should rethink their whole understanding of sex and gender (Cornwall 2010).

Transgender and intersex both pose particularly important questions when it comes to theological teachings about marriage. Transgender and intersex people might be homosexual or heterosexual, just like anyone else. However, it's not always obvious whether they should be considered male or female for the purposes of marriage. According to many Christians, and legally in many jurisdictions, marriage can happen only between a male and a female.

We began this chapter by noting that people can be understood as having three interrelated facets: sex, gender, and sexuality. We observed that Christian theologians have often endorsed only some combinations of these three facets as legitimate or good – and that variations from the norm, such as intersex, transgender and homosexuality, have sometimes been figured as imperfect or fallen.

We then examined New Testament passages on gender relations, noting disagreement between scholars about whether these passages were written by Paul, whether they should be considered normative for today, and whether they represent a central truth for Christianity or distract from Christianity's message of equality. We considered the notion of gender complementarity and saw that some critics have considered it a formalization of inequality.

Next, we asked whether unusual states such as intersex and transgender mean that ideas of gender complementarity in Christianity should be questioned and whether Christian theologies of sexuality which do not take account of the embodied experiences of intersex and transgender people are likely to be inadequate.

In recent years, doctors, social scientists and others have begun to suggest that the two-sex model of human sex isn't perfect, any more than the one-sex model was, because there are people whose bodies don't fit into it: most obviously, intersex people. The question for theologians and other Christians, then, is whether Christianity is also operating according to a 'two-sex' model of human sex, and, if so, to what extent this is justifiable. What does theological belief in a two-sex model – and, more importantly, the belief that God intended everyone to fit into the two-sex system – mean for intersex people, and for theologies of sex in general?

In Chapter 4, we'll move on to considering how sexuality plays out in the lives of people who are not physically sexually active, and how Christian theologians have understood celibacy and virginity within the tradition.

Questions for study and reflection

1 Theologically, does it matter whether someone identifies as masculine, feminine or neither? Does it matter whether their gender identity 'matches' their biological sex? Why?

2 Virginia Ramey Mollenkott argues, 'God made no mistake by creating intersexuals.' How might a Christian theologian agree or disagree with this statement?

Further reading

Althaus-Reid, Marcella and Lisa Isherwood (eds), 2009, *Trans/Formations, Controversies in Contextual Theology*, London: SCM Press.

Cornwall, Susannah, 2010, *Sex and Uncertainty in the Body of Christ: Intersex Conditions and Christian Theology*, London: Equinox.

Sytsma, Sharon E. (ed.), 2006, *Ethics and Intersex*, Dordrecht: Springer.

Tanis, Justin Edward, 2003, *Trans-Gendered: Theology, Ministry, and Communities of Faith*, Cleveland, OH: Pilgrim Press.

4

Celibacy and Virginity in Christianity

The community needs some who are called beyond or aside from the ordinary patterns of sexual relation to put their identities directly into the hands of God in the single life. This is not an alternative to the discovery of the body's grace. All those taking up the single vocation must know something about desiring and being desired if their single vocation is not to be sterile and evasive. (Williams 2002, p. 317)

Celibacy ... is not 'no sexuality', not a renunciation of being sexual ... – it is another way of being sexual, of being embodied. Celibate living that positively values sexuality finds that sexual attraction, warmth, and energy permeate all human relationships, all encounters with the 'other who is not one'. (Gray 1997, p. 151)

All human beings have a sexuality of some kind, whether or not they ever have a physically sexual relationship with another person. Although around 90 per cent of adults will be sexually active at some point in their lives, some have either never had a genital sexual relationship or have had a sexual relationship in the past but choose not to have sex again either for a limited time or permanently. In this chapter, we'll consider some of the ways in which virginity has been understood theologically and the broader interactions between celibacy and sexuality.

What is virginity?

The word 'virgin' doesn't have an uncontested definition. It usually refers to someone who has never had sexual intercourse. However, this assumes that sexual intercourse is always easy to classify and define. Studies of the virginity pledge movement in the USA suggest that some teenagers who promise to remain virgins until they get married still engage in sexual activity such as oral and anal sex, since they don't consider that these affect their 'real' virginity, which is only lost through penetrative vaginal sex (see, for example, Bearman and Brückner 2005; Bersamin et al. 2007; Rosenbaum 2009).[1] But is this the best definition of sexual intercourse? If sexual inter-

---

1 Some studies suggest that virginity pledgers are as likely to have had premarital sex

course always means penetrative sexual intercourse involving a penis and a vagina, do people who have never had a heterosexual relationship never lose their virginity, even if they have been genitally sexually intimate with people of the same sex? Can people who have unusual genital anatomy (maybe because of an intersex condition, or maybe because their genitals have been damaged in an accident) never lose their virginity? These questions make clear that, from the outset, virginity is not such a clear, yes-you-are-or-no-you-aren't state as we often assume.

In some cultures, virginity is considered to have been lost when a woman's hymen (the skin partially covering the vaginal opening) has been broken. Although the hymen can be broken through exercise, masturbation or using tampons as well as through penetrative sex, blood on the sheets after a wedding night is considered 'proof' that the hymen has been intact until that point. Adrian Thatcher comments, 'The hymen, on this view, was a sort of kitemark of virginal quality assurance' (1993, p. 85). In cultures where not being a virgin at marriage is considered shameful or undesirable, some women whose hymens have already been broken (either through sex or some other activity) undergo 'reconstructive' surgery, so they will bleed on their wedding nights.

This exclusive focus on the hymen might seem rather essentialist. It's obviously not a perfect marker of whether or not someone is a virgin (especially since it's possible to have had penetrative sex without the hymen breaking). It also focuses solely on the woman's body: there's no equivalent physical change which penetrative sex causes to a man's body. For this reason, many scholars, including Thatcher and L. William Countryman, have criticized it for its repetition of the idea that female bodies and female sexualities are reducible to property to be exchanged between men (Thatcher 1993, pp. 84–5; Countryman 1989, pp. 261–3): insisting that women are virgins at marriage ensures that no man will find himself in the position of unwittingly bringing up and providing for a child of whom he is not the biological father.

Celibacy and virginity in early Christianity

Biblical ambivalence

There are hints in the New Testament of an ascetic attitude toward sex, and Paul seems to assert that celibacy is a 'higher' state than marriage (1 Cor. 7.8–35). Many scholars have suggested that this was probably because Paul

---

five years after pledging than non-pledgers, and are less likely to use contraception when they do have sex (Thomas 2009, p. 63; cf. Rosenbaum 2009). Bearman and Brückner suggest that this is because 'sexually active pledgers have a greater incentive than nonpledgers to hide that they are having sex' (2005, p. 272) and note that this lack of contraceptive use increases the risk of contracting sexually transmitted infections.

believed Jesus would return very soon (1 Cor. 7.29) – sex and reproduction were therefore distractions from the more pressing business of preparing for his return. However, Paul's championing of celibacy would have sat oddly against both the Jewish tradition, in which offspring were considered a sign of God's blessing, and the contemporary Roman context in which low life expectancy meant that people were strongly encouraged to marry early and have lots of children in order to maintain adequate population levels (Brown 1988, pp. 6–7). In the Synoptic Gospels, Jesus responds to a question about marriage in the new creation by saying that there will be no marrying or giving in marriage in heaven. Luke adds that this is because, in the new creation, people will be like angels (Luke 20.34–6). William Loader comments,

> The implication is clear. If no one dies, then no one needs to be born. If no one needs to be born, then no one needs to have sex. The underlying assumption which Luke shares with many in his world is that the only purpose of sexual intercourse is begetting children. (2010, p. 100)

As we'll see in Chapter 5, the association between sex and procreation has remained very important for Christian theologians.

In the early centuries of the Christian era, Christians were also influenced by the Stoic tradition, making them keen to advocate asceticism and to show Christianity's compatibility with the best of Greco-Roman thought. Having sex simply because it felt good was deemed self-indulgent, focusing too much on the body rather than on 'higher' spiritual pleasures. Some early theologians took extreme views: Jerome (c.347–420), in the late fourth century, for example, believed that virginity was so blessed that it would be extremely difficult for even a married sexually active person to lead a properly Christian life (Dormor 2004, p. 21). However, Duncan Dormor notes that this extreme asceticism post-dates the biblical era. The Bible itself seems far more positive about sexuality and eroticism – the Song of Songs is often cited as an example of a book which endorses the positivity of human sexuality. While imprisoned in Tegel prison in Berlin in 1944, the German Lutheran theologian Dietrich Bonhoeffer (1906–45) wrote to his friend Eberhard Bethge, 'Even in the Bible we have the Song of Songs; and really one can imagine no more ardent, passionate, sensual love than is portrayed there. It's a good thing that the book is in the Bible, in face of all those who believe that the restraint of passion is Christian' (2001, p. 106).

Asceticism in the Church Fathers

Even so, in the first few centuries of the Church, ascetic virginity increasingly came to be affirmed, with some people entering orders of perpetual virginity, pledging to remain virgins and dedicate their lives to God. Augustine of Hippo (354–430) echoed Paul's belief that virginity was preferable to marriage (though he also noted in chapter 28 of his treatise *On the Good of Marriage* that it was better to be an obedient, faithful married person than a disobedient, unruly virgin). For some of the Church Fathers, such as Gregory of Nyssa (c.335–c.395), virginity echoed God's unchangingness and incorruptibility: 'Whereas marriage involved humans in an ongoing succession of births and deaths, Gregory argues, virginity enables us to by-pass that succession and associate ourselves with heavenly realities that do not perish' (Clark 1983, p. 118). Sexual intercourse meant a change from a virgin to a non-virgin state. God was believed to be perfect and unchanging (because any change in a being who was already perfect could only be a change for the worse), so it was thought that those who sought to be like God should value unchanging constancy too. Gregory also argued that the generation of new life could only lead to subsequent death:

> A virginal life should ... be preferred, at least by rational people, since it is stronger than the power of death. For physical procreation ... is more the occasion of death than of life for human beings. Corruption has its origin in generation; those who cease from procreation through virginity set a limit within themselves for death, preventing it from advancing further because of them. (Gregory of Nyssa, *On Virginity*, 14.1; quoted in Clark 1983, p. 121)

Other early Christian theologians held similar views. Tertullian (c.160–c.225) believed that virginity was a sign of the overcoming of sexual differentiation which would occur in the new creation (Brown 1988, p. 81), and, for Origen (c.185–c.254), this signified and anticipated a heavenly return to human souls' original unsexed states before they became 'trapped' in sexed bodies (p. 167). In short, sex and reproduction were linked strongly with physical life on earth, whereas to remain a virgin could be seen as anticipating heaven or the end times (Elliott 1993, p. 25).

Strongly ascetic exhortations of virginity sit slightly oddly next to Christian assertions about the goodness of incarnation, the body, and the created, material realm. Indeed, the Church Fathers were such keen advocates of virginity that some of them began to be accused of being heretics, particularly given the strong links between virginity and Gnosticism (Clark 1983, p. 126). Jerome tried to rebut these accusations by saying that he and his sympathizers didn't disparage sex and marriage as such, but merely believed virginity to be even better.[2] Jerome seems to have believed that virgins had

---

2 Part of his argument in favour of virginity rests on the fact that there is no danger of the population dying out (as some opponents of virginity suggested) in any case, because virginity is so difficult to stick to and most people are not up to the task: there will, he says, always be 'prostitutes' and 'adulterous women' whose activities produce 'squalling infants' (Jerome, *Against Jovinian* 1.36; quoted in Clark 1983, p. 129). In other words,

somehow transcended their maleness or femaleness. However, even Jerome rejected Origen's strong account of sex transcendence, and came to affirm that the sexed differences between men and women were good: Jesus, though celibate, had male body parts, a sign of his humanity. Even if they were not to be used for reproduction, sexual organs were to be part of humans' resurrection bodies; therefore, since the genitals were to exist without being used for reproduction in heaven, it was also right and appropriate for virgins' genitals to exist without being used for reproduction on earth too.

Augustine, who was almost contemporary with Jerome, had a much less negative view of sexual intercourse, even though he wished it could occur without feelings of lust. Lust, for Augustine, was a corrupt addition to sex and reproduction which had come about as a result of the Fall (prior to this, Augustine believed, although humans did have genitals, they were able to control and use them without lust, as they could do any other body part). However, this didn't mean that sex and reproduction themselves should be denigrated. Augustine asserted in *The City of God* that bodies in themselves were not bad; it was the corruption of bodies, via sin, that was the problem. Sexed bodies were needed in order to produce more humans to populate God's holy 'city'.

It is important to note that in his book *De Sancta Virginitate*, Augustine 'never argues that one should become a virgin because sexual difference is bad. Augustine never suggests, as some of his predecessors do, that sexual difference is not part of God's good creation and is something we should aspire to flee' (Roberts 2007, p. 51). Even so, Augustine was suspicious of sexuality's tendency to lust, and therefore advocated virginity as a good for both women and men. Unlike Origen, Jerome and others, Augustine was not persuaded that true spiritual freedom was possible on earth, because of 'the bondage of the will to sexual desire' (Brown 1988, p. 442).

Kathryn Wehr draws a comparison between accounts of virginity in John Chrysostom (c.347–407), Gregory of Nyssa and Ambrose of Milan (c.330–97), and accounts of virginity in contemporary evangelical Christian writers in the USA. She concludes,

> One of the most striking features of the Patristic vision is the unabashed preference for virginity over the married state. This can sound very foreign today in a culture that, though declining in number and length of marriages, is nonetheless still centred on coupling and sexuality. Within the Evangelical Church many feel on the defensive to support marriage while unmarried people often feel either shamed or ignored by those seeking to promote a traditional view of marriage ... The preference for virginity found in the works of Chrysostom, Gregory, and Ambrose ... catches today's readers off-guard. Evangelicals may not be brought

holy people do not need to bother themselves about the pragmatic, inconvenient business of keeping the species going: there are sinners to do that.

wholly over to the Patristic point of view, but it may help correct some of the distortions maintained on the other extreme. This in turn may help single people value their own state and find their place within their community, their church and even their own skin. (2011, pp. 97–8)

Asceticism and female sexuality

Many of the Church Fathers felt that virginity was positive for both men and women. Nonetheless, Muriel Porter notes that there was also a sense during this period that female sexuality was especially dangerous and an incitement to sin:

> Because women were believed to inflame men's passions against the male will, they were consistently required by the early Church fathers to refrain from all adornment, and to veil themselves in church. Because of the threat they posed, they were carefully segregated from men in worship, as they were in many other aspects of their lives. They were fully respected only if they remained virgins or at least renounced sexual activity after marriage; in other words, the only women fully accepted were women who denied their sexuality. (1996, p. 18)

This seems to stem from the notion, propounded by Augustine, Ambrose and Tertullian among others, that women were especially culpable for sin because it was Eve who had incited Adam to disobey God in the Garden of Eden. Addressing women, Tertullian says,

> God's judgment on this sex lives on in our age; the guilt necessarily lives on as well. *You* are the Devil's gateway; *you* are the unsealer of that tree; *you* are the first forsaker of the divine law; *you* are the one who persuaded him whom the Devil was not brave enough to approach; *you* so lightly crushed the image of God, the man Adam; because of *your* punishment, that is, death, even the Son of God had to die. (Tertullian, *On the Dress of Women* 1.1.2; quoted in Clark 1983, p. 39)

Porter notes that, in the early Church through to the medieval period, women also often engaged in extreme fasting, with both fasting and virginity signifying self-denial and self-sacrifice. This asceticism further asexualized them, since many women became so thin and undernourished that their periods stopped – a cessation of one of the most obvious manifestations of fertile female sexuality (1996, p. 21). Ascetic virginity was, therefore, she argues, hostile to women's sexuality in particular.

Nonetheless, others have suggested that both fasting and virginity might have several purposes considered positive by those who practised them, including women; for example:

- affirming that the needs of the spirit are more important than the needs of the body;
- focusing the mind or spirit on God, giving up the time when one might have been eating or having sex, in order to dedicate to prayer or meditation;
- being a means of self-discipline, using the practice of resisting physical desire as a way to rehearse resisting temptations to sin;
- affirming belief in heaven – since heavenly bodies may not have the same needs and desires as earthly bodies. The Bible says that there will be no marrying in heaven, so abstaining from sex on earth could be seen as a way of anticipating (and even helping to hasten) the heavenly order (Shaw 1997, p. 583). Summarizing Christian exhortations of virginity and asceticism up to the fourth century, Peter Brown notes,

> In Christian circles, concern with sexual renunciation had never been limited solely to an anxious striving to maximize control over the body. It had been connected with a heroic and sustained attempt ... to map out the horizons of human freedom ... To many, continence had declared the end of the tyranny of the 'present age.' In the words of John Chrysostom, virginity made plain that 'the things of the resurrection stand at the door.' (1988, p. 442)

John Chrysostom believed that, after Christ, humans could begin to live the life of heavenly beings: sexless, like the angels.

Virginity, monasticism and female empowerment

Early on in the Christian era, single-sex monastic communities were formed, with virgin women or men living celibate, ascetic lives in orders. Elm notes that, in some respects, virgin women and virgin men were equals in these communities, at a time when women and men outside were not (1994, pp. 164–5). Even if the lives of female virgins living in monastic communities at these times were fairly prescribed, then, it's possible that for some women this was still deemed preferable to the alternative – marriage, sexual activity with men, and bearing children – especially at a time when maternal and infant mortality were high and many women died in childbirth. Ambrose wrote,

> Let us compare, if it pleases you, the advantages of married women with that which awaits virgins. Though the noble woman boasts of her abundant offspring, yet the more she bears the more she endures. Let her count up the comforts of her children, but let her likewise count up the troubles. She marries and weeps. How many vows does she make with tears. She conceives, and her fruitfulness brings her trouble before offspring. She brings forth and is ill. How sweet a pledge which begins with danger and ends in danger, which will cause pain before pleasure! It is purchased by

perils, and is not possessed at her own will. (Ambrose of Milan, *Three Books Concerning Virgins*, 1.6; Schaff and Wallace 2007, p. 367)

This might also have gone for other women who chose to remain virgins, whether or not they entered monastic orders. Ambrose recounted the tale of a young woman from a noble family who was being urged by her parents and other relatives to marry. The girl sought refuge with a priest and told her parents that she would not marry, unless they could find her a husband who would be a better bridegroom for her than Christ himself:

'Can any better veil,' she said, 'cover me better than the altar which consecrates the veils themselves? Such a bridal veil is most suitable on which Christ, the Head of all, is daily consecrated. What are you doing, my kinsfolk? Why do you still trouble my mind with seeking marriage? I have long since provided for that. Do you offer me a bridegroom? I have found a better. Make the most you can of my wealth, boast of his nobility, extol his power, I have Him with Whom no one can compare himself, rich in the world, powerful in empire, noble in heaven. If you have such an one, I do not reject the choice; if you do not find such, you do me not a kindness, my relatives, but an injury. (Ambrose of Milan, *Three Books Concerning Virgins*, 1.12; Schaff and Wallace 2007, p. 373)

Ambrose noted that this choice was one which incurred financial loss for the girl's family, since her marriage would have given her property, possessions and financial security, but remaining unmarried would mean her family needed to continue supporting her themselves.

Nonetheless, Marion Grau notes that the imagery of avowed virgins being 'brides of Christ' is ambivalent and suggests that virgins were *not* wholly free from male control:

Does Christ simply replace the woman's ... human head of the household, with a divine husband? And does this new structure of hierarchy ... merely serve to reinforce with transcendent power the repression and control of men over woman's economic status on both the metaphorical and material level? ... Though they have not given their bodies to a man, their male advisers, standing in for the heavenly bridegroom and the heavenly father, continue to discipline the virgins' bodies and minds. (2004, p. 129–30)

Furthermore, virgins in monastic communities who ostensibly gave their loyalty only to Christ might still find themselves in a position of enforced allegiance to a male priest or bishop (p. 125). Grau argues that the fact that so many extant stories of female virgins appear in works by men is also significant, since their voices are 'ventriloquized' and mediated: 'The tropes of virgin and bride are ... assumed and managed by patristic authors to more strongly inscribe masculine authority and their own claims to orthodoxy' (p. 123).

The theological significance of virginity

The Virgin Mary

Virginity is praised on many grounds, but chiefly because it brought down the Word from heaven. (Ambrose of Milan, *Three Books Concerning Virgins*, 1.3; Schaff and Wallace 2007, p. 365)

An important association of virginity within Christianity right up to the present day, particularly in Roman Catholicism, has been with the Virgin Mary, the mother of Christ. In the Nicene Creed, Christians affirm that Jesus 'was incarnate by the Holy Spirit of the Virgin Mary, and was made man'. The supposed miraculous conception of Jesus, without any human male participation, has been taken as evidence of his uniqueness and the specificity of his simultaneously divine–human nature. The Roman Catholic and Orthodox Churches also affirm that Mary was a perpetual virgin: that is, that she remained a virgin after the birth of Jesus, and throughout her life. Other denominations reject this teaching, some noting the biblical verses (such as Mark 6.3) which suggest that Mary gave birth to other children after Jesus. Some linguists and biblical scholars argue that the Greek word *parthenos*, used in reference to Mary and usually translated 'virgin', can simply mean a young or unmarried woman, not necessarily one who has never had sexual intercourse. Similarly, the Hebrew word *almah*, often translated 'virgin', which appears in texts like Isaiah 7.14, which have been taken as prophecies of the birth of Jesus, can also mean a young, unmarried or recently married woman. Nonetheless, the Virgin Mary has been venerated and held up as an example of feminine obedience and purity on the grounds of her virginity.

In some accounts, Mary's virginity is understood as an important reversal of Eve's disobedience. Some typological theologies interpret particular characters or individuals as foreshadowing or echoing other characters or individuals within salvation history. For example, Jesus is often figured as a 'Second Adam', following Paul's assertion in 1 Corinthians 15.22 that all humans die in Adam, but all will be made alive in Christ. Similarly, Mary is sometimes figured as a completion of or correction to Eve. It sometimes appears as though Mary's virginity is being used as a 'corrective' to Eve's sexuality – given the associations, after Augustine, between sexuality and Original Sin. Augustine also believed that Mary had dedicated herself to God as a virgin even before she conceived Jesus by the power of the Holy Spirit, an assertion he may have taken from an early extracanonical text called the Protoevangelium of James. For Augustine, Mary therefore became an exemplar for other consecrated virgins.

Peter Brown comments that Mary's virginity was significant to early Christians, because it meant her body was free of the marks of the Fall and therefore testified to how other virgins' bodies could also be 'reformed': 'Virgins of the church bore bodies analogous to that of Mary: unshaken by intercourse and childbirth, here was a body "that has the marks of sex without its dire constraint"' (1988, p. 444). Virgin bodies were both continuous and discontinuous with other human bodies and the violence they faced even in everyday occurrences such as giving birth.

Mary F. Foskett comments,

> Some feminist readers have associated Mary's virginity with a misogyny that reifies male power over women, subordinates female sexuality and creativity to a virginal ideal, and perpetuates the notion of femininity as passive receptivity. Others have found in Mary's virginity a positive expression of female autonomy and power. (2002, p. 2)

As Foskett notes, Mary's virginity has also sometimes been understood as subversive. For some commentators, the fact that Jesus' conception is said to have taken place without sexual intercourse having occurred is a strong affirmation that women's dignity and worth exists distinctly from their experiences as sexually active wives and mothers. This does not mean that sex, marriage and motherhood are negative things, but rather that they are not the only path open to women, or the only way for women to gain acceptance in the eyes of God.

QUESTION BOX

What difference, if any, would it make to Christian theology and, in particular, Christology (doctrines about Jesus Christ), if Mary the mother of Jesus had not been a virgin at the time of his birth?

Purity and the contemporary virginity movement

Within contemporary Christianity, particularly the evangelical and Pentecostal wings of the Church, there is much emphasis on virginity as signifying purity. In the USA in particular, many young Christians pledge to remain virgins until they marry, and sometimes wear a ring or other token as a sign of their promise. Advocates argue that this might give young people who don't feel ready to have sex a framework on which to pin their refusal, and might also help young people to develop romantic relationships which are not simply goal-oriented or based on just physical attraction. Sexual abstinence is also one way to avoid unwanted pregnancy and sexually transmitted infections. Virginity pledges might therefore be interpreted as a positive affirmation of one's value and worth even if one is not sexually active, and might be considered a rejection of cultural norms which privilege early and extensive sexual experience.

However, such a strong emphasis on virginity might also be considered to repeat some of the older Gnostic-type ideas which demonized sex and considered it and bodies inherently sinful. More troublingly, some commentators have suggested that the contemporary virginity movement focuses too much on *female* virginity specifically and portrays female sexuality as something which needs to be 'guarded', 'protected' and eventually passed from the control of the woman's father to her husband. This, they argue, seems to undermine the woman's own agency and capacity to make her own decisions about her body and whether or not to be genitally sexually active (Valenti 2009; Browning 2010). The fact that virginity pledges focus exclusively on male–female sex might be considered to exclude young lesbian and gay people, or to assume that homosexual relationships are not 'real' sex or morally significant in the same way.

Andy Smith argues that conservative evangelical overemphasis on virginity as equalling purity can be deeply damaging to people who have experienced sexual abuse, and she problematizes a narrow, black-and-white definition of virginity:

> I have heard evangelical women say they would kill themselves if they were raped because it would mean that they were no longer 'pure'. Virginity needs to be redefined as something you choose to give away; it cannot be taken from you. Sexual assault does not take away your virginity. (1995, p. 345)

A new feminization of virginity?

Some commentators have noted that contemporary Christian teachings on celibacy for unmarried people might also disproportionately be applied to women, since there are more women than men in most church congregations. The sociologist Kristin Aune wrote in 2002 that, at the time, over a quarter of church attendees in Britain were single women, whereas only one-tenth were single men (2002). As a result, women who believed that they should only be sexually active within marriage, and that they should only marry a man who was a Christian, were likely either to remain celibate against their will or to become sexually active in secret with non-Christian men and to experience profound guilt as a result.

ACTIVITY

Read these excerpts from two articles on celibacy by Christian women in their forties: the first by Catherine von Ruhland, who was celibate against her will, and the second by Jenny Taylor, who had been sexually active in the past but had come to see celibacy as empowering and had been celibate since her twenties. What theological and moral 'goods' is each writer appealing to?

I'm an unmarried Christian woman who's hit the Big 4-0 and the idea that someone such as myself might have any sexual dreams and desires, let alone want to fulfil them, is rarely acknowledged within the Christian community. Yes, last year I reached my 40th birthday – and, reluctantly, I'm still a virgin … Like a lot of fellow reluctant celibates, I only remained a virgin because I was willing to wait. In my thirties I realised I had grown out of that teaching. After all, if a hoped-for marriage is the reason for abstaining, then does not the continual lack of a wedding invalidate such a choice? … I don't doubt that promiscuity can lead to deep emotional pain – but is it really any worse than that experienced by so many Christians who would dearly love to be married but are not and fear growing old alone? (Von Ruhland 2004, pp. 12–13)

The truth is my body is not my own … It is held in trust for others, for whatever reason God may decide and as I get older, it's easier to see the value in that … Purity and availability for God's work and for others: these were increasingly attractive ideas that gave my life some structure. I once lived in a community. It was Christian but mixed – and all the couples were there enduring their marriages. The tension was often palpable. Yet I could be available to all of them; could perhaps remind them of what they had! There was a point to Jesus' singleness … We need not more sex but more celibates. We need more of a counter-culture that values our struggle. (Taylor 2004, pp. 12–13)

Celibacy in the theological tradition

Many people understand virginity as a state which precedes something: one is a virgin *before* or *until* one has had sexual intercourse. It is not a permanent state. When the state of not having sexual intercourse *is* a longer or permanent one, however, especially when this has come about as a result of deliberate choice, the term celibacy is more often used. Some people, particularly those who enter the priesthood or monastic orders, consider celibacy part of their vocation to serve God. Others may consider celibacy their call even if they take no formal vows. However, there are also people for whom celibacy is something of a default state: they haven't actively chosen not to be sexually active, but they may simply not have had the opportunity to engage in a genital sexual relationship. For some, this unchosen celibacy can be a deeply painful and unsatisfying state; for others, it may become empowering. Importantly, Donald Goergen and others note that a celibate person is not necessarily a virgin; celibates may have been (genitally) sexually active at earlier times in their lives (1974, p. 120).

Celibacy and marriage in the New Testament

Many Christians believe that the Bible teaches that it's wrong to have sexual intercourse before one is married. The Bible doesn't actually say anything as direct as this: it often bans *porneia*, usually translated as 'fornication' or 'sexual immorality' – but it's not clear exactly what the biblical writers meant when they used this word, and there is no specific textual evidence that it refers to sex outside marriage.

Nonetheless, there are certainly biblical allusions to the power and spiritual significance bound up in sexual activity: in 1 Corinthians 6.15, Paul asserts that someone who is 'united' to a prostitute becomes 'one body' with the prostitute. This is grounded in the assertion in Genesis 2.24 that 'a man leaves his father and his mother and clings to his wife, and they become one flesh' – though it's important to note that there's no distinction in Hebrew between the words for woman and for wife, so while this might indeed be an assertion that sexual intercourse changes a relationship, there's not a clear sense in Genesis that this is only to happen within marriage.

ACTIVITY

Look up these New Testament verses, often cited by people who say that the Bible teaches that sex before marriage is wrong, in several English translations if possible. If you have access to one, try looking at a Greek–English interlinear version of the text. How do the translations vary? Are these texts clearly outlawing sex before marriage?

Mark 10.2–12	Ephesians 5.3
Acts 15.20	Colossians 3.5
1 Corinthians 5.1; 6.13, 6.18;	1 Thessalonians 4.3
10.8	Hebrews 13.4
2 Corinthians 12.21	Jude 7
Galatians 5.19	

Paul seems himself to have been influenced by ascetic Greek philosophical ideas. In 1 Corinthians 7.8–9, Paul suggests that it would be best for un-married people and widows 'to remain unmarried as I am'. Later in the same chapter, Paul says that although it's not wrong to marry, married peo-ple are likely to experience distress, and that married people are likely to be so concerned about their spouses and the world that they have little energy to give to 'the affairs of the Lord'. Some commentators have suggested that these remarks may have been prompted by Paul's belief that Jesus would re-turn imminently, rather than by a negative view of marriage per se: later on, at a time when Jesus had not yet returned and the Christian communities were working out how to live settled lives within their wider societies, either Paul or someone writing in his name sets out guidelines for good order in families and marriage relationships, and suggests that women will be saved from their sin via bearing children (see, for example, Eph. 5.22—6.4 and 1 Tim. 2.14–15, which were discussed in Chapter 3). It's possible, therefore, that Paul would not have advocated singleness (and presumably celibacy) in the way that he did if he had known that Christian interpreters centuries later would interpret his writings as long-term ethical instructions. How-ever, in the letters which most scholars agree were written by Paul, Paul certainly doesn't seem to see marriage as a necessity, or celibacy as a second-best option for Christians.

Clerical celibacy

Although some parts of the New Testament (such as Titus 1 and 1 Timothy 3) seem to suggest that those men worthy to be church leaders are those who have already demonstrated they can be good husbands and fathers (Porter 1996, p. 26), it's clear that from fairly early on in Christian history, there was a strong stream encouraging either celibacy or sexless marriage for clergy. In part, this was to help clergy remain 'set apart' from lay people, emphasiz-ing their status as having a special role or ministry. Adrian Thatcher notes that early Christian ascetic celibacy also perpetuated the idea that women (associated with earthiness and materiality) were 'the cause and tempta-tion of disorder in men' (1993, p. 177). Later, this also became one of the reasons for advocating celibacy for male clergy (Porter 1996, p. 17).

Jane Shaw (2007) argues that it was the Reformation many centuries later, and Martin Luther's suspicion of monastic communities because of their associations with Catholicism, which eventually led to the accept-ance of marriage for clergy in Protestant denominations. Martin Luther (1483–1546) interpreted Paul as saying that celibacy, and therefore virgin singleness, was the vocation of only a very few people, and that marriage is a gift of God as much as it is a pragmatic necessity for the ardent who would otherwise burn with passion. Christopher Chenault Roberts agrees that, according to Luther, a few are called to virginity, but, post-Fall, most humans' sexualities are subject to desire, and it would be foolish for a passionate person not to marry in order to give these desires an appropriate outlet (2007, p. 117). Indeed, Luther believed nuns were 'showing off' their peculiar gift of chastity, relying vainly on their own work of purity rather than trusting in God for their salvation, and that these women were thereby more like 'brides of the devil' than brides of Christ (Shaw 2007, p. 220).

The move to a married priesthood was not universal or one-directional: the Roman Catholic Church today still requires its priests to be unmarried, and in the Orthodox churches, although deacons and priests may marry, bishops may not (Cahill 1996, p. 169). In recent years, critics of the Roman Catholic policy of celibacy for all clergy have suggested that denying priests an appropriate outlet for their sexual desires makes it more likely that clergy will sexually abuse the children in their care, and some Roman Catholics are campaigning for priests to be allowed to marry.

Gray: a sexually embodied celibacy

Janette Gray, a member of the Roman Catholic order of the Sisters of Mercy, notes that celibacy has often been understood rather negatively in the Christian tradition. This has sometimes occurred because celibacy has been associated with a complete renouncement of sexuality – a tradition stemming, as we saw in Chapter 1, from Gnostic and Manichaean thought, which fed into a Christian model of celibacy whereby sex and sensuality were understood as worldly and negative. Gray says, 'This view of celibacy denigrates all that is physical and of the senses – sex, marriage and the world – because it only discerns Godlikeness as spiritual and other-worldly, pure and detached' (1997, p. 146).

However, notes Gray, this negative picture isn't the only way to understand celibacy. Celibacy need not deny the goodness and grace of being an embodied, sexual person, even if celibate people choose to live all or part of their lives without actually having physical sexual intercourse. Nor need it demonize feminine embodiment or sexuality in particular. Celibacy does not need to be about trying to 'escape' the body or matter in general, as it was for the Gnostics and Manichaeans. Gray explains:

A sexually embodied celibacy is the search for union with God, mediated in human relationships other than sexual partnership. This happens through being sexual, not by imagining that sexuality can be abandoned as a zone of sin beyond God's saving action. This celibacy is a way of being sexual. It recognizes the body as constitutive of our being, not merely as a vessel for the spirit. (1997, pp. 149–50)

Celibacy might be particularly empowering for women, since their sexuality can be understood outside the context of sex with other people (especially men). Their sexuality does not have to be about having babies, or pleasing someone else; it can be about using their creative energy for themselves, for helping a range of other people, and for their relationship with God. Rather than seeking love and acceptance through sexual relationships, celibates can affirm that they *already* are – just as all of us already are – loved and affirmed by God (1997, p. 158). For this reason, among others, monastic communities (communities of monks or of nuns – which are almost always single-sex, and usually comprised of people who have taken vows of celibacy) should not be considered communities where sexuality does not exist.

Goergen: celibacy as sexuality beyond genitality

Nonetheless, celibates have chosen to channel their sexuality in a particular, usually non-genital way. For many celibate people, this is an affirmation of human beings' existence as more than genitally active creatures. Donald Goergen affirms that celibacy is 'an invitation to a society where love and not orgasm is the goal of sexuality' (1974, p. 113). Crucial to a healthy account of human sexuality, be it expressed in celibacy or in genital sexual activity, is the affirmation that 'sexuality and spirituality are not enemies but friends' (p. 224). Celibacy isn't 'better' than genitally active sexuality, but a different vocation, to which some people may be called for all or part of their lives. In fact, says Goergen, 'Celibacy and [genital] sexuality both have the same ultimate goals – the fullness of life' (p. 227). However, Goergen affirms celibacy as pointing to a counter-cultural value system, where sexuality is deemed too powerful and too important to limit to **genitality** alone. Whereas sexual love in marriage is most properly expressed in genital love for only one other person, he suggests, the absence of genital sex in the life of the celibate means that their sexual love can exist more broadly, with this energy available for loving many other people as well as God (p. 116). Celibacy is a rejection of the idea that genital sex is the highest form of happiness we can experience, or the deepest way to experience intimacy (p. 118).

Cahill: celibacy and community

From a slightly different angle, Lisa Sowle Cahill points to celibacy's capacity to build up communities; she believes that even more important than celibacy's witness to the non-ultimacy of sexuality as defining identity is 'its role in building up discipleship community' (1996, p. 182). Celibates, she notes, aren't usually called to live in isolation from the rest of society. Rather, precisely because they don't have their own sexual or romantic partners, or their own children, they have time and energy to focus on the broader family of God, the Church community.

Summary

Concerns about asceticism and virginity often seem to echo broader concerns about values and goods for Christians. Eugene F. Rogers argues that marriage and monasticism aren't actually as different from each other as they might appear. He says,

> Theologically understood, marriage is ... a discipline whereby we give ourselves to another for the sake of growing in holiness – for, more precisely, the sake of God. In this respect marriage and monasticism are two forms of the same discipline ... They are both ways of committing ourselves to others – a spouse or a monastic community – from whom we cannot easily escape. Both the monastic and the married give themselves over to be transformed by the perceptions of others; both seek to learn, over time, by the discipline of living with others something about how God perceives human beings. (2004, p. 26)

The principles of marriage and celibacy are, in theological terms, not dissimilar.

Indeed, they might both be summed up under the heading 'chastity'. Significant particularly in the thought of Thomas Aquinas (1225–74), 'Chastity is one of the virtues associated with temperance; more specifically, the chaste person exhibits a stable disposition of appropriate desire with respect to sexual matters' (Porter 2005, p. 288). To be chaste is to exhibit judgement and discernment in sexual behaviour as well as other aspects of one's life, not rejecting sexual desire, but acknowledging that sexual desire can be expressed in more and less appropriate ways.

Aquinas' own understanding of chastity, and the norms of his age, meant that he endorsed only heterosexual marriage as a right context for sexual activity. But Jean Porter suggests that Aquinas' principles might be used in a new account of chastity, one which would allow 'considerable room for adaptation to one's individual circumstances and dispositions. Thus, it would be flexible enough to allow for differences in sexual orientation, as well as for more diffuse factors such as one's natural level of sexual desire, the practical possibilities of forming a long-term partnership, and the like' (2005, p. 289). Porter draws an analogy with food, suggesting that people might be able to agree a general principle that moderation (the equivalent of 'chastity') in eating and drinking is a good thing, but not thereby spelling out exactly what foods must be eaten and in precisely what quantities, since this will inevitably vary according to culture, needs, and personal likes and dislikes (p. 291). Chastity as a principle for sexual ethics might do well to be similarly adaptable.

Adrian Thatcher believes that justice and chastity in both sexual relationships and in embodied celibacy can be summed up by five principles.

These are the principle of positive waiting; the principle of proportion; the principle of loving commitment; the principle of exclusion; and the principle of honouring states of life (2011, p. 205). Positive waiting, for example, means that both sexual activity and celibacy should be set in a context of challenge to a social norm of immediate gratification: just, ethical sexuality necessitates restraint and patience, whether this means not having sexual intercourse very early on in a relationship, or contextualizing all sexual conduct as occurring in the 'between times' when creation is awaiting God's return and new order (p. 206). Proportion means that any sexual intimacy in a relationship should correspond to the intimacy in other aspects of the relationship: 'The more intimacy negotiated, the greater must be the commitment to match it' (p. 206). Honouring states of life is particularly important to Thatcher, since it allows for an acknowledgment that the sexual ethics appropriate to a fifteen-year-old may not be identical with those appropriate to a couple in their thirties or to a widower in his seventies. Chastity means restraint and a commitment to justice in all sexual activity, but for Thatcher this does not necessarily mean mandating against all sexual activity outside marriage.

In this chapter, we have seen that celibacy refers to a state in which someone has made a commitment to abstain from sexual activity, either for a limited period of time or for life. Usually, though not always, celibacy is understood as a permanent state (and Goergen notes that celibates who do experience occasional genital sexual activity are not thereby forgoing their entire celibate vocation – 1974, pp. 185–6). By contrast, when we think about the term 'virginity' in contemporary society, we usually mean a state someone is in *before* they have entered into a physical sexual relationship, but without the sense that this will necessarily be permanent.

At the beginning of the chapter we noted that the definitions of virginity and sexual intercourse are not obvious or uncontested. We saw that there was an ambivalence about sex in early Christianity, and that sexual activity didn't seem to sit easily with the asceticism promoted by the Church Fathers, who were concerned to anticipate the goods of the next world. We noted that some critics have seen this strong asceticism as evidence of fear of or negativity about female sexuality, while other commentators have shown that virginity might have been subversive or empowering for women in particular. We went on to explore snapshots of the significance of virginity from the theological tradition, including the importance of the figure of the Virgin Mary, and the contemporary revival of purity and virginity movements in conservative evangelical Christianity.

Next, we explored the co-existence of celibacy and marriage as goods in the Christian tradition, noting an ambivalence about marriage in the New Testament which may have stemmed from fear that it was a distraction from the work of the Kingdom. We touched on the issue of clerical celibacy, then engaged with work by scholars including Gray, Goergen and

Cahill who suggest that celibacy is not a suppression of human sexuality, but rather a focusing of sexuality in a different direction.

In Chapter 5, we'll move on to considering marriage in more detail, with particular reference to the place and theological significance of sexual intercourse within marriage.

Questions for study and reflection

1 Are celibacy and virginity meaningful 'goods' for Christian theologians in the twenty-first century? Why or why not?

2 To what extent is the association between physical purity and spiritual or moral purity a positive one? To what extent is it problematic?

3 Should unmarried Christians always remain celibate? Why or why not?

Further reading

Brown, Peter, 1988, *The Body and Society: Men, Women, and Sexual Renunciation in Early Christianity*, New York, NY: Columbia University Press.

Castelli, Elizabeth A., 2008, 'Virginity and its Meaning for Women's Sexuality in Early Christianity', in Levine, Amy-Jill with Maria Mayo Robbins (eds), *A Feminist Companion to Patristic Literature*, London and New York: T&T Clark, pp. 72–100.

Elm, Susanna, 1994, *Virgins of God: The Making of Asceticism in Late Antiquity*, Oxford: Clarendon Press.

Evans, Roger Steven, 2003, *Sex and Salvation: Virginity as a Soteriological Paradigm in Early Christianity*, Lanham, MD: University Press of America.

5

Sex and Marriage

Sexual intercourse, as an expression of faithful intimacy, properly belongs with marriage exclusively. (House of Bishops of the Church of England 1999, p. 8)

The effective framework for sexual intercourse is a committed, permanent and faithful relationship and that is what marriage is ... The point is not that sex is wrong before marriage and right after. The point is that sexual intercourse can only have justice done to its richness in a relationship we call marriage. (Dominian and Montefiore 1989, p. 32)

When engaged in improperly, sexual intercourse is no longer the positively meaningful, beautiful act it is designed to be, but becomes instead an expression of self-gratification, adultery, infidelity, or exploitation. The divinely intended, positive meaning of this act is found only when it is enjoyed within its divinely given, proper context, namely, marriage. (Grenz 1990, p. 82)

These quotations – from Anglican, Roman Catholic and evangelical Baptist perspectives – make clear that their authors understand sex as properly belonging within a marriage relationship. Their affirmation of marriage as the only appropriate setting for sexual intercourse is grounded in the belief that marriage provides a context *different* from that of other kinds of relationship and that sex can only have justice done to it in this special context.

Later I'll explore some reasons why theologians might believe this to be the case, and will return more fully to examining teachings on marriage from the Church of England and the Roman Catholic Church. First, however, we must consider what theologians actually mean when they talk about marriage.

ACTIVITY

Eugene F. Rogers, who has taught many university courses on theology and sexuality, says, 'I have found students often at a loss to say what marriage might be for. They tend not to believe that it is practically necessary any more to legitimate sexual intercourse or children, and they cannot imagine more for it to mean.' (2002c, p. xix)

What 'more' might there be for marriage to mean – for Christians? For people of other faiths? For people of no faith? Construct a diagram showing how the meanings of marriage might overlap for these groups.

Models of marriage

'Biblical marriage'?

Marriage has been understood variously at different times and in different places. Christians sometimes talk about 'biblical marriage' as a standard to which all marriages should aspire. However, marriage is not presented consistently, or exactly as we would now understand it, even throughout the biblical texts. For example, the Bible contains references to marriages which are:

- POLYGAMOUS. Many men in the Hebrew Bible are portrayed as having several wives simultaneously. The books of Samuel and Chronicles mention at least ten wives of David. 1 Kings claims that Solomon had 700 wives and 300 concubines[1] – and although the text says these women 'turned his heart from God', this seems to be because they were from non-Israelite tribes and nations rather than because of their number.
- BETWEEN FAMILY MEMBERS. In the biblical practice of Levirate marriage, it was expected for men to marry and father children by their dead brothers' widows (Deut. 25.5–6). Some marriages in the Bible occur between blood relations: Abraham was the half-brother of his wife Sarah (Gen. 20.11–12).
- NON-CONSENSUAL. Women often have little or no choice about who they marry. Wives are sometimes taken as spoils of war. In Judges 21, the Benjaminite men abduct the women of Shiloh to take as their wives.
- CONTRACTED BETWEEN CHILDREN. Although the Bible does not give a specific age of consent for marriage, early Jewish commentaries

---

1 A concubine was a slave-woman with whom a man had a sexual relationship and often children. Concubines did not have the same legal rights as wives, and their children did not usually inherit money, property or titles in the same way as children of a marriage.

suggest that marriages were often contracted between people who would now be considered too young to consent to marriage (about 12 years old). Early marriage may have been more common in the biblical era because of shorter life expectancies.

- FINANCIAL TRANSACTIONS. In the landscape of the Hebrew Bible, men commonly arrange marriages, and women are considered property to be transferred from their fathers to their husbands (Tobit 6—7). Genesis 34.12, Exodus 22.16–17, and Tobit 8.21 (in the **Apocrypha**) are examples of references to 'bride-prices' – an amount of money given to the bride's family by the groom in exchange for the bride.

Christians and theologians who appeal to the Bible for evidence that marriage should only ever take place between one man and one woman are therefore already selective about *which* biblical references to sex and marriage they favour. Making the Bible seem more unified in its presentation of marriage than it actually is, argues Adrian Thatcher, does a disservice to the texts:

> Is marriage a great mystery signifying the union between Christ and the Church? (Eph. 5.32). Yes. Is it a concession to the randy, to be avoided if possible? (1 Cor. 7). Yes. Is it an imperilment of one's eternal destiny? (Luke 20.34–36). Yes (though no one will say so publicly). Living with diversity can sometimes provoke more insight than harmonization when it may in any case not be there. (2005, p. 17)

Sacrament, covenant, contract? Post-biblical models of marriage

Marriage is not solely a religious institution. In most jurisdictions, marriage is a *legal* phenomenon, which may or may not also have religious significance. Importantly, the legal status of marriage may have implications for the standing of those associated with it. For example, children born outside marriage used to be called 'illegitimate', a hint that they did not usually have the same inheritance rights as children of married parents. In some countries, unmarried couples don't have the same tax benefits as married couples and may not be recognized as their partners' next of kin. For this reason, many campaigners believe it's unfair that same-sex couples often cannot benefit from the legal recognition attached to marriage.

Other commentators argue that marriage is primarily a capitalist institution, which is about safeguarding male property rights, and is therefore an outmoded phenomenon which no one should endorse. Marriage has been criticized for figuring women and children as commodities, to be protected not for their own sake but because they 'belong' to husband–fathers.

John Witte Jr suggests that the ways in which the Western Christian Church has understood marriage might be divided into five categories (outlined below). These are not necessarily mutually exclusive, and, as Witte argues, it's possible to hold more than one of them simultaneously. For example, most Christians in Britain who marry understand marriage as *both* a legal contract *and* a religious joining of two people.[2] However, says Witte, 'These perspectives ... have also come to stand in considerable tension, for they are linked to competing claims over the form and function of marriage' (1997, p. 2).

The sacramental model

The *sacramental* understanding of marriage is particularly linked to Catholic theology as it arose in the twelfth century. In Christian theology, a **sacrament** is a ritual practice or outward sign which signifies the presence or inner activity of God; it is a means of mediating grace. In the sacramental account, marriage echoes the mystical relationship between Christ and the Church, and is a way to bring about grace for both the spouses and their wider community (Witte 1997, p. 4). Sacramentalists sometimes assert that this power is so strong that marriage should be considered unbreakable – divorce is not really possible, and any remarriage is a form of adultery.

The sacramental account appears from early on in Christian history, with Augustine of Hippo (354–430) arguing in chapter 21 of his treatise *On the Good of Marriage* that the sacramental aspect was the greatest aspect of marriage, and that marriage's exclusivity (that is, the fact that it involved two and only two people and was entered into for life and that each person had only one spouse) symbolized the unity of all those who had become children of God.

In the sacramental account, something happens at marriage which profoundly changes the nature of the relationship between the partners. Marriage also symbolizes the relationship between God and humanity. As a sacrament, marriage imparts something of God's grace to the spouses. It's this cosmic significance which is believed to render marriage unique, and therefore a more appropriate context than other kinds of relationship for sex.

'Imparting grace' might sound rather abstract, but the Church of England bishops who authored *Issues in Human Sexuality*, and are sympathetic to the sacramental model, argue that, in marriage,

> We learn to break down our pride and self-concern, to be open to our partner as he or she really is, to treasure what is good and forgive faults, to sacrifice ourselves for the sake of the other, to be loyal whatever the

---

2 The fact that it is legal *and* religious is demonstrated by the fact that religious wedding ceremonies at which the officiant is not legally recognized as a marriage celebrant are not legally binding, and the couple will have to go through a separate legal ceremony with a registrar.

price. In these ways marriage becomes a means of grace, making us more like Christ both in ourselves and in our dealings with the world around us. (House of Bishops 1991, pp. 20–1)

This is expanded in *Marriage: A Teaching Document*:

The description of Christian marriage as a 'sacrament' is valued because it has its source in the New Testament (the 'great mystery' of Eph. 5.32) ... It means that the pledged relation of husband and wife is a sign of the pledge of love that Christ has for his Church, the promises he has made to it, the faithfulness, forgiveness, and patience that he has shown it, the delight he takes in it. The grace of God in the Holy Spirit is given to all who enter marriage in the conscious desire to hear his call, seeking his strength to live together as they have promised. (House of Bishops 1999)

Importantly, Vincent J. Genovesi, the Roman Catholic ethicist, argues that marriage actually makes the *spouses themselves* sacramental:

A couple who enter into a sacramental union of love want their love for each other not only to reflect but also to embody God's love. They want the reality of Christ and his love to be mediated by husband to wife and by wife to husband ... In a deeply theological sense, it is more accurate and closer to the reality of things to say that on their wedding day a man and woman start to *become sacraments*, or living and effective signs of God's love, rather than to say simply that they *receive* the sacrament of matrimony ... They do strive to become sacraments or signs, first to each other and then to all the believing community, of God's abiding love. (1996, pp. 164–5)

Witte focuses on the Western tradition, but the sacramental model of marriage is also particularly important within the Eastern Orthodox Churches. Orthodox marriage services have much in common with the sacrament of baptism. Thomas Hopko comments, 'There is no "legalism" in the Orthodox sacrament of marriage. It is not a juridical contract. It contains no vows or oaths. It is, in essence, the "baptizing and confirming" of human love in God by Christ in the Holy Spirit' (1997).

The social model

The *social* understanding of marriage is linked in particular to the Lutheran tradition. Martin Luther (1483–1546), the sixteenth-century theological reformer, believed that, rather than being a heavenly sacrament, marriage was basically an earthly phenomenon, a pragmatic way to order society and provide a legitimate arena for sexual activity. In this account, marriage is more to do with the state than the Church, and the legal rather than the spiritual (Witte 1997, pp. 5–6). Unlike in the sacramental account of marriage, in the social model, marriage is not believed to change the spouses' relationships with God, or impart any kind of special grace.

Indeed, Karl Barth (1886–1968), the Swiss Reformed theologian, who was influenced by Luther's thought, expressed suspicion about the sacramental model of marriage, as he believed that it tended to say too much for the capacity of the marriage relationship to confer grace on the spouses. Understanding the spouses as 'gracing' each other would, feared Barth, make them Godly rather than truly creaturely, detracting both from their true status as human and from the uniqueness of God's grace and saving power. He says,

> [The] exaltation of marriage is dearly bought. Its consequence is that man[3] has no longer any God to whom he can look and from whom he can expect help as man expects it from God, the transcendent, strange and only Helper. No longer can we turn and cling to Him if we ourselves are participants in an **apotheosis** and dispensers of sacramental grace. (1961, p. 125)

The covenantal model

The *covenantal* model depicts marriage as bonding and binding for whole communities, not just individual people or families. Marriage involves not just the spouses, but also those who witness to their relationship. The covenantal understanding is grounded in biblical accounts of the formal covenant relationship between God and the people of Israel, governed by certain rules and expectations about the behaviour and duties of each party. However, while this model portrays marriage as sacred, it's not considered sacramental as such: marriage can't, in itself, confer grace on those involved (Witte 1997, p. 8).

More broadly, we might characterize the covenantal model of marriage as implying a bond between the spouses witnessed to *by God* as well as by the broader community, which sets up further expectations and responsibilities. The Bible describes marriage in covenantal terms in Malachi 2.14: 'The Lord was a witness between you and the wife of your youth, to whom you have been faithless, though she is your companion and your wife by covenant.' There is an extended metaphor of God's love for Jerusalem as a marriage covenant in Ezekiel 16.

---

3 At the time Barth was writing, and at the time his writings were translated into English, it was common for the word 'man' to be used to refer to all humans. Barth is not just talking about males here.

John Calvin (1509–64), in his commentary on the book of Malachi, says,

[Malachi] calls ... attention to the fact that God is the founder of marriage, *Testified has Jehovah*, he says, *between thee and thy wife*. He intimates in these words, that when a marriage takes place between a man and a woman, God presides and requires a mutual pledge from both. Hence Solomon, in [Proverbs 2:17], calls marriage the covenant of God, for it is superior to all human contracts. So also Malachi declares, that God is as it were the stipulator, who by his authority joins the man to the woman, and sanctions the alliance. (1849, pp. 552–3)

The commonwealth model

The *commonwealth* model of marriage was particularly popular during the sixteenth and seventeenth centuries in England, when families were understood to be microcosms of nation-states. Husbands and wives were 'kings' and 'queens' of their own miniature 'countries'. Families were understood as the contexts in which the common good of all members could be nurtured. This was, in some senses, fairly reactionary and hierarchical, since although it purported to be for everyone's good, it tended to privilege the concerns and 'goods' of men and those in positions of authority in particular.

Subsequently, however, this shifted to a model in which commonwealth became more genuinely 'common': 'The traditional hierarchies of husband over wife, parent over child, and church over family were challenged with a revolutionary new principle of equality. The biblical duties of husband and wife and of parent and child were recast as the natural rights of each household member against the other' (Witte 1997, p. 9).

The contract model

The *contract* model of marriage portrays it basically as a voluntary bargain, in which the terms should be set by the couple themselves rather than by external legal, religious or social norms. In most cases, this will be limited to some extent by 'the general norms of civil society' (Witte 1997, p. 10), but in large part, it's up to the spouses themselves to define and live out what they want their marriage to be, based on their own private choices. Witte suggests that this final model prevails in the contemporary USA (the context in which he lives and works) in particular. The contract model might be understood as fairly weak in theological terms because it doesn't carry an inherent sense of permanence or sacredness, and is vulnerable to being broken.

QUESTION BOX

1 Which model of marriage outlined above accords most strongly with the way marriage is represented in a) your society and b) the church or other faith community, if any, to which you belong?
2 Do you think Christian theologians should endorse one model over the others? Why?

Sex and procreation

The way theologians understand marriage affects the way they understand the significance of sex within and outside marriage. Theologians have often understood sexual activity within marriage as serving several functions. We will come on to these in a moment.

Interestingly, however, there have been times at which even married Christian couples were praised for *not* having sex. Spiritual or 'Josephite' marriages (named after Joseph the husband of Mary, whom Roman Catholic and Orthodox Christians believe didn't have sexual intercourse with Mary even after Jesus' birth) were most prevalent during the medieval period, and were a legal institution in which couples pledged to abstain from sex in order to dedicate themselves more fully to God. Dyan Elliott suggests that spiritual marriages were in some senses subversive, since they allowed spouses, especially wives, to disrupt expected gender roles and separate marriage from patriarchy and procreation (Elliott 1993, p. 17), in a way not possible for other married people until the advent of safe and widespread contraception.

The existence of spiritual marriage even as a somewhat minor anomaly might be rather surprising, given that the procreation of children often seems the most 'obvious' explanation for the existence of sex in marriage. However, it's clear that marriage and sexual intercourse don't always map onto each other.

Indeed, if the link between sex and procreation seems obvious now, it hasn't always done so. Paul's own treatment of marriage, argues Elliott, 'obliterates' its reproductive function, placing sex but *not* procreation firmly at the centre of the couple's bond (1993, p. 22). Paul calls for spouses to give up their sexual rights over their bodies to each other (1 Cor. 7.3–4),[4]

---

4 Some commentators believe this injunction might undermine the agency of both partners, but especially women, to decide what happens to their bodies sexually. Loader says, 'Putting sexual intercourse into the context of rights creates a basis for potential abuse, including marital rape, though clearly that is not Paul's intent' (2010, p. 47).

but does not mention having children as a reason to marry, focusing rather on the sexual 'burning with desire' that many people experience. Furthermore, John Chrysostom (c.347–407), the fourth-century Archbishop of Constantinople, believed that it was always the will of God, rather than sexual intercourse in its own right, which led to the creation of new people, and that if God willed it, reproduction could take place by some other, non-sexual means (Clark 1983, p. 122).

Rowan Williams notes that, even within the Bible itself, there's plenty of evidence that marriage and heterosexual relationships are not all about the procreation of children. Only two verses, both in the Hebrew Bible (Gen. 1.28 and Mal. 2.15), make a direct connection between having sex and having children, and, in the New Testament, both Paul and Jesus seem to challenge conventional first-century Jewish notions of family and kinship. Williams notes that homosexual relationships also disrupt the link between sex and procreation: 'Same-sex love annoyingly poses the question of what the meaning of desire is – in itself, not considered as instrumental to some other process, such as the peopling of the world' (2002, p. 318). In other words, even if heterosexual people might run the risk of forgetting that sex is not all about reproduction, the existence of homosexuality is a reminder that humans also have sex for other reasons.

Nonetheless, many Christians affirm procreation as one of the main purposes of sex in marriage. Some Christians follow Augustine, who believed that sex which took place as a result of lust rather than a conscious and dispassionate awareness that it was necessary in order to perpetuate the species was wrong.

This strong link between sex and procreation recurs in contemporary movements which appeal to the injunction in Genesis 1.28 to go forth and multiply, and to fill the earth. This is a central tenet of the Quiverfull movement in contemporary conservative evangelical Christianity, which counsels married couples that they shouldn't plan whether or when they have children, or try to limit the number they have, but should allow God to 'open and close the womb'. There are some similarities here with the Roman Catholic Church's continued prohibition of contraception, but differences include the sense in some parts of the Quiverfull movement that it is important for Christians to have many children so that the total number and proportion of Christians in the world will increase, and the strong associations with patriarchy and anti-feminism (Joyce 2009).

Teaching on sex in marriage from two denominations

Church of England

ACTIVITY

Read these two excerpts from the Church of England marriage service – the first from the Book of Common Prayer (BCP) (1928 version), and the second from the Common Worship (CW) liturgy (from 2000). What similarities and differences do you notice between the ways in which they set out the purposes of marriage?

> BCP: First, [marriage] was ordained for the procreation of children, to be brought up in the fear and nurture of the Lord, and to the praise of his holy Name.
>
> Secondly, [marriage] was ordained for a remedy against sin, and to avoid fornication; that such persons as have not the gift of continency might marry, and keep themselves undefiled members of Christ's body.
>
> Thirdly, [marriage] was ordained for the mutual society, help, and comfort, that the one ought to have of the other, both in prosperity and adversity.

> CW: Marriage is a gift of God in creation
> through which husband and wife may know the grace of God.
> It is given
> that as man and woman grow together in love and trust,
> they shall be united with one another in heart, body and mind,
> as Christ is united with his bride, the Church.

> The gift of marriage brings husband and wife together
> in the delight and tenderness of sexual union
> and joyful commitment to the end of their lives.
> It is given as the foundation of family life
> in which children are [born and] nurtured[5]
> and in which each member of the family, in good times and in bad,
> may find strength, companionship and comfort,
> and grow to maturity in love.

Three things are happening in the marriage relationship, in this Anglican understanding:

---

5 The brackets here are an acknowledgement that physical birth is not the only way children enter into families: some are adopted.

1 It becomes the context within which sexual activity takes place. Sexual activity unites the spouses (CW), and happens within marriage as a remedy against sin (BCP).
2 It becomes a location for rearing children. In most cases, children are born as a direct result of the spouses' sexual activity. The BCP gives the procreation of children as the first purpose of marriage, and CW as the third, suggesting a shift in emphasis.
3 It becomes a location for 'strength, companionship and comfort' (CW) or 'mutual society, help and comfort' (BCP). Sexual activity is affirmed as bringing about and cementing this companionship and comfort.

These three facets are affirmed in the Church of England's teaching on marriage. In *Issues in Human Sexuality*, the bishops assert that, since sex requires such strong intimacy, it should happen in the context of strong commitment. Sharing intimacy at a solely bodily level without all the other intimacies of committed relationship 'is to make a relationship far less than it could be' (House of Bishops 1991, p. 19). The intimacy in other, non-marital sexual relationships is good to an extent – but, say the bishops,

> Christian teaching about marriage ... offers two things: first, guidance, based on God's revelation in Scripture and Christian experience, as to the way of life within which full physical expression of our sexuality can best contribute to our own maturity and sanctification and that of others; and secondly, a direction in which other sexual relationships can and should move, if they are to serve more effectually the true fulfilment of those concerned. (House of Bishops 1991, p. 20)

This argument suggests that sex outside marriage is good to the extent that it is *like* sex within marriage, or *gestures toward* sex within marriage, but that its good-in-itself will always be limited. For these reasons, 'God's perfect will for married people is chastity before marriage, and then a lifelong relationship of fidelity and mutual sharing at all levels' (House of Bishops 1991, p. 22).

In *Some Issues in Human Sexuality*, the bishops reassert that 'the original purpose for sexual relationships given in Genesis 1 is in order to have children. To this extent we have to agree with the continuing Roman Catholic emphasis on the fact that procreation is a central part of what the sexual act is about' (House of Bishops 2003, p. 82). Nonetheless, they recognize that 'it may be legitimate for a couple to seek to limit the number of children they have because of their own particular circumstances, the effect of further children upon any existing children they may have, or because of the need to avoid overpopulation' (House of Bishops 2003, p. 82). Importantly, this is represented as being an example of the way in which the development of tradition is dynamic, with the Bible being continually re-interpreted in light of changing social and cultural norms: overpopulation was not a problem at the time the biblical texts were produced, but it might be necessary to read the injunction to 'go forth and multiply' cautiously given the current strain on the earth's resources.

It was less than one hundred years ago, at the 1930 **Lambeth Conference**, that the Church of England's bishops legitimated the use of artificial contraception if, for some reason, it was prudent to avoid conception but abstinence from sex wasn't an option. As recently as 1908, the bishops had stated that artificially restricting family size was 'demoralising to character and hostile to national welfare' (quoted in House of Bishops 2003, p. 20). This assertion was made at a time when Britain was at the height of its colonial powers, and was considered to need a strong and stable population to continue the work of governance. Infant mortality in 1908 was high, with around 115 of every 1,000 babies dying in their first year (this had fallen to 63 of every 1,000 babies in 1930, and only around 6 in every 1,000 babies by 2000) (Hicks and Allen 1999, p. 8). The Book of Common Prayer listed the procreation of children as the first or primary aim of marriage; in this light, contraception would have frustrated its purpose. However, attitudes shifted throughout the first half of the twentieth century, influenced by changing social and gender norms after World War 1 and World War 2. At the 1958 Lambeth Conference, the bishops asserted that the use of contraception was a matter to be settled between husbands and wives, and in 1968 the bishops explicitly opposed the Roman Catholic ban on contraception as expressed in the **encyclical letter** *Humanae Vitae* (House of Bishops 2003, p. 21).

For many heterosexual couples, the procreative capacity of sexual intercourse continues to be a joyous and delightful aspect of their relationship, in which their relationship of love is expanded to include their own children, and they come to share in something of the creativity of God. Nonetheless, not every heterosexual relationship – even every heterosexual marriage relationship – can support the possibility of conception arising from every single sexual encounter. Furthermore, human creativity and the expansion of communities are not limited to the creation of more biological children.

Roman Catholic Church

Official teachings

In Roman Catholicism, too, marriage is deemed to be for the creation and nurturing of children; mutual love, help and affirmation; and a means for avoiding concupiscence (providing the spouses with an arena in which their sexual urges can be expressed, so that they do not have to commit sin by expressing them outside marriage). The sacramental model of marriage is particularly important within Roman Catholicism: Pope John Paul II, in his lectures on body theology, held that human males' and females' natures as physically directed toward each other signified and revealed the broader gift and grace conferred in marriage, and the even greater love of Christ for the Church, which is also 'spousal' (John Paul II 1979–84). As such, he said, human spouses should not do anything, in their sexual relationship or any other aspect of their marriage, to frustrate the way in which marriage images and reveals the divine–human relationship.

Much Roman Catholic teaching on sex and marriage has affirmed that married sexual activity should be open to the possibility of conception. Stuart and Thatcher note that, from the time of Augustine until the **Second Vatican Council (Vatican II)** in the 1960s, the procreation of children was considered the primary purpose of marriage, and the other purposes were considered secondary. However, Vatican II made all three purposes equally important and explicitly emphasized that procreation is *not* all that marriage (or sex within marriage) is for (Stuart and Thatcher 1997, p. 65; cf. *Gaudium et Spes* part 2 ch. 1). The unitive function of sex is no longer considered secondary to the procreative one. Michael G. Lawler concurs: 'The history of marriage in the Catholic tradition has progressed from a model of *procreative institution*, in which procreation is everything, to a model of *interpersonal union*, in which the relationship and love between the spouses is the foundation of the marriage and family' (2002, pp. 178–9). This represents a significant shift in Roman Catholic theology.

Nonetheless, the emphasis on procreativity in Roman Catholic teaching on sex and marriage means that the deliberate prevention of the conception of a child is still considered illegitimate. One of the most important documents on the matter is Pope Paul VI's 1968 encyclical letter *Humanae Vitae* ('concerning human life') (Paul VI 1968). In it, he affirms that sex within marriage is good, even if it does not lead to conception, but that sex and procreation must not be deliberately separated. This is grounded in Natural Law teaching, in which 'frustrating' or blocking the natural purpose of sexual intercourse goes against reason and is therefore illegitimate.[6]

Humanae Vitae has been criticized by Genovesi and others for its apparent inconsistency. On the one hand, the document acknowledges that even

---

6 The commission set up to investigate population and birth by Paul VI's predecessor, John XXIII, was expected to recommend that the Church should change its stance on contraception in light of overpopulation in the Global South (Genovesi 1996, pp. 190–1). However, Paul VI reaffirmed the prohibition of artificial contraception, and argued that the unitive and procreative aspects of sex were inseparable. This meant that Paul VI could not allow for the possibility of conception to be removed from any act of marital sexual intercourse whatever the circumstances. Paul VI was succeeded by John Paul I, whom many believed would be a more liberal pontiff and would interpret *Humanae Vitae* broadly. Prior to becoming pope, John Paul I had written and spoken on several occasions of his sympathy for married couples who wished to limit the size of their families (Allen 2003). However, John Paul I himself died only 33 days after his installation, and was succeeded by John Paul II, who reiterated Paul VI's teachings from *Humanae Vitae*.

God has separated the unitive and procreative aspects of sex, since there are times during a woman's menstrual cycle when she is unable to conceive. Having sex during these times is not illegitimate, since the unitive 'meaning' of sex is still present and good even when no conception can take place. On the other hand, to deliberately have sex during these infertile times with the *intention* of avoiding conception is condemned, because it attempts to separate sex's unitive and procreative functions (Genovesi 1996, pp. 193–4). Using artificial contraception pushes this even further. Paragraph 16 of *Humanae Vitae* asserts that abstaining from sex during fertile times to avoid conception is more justifiable than using contraception during these times.

Pope John Paul II rigorously followed Paul VI's teachings from *Humanae Vitae*. In his lectures on body theology (John Paul II 1979–84), John Paul II reiterated and amplified the teaching that, in order to reflect and mediate God's love for humanity, sex must always be open to the transmission of life. Later, he argued that the use of contraception led to consumerist attitudes, with people caring more about material possessions than the spiritual gift of children (Thatcher 1999, p. 200). Being unable to afford children was not a good enough reason to prevent their conception. However, counters Thatcher, having children is not always unselfish, and not having them is not always selfish. Thatcher criticizes the idea that every act of sex must be open to conception; he asks, 'Why could not the couple cooperate with God in the mission of procreation by *sometimes* being open to new life?' (p. 195). Indeed, Thatcher suggests, making sex *always* potentially procreative might actually undermine sex's other purposes and the other ways in which it is good: a couple is less likely to be able to enjoy sex freely, and rejoice in the way it unites them as a couple, if they are also worrying about conceiving a child that they could not support. Furthermore, 'The Church has never insisted that the intention to have children is a condition of marriage, and couples who are known to be infertile or are no longer fertile are not forbidden to marry' (p. 299).

Contemporary Roman Catholic theologians

The Roman Catholic ethicist Kevin T. Kelly suggests that a couple's motivation for not having children for the first few years of their marriage, or for not adding to their existing family, could itself be 'life-giving', even if the couple is not creating further biological life (1997, p. 86). A couple may wish to do rightly by their existing children, who might be adversely affected by the arrival of another sibling. Even if the conception of children is one important aspect of sex within marriage, says Kelly, it's not the only one, and shouldn't be made absolute.

This is especially the case given that, in some sense, the Church recognizes its future as being eschatological. If the Church is more concerned with its future in God's new order than with preserving the existing order, suggests Gerard Loughlin, then it is odd that there has been so much emphasis on procreation and the perpetuation of social norms. Loughlin doesn't degrade the goodness of children, but, rather, affirms that they are children of *Christ*, and the whole Christian community, not just individual mothers and fathers. All Christians are involved in nurturing all the children of the community. Therefore, concludes Loughlin, not every sexual relationship must be procreative:

> Children [are] born to the Church, and not merely to their parents ... This is why ... not everyone in the Church has to look for the gift of children, why not every particular relationship or sexual act has to be open to the gift of children, in short, why there can be infertile straight couples and gay couples; why there can be celibates, consecrated virgins and single people. For in the imagination of the Church, children are first and foremost gifts that arrive through the nuptial union of the Church with her beloved, Jesus Christ. (2004b, p. 97)

Similarly, the Roman Catholic lesbian theologian, Elizabeth Stuart, has argued that sex's unitive purpose means that it *cannot* be understood as occurring solely within marriage:

> Christians are not called into a sexual community but an ecclesial one. Sexual relationships must themselves be permeable to the Church and spill over into the Church. Only if our relationships build up the body of Christ by proclaiming the gospel and challenging the Church to be faithful to that gospel can they be deemed to be unitive. (1999, p. 18)

Sex, in this account, is not only about a couple and their own children, but about the broader community. For Christians, the uniting which sex brings about must include drawing people into Christ's body, the community of the Church. God's new order is about hospitality to strangers, those outside the biological kinship group, rather than care only for biological children and 'insiders' (2003, p. 95).

Gareth Moore believes that Pope John Paul II was wrong to suggest both that *all* sex is self-giving, and that *all* sex outside marriage is therefore wrong because the partners' capacity for self-giving is limited. Moore suggests that sex outside marriage is only a 'lie' or 'deceitful' if it *intends* to deceive, that is, if one partner believes it to signify more than it does and the other partner colludes in this misapprehension. If everyone involved knows the act of sex to be context-specific, this is not in itself illegitimate, because sex can 'mean' a range of things and, like an unfamiliar word or phrase, acquires meaning according to its context (1998, p. 240). We'll return to this aspect of Moore's argument in the Conclusion.

Sex, divorce and remarriage

If a cosmic change takes place at intercourse which somehow permanently bonds the partners together, argue some theologians, divorce is not really possible. It cannot undo the permanent change that has taken place. Any subsequent marriage or sexual relationship, therefore, will be adulterous. Sometimes people who make this kind of argument point to Paul's question in 1 Corinthians 6.15–16:

> Do you not know that your bodies are members of Christ? Should I therefore take the members of Christ and make them members of a prostitute? Never! Do you not know that whoever is united to a prostitute becomes one body with her? For it is said, 'The two shall be one flesh.'

William Loader says, 'The assumption in Paul's argument is that sexual intercourse actually does something of a permanent nature to people' (2010, p. 73).

This, however, raises questions: if all sexual intercourse permanently and forever 'joins' the participants in some way, does this mean someone who has been raped is permanently and forever 'joined' to their rapist and is committing adultery in any other sexual relationship they have? The question is whether sexual intercourse always has a cosmic significance such that sexual relationships with more than one person (or during a remarriage after divorce) can never be legitimate. It is important to read Paul's assertion in the context of the following verse: 'But anyone united to the Lord becomes one spirit with him' (1 Cor. 6.17). Paul understands spirits to be as important as bodies: the significance of bodily actions must therefore be contextualized within the significance of attitudes. As Loader goes on to say, 'Sexual intercourse ... sets up a rival sphere of influence to that created by our having been joined to Christ' (p. 73). It is for this reason that sex with a prostitute is inappropriate: it represents loyalty to the things of the world, not the things of God (p. 74).

In Mark 10.11–12, Jesus says, 'Whoever divorces his wife and remarries commits adultery against her; so too, if she divorces her husband and re-marries, she commits adultery.' Matthew's version of the passage tempers it by adding a disclaimer: 'Except in the case of infidelity'. It seems, then, that Jesus *is* pointing to some kind of cosmic bond between spouses, but that this bond is revoked or threatened when one partner has been sexually unfaithful. Since adultery was deemed to violate men's property rights over their wives, slaves and children, adultery by women was considered a legitimate reason for divorce. Like sex before marriage, it could otherwise lead to men bringing up, and giving their resources to, children who were not their own. As a result, in the Bible, 'Adultery was rarely depicted as wronging a woman or as emotional hurt to either partner' (Loader 2010, p. 61). Thatcher suggests that Jesus' words should be interpreted as protecting vulnerable people whose relationships have ended against their will, not preventing divorce and remarriage where both partners desire it (1999, p. 257). He also suggests that *porneia*, the word usually translated 'adultery' in these passages, might be understood as a broader kind of offence which threatens a marriage relationship (for example, marital rape or domestic abuse), not just sex with someone else (p. 263).[7]

In the Church of England marriage service, the spouses make their promises to each other 'until death parts us'; in the Roman Catholic liturgy, 'all the days of my life'. Death changes a relationship; in both these denominations, one may remarry if one's spouse has died. Interestingly, though, there is also an Orthodox tradition which understands that the 'death' which 'parts' the spouses could also be the death of the relationship itself. If the relationship has died, the marriage is effectively over; divorce does not bring about the end of the marriage but merely formalizes it. The question is whether a subsequent sexual relationship within another marriage can be legitimate, and this seems to hinge on whether the 'sacramental' element of a marriage – the element which, in some accounts, makes a marriage indissoluble – coincides with sexual intercourse having occurred.

Kelly believes that the indissolubility of a marriage, and the fact that sexual intercourse has taken place within it, are not the same thing. The Roman Catholic Church has privileged **consummation** (first sexual intercourse) as the marker for when a marriage has really taken place: marriages can be annulled provided that the spouses have not had sex (1997, p. 35). However, says Kelly,

> I reject an excessively physical interpretation of being 'two in one flesh', even though I would not want to deny importance to the act of intercourse ... Being 'two in one flesh' is more than an interpenetration of two bodies; it is about two persons becoming one in a very real sense. According to this interpretation a marriage is consummated when the husband and wife really experience themselves as a 'couple'. (p. 35)

If all love and relationship has disappeared, suggests Kelly, there is a sense in which the marriage is no longer sacramental (p. 37). Given that not every

---

7 *Porneia* is condemned on several occasions in Paul's writings, but he never defines exactly what it is. David H. Jensen notes that, for readers who already assume that the only legitimate kind of sex is penetrative vaginal sex between married people, *porneia* comes to mean any behaviour which does not fit this mould: masturbation, oral sex, anal sex, and so on. However, says Jensen, 'In 1 Corinthians, Paul mentions *porneia* in reference to prostitution and illicit marriages; in Galatians 5.19 he seems to use it more generally, without connection to specific sexual behaviors. This vagueness has allowed each generation to redefine the meaning of *porneia* to be whatever departs from the supposedly self-evident mores of each era' (Jensen 2010, p. 17).

married couple who have had sexual intercourse experience a true depth of love and indissolubility in their relationship, it cannot be sexual intercourse which renders a marriage indissoluble. Kelly concludes that the existence of a previous marriage does *not* inherently preclude a subsequent sexual relationship within a second marriage from being sacramental or a means of grace.

Moore suggests that the act of sexual intercourse doesn't in itself carry an inherent meaning but rather, like a unit of language, acquires its meaning according to how it's used. Sex used lovingly in a committed relationship will come to mean love and commitment; sex used violently in a context of rape will come to mean violence and violation. He says, 'Sexual intercourse does not have any great unitive significance in itself, but ... it bears what significance it does have by virtue of the context in which it takes place' (1998, p. 240). We might therefore want to say that sex can *stop* meaning things as well as *start* meaning them. Sexual activity after divorce, then, might be interpreted as non-adulterous, if the prior relationship has ceased to carry loving, life-affirming meaning.

Can same-sex covenants ever be marriages?

The way that theologians answer this question will depend on how they define marriage. We saw above that, in the Church of England and Roman Catholic traditions, the purposes of marriage are threefold:

1 to provide a stable context in which children can be born and/or brought up;
2 to provide a context for committed sexual activity;
3 to provide strength, comfort and companionship for the spouses.

If marriage is understood as a relationship in which it's necessarily possible to procreate biological children via sexual intercourse, then same-sex relationships can't be considered marriages. However, if children can enter families through adoption as well as biological birth, same-sex covenants need not be ruled out of being considered marriages on this account. Same-sex relationships might also fulfil the second and third purposes of marriage.

But those who argue that same-sex covenants cannot properly be called marriages believe that there are other reasons why they fall short. One of the most significant is that the relationship between human husbands and wives is considered, by many theologians, to echo the relationship between God and human beings. Karl Barth, the twentieth-century Swiss theologian, held that the structure of authority of humans as male and female mirrored the structure of authority from God to Christ to the Church. Humans must therefore also be 'appropriately' masculine and feminine in their marriage relationships. For Barth, the relationship between men and women and its power to echo the relationship between God and humans depended on men's and women's mixture of similarity and difference. This happened along specifically gendered lines, with men called to initiate and women to respond (1961, pp. 169–71). A same-sex relationship could not be a marriage because it would not adequately hold together similarity and difference: two spouses of the same sex would be too alike. Barth and many other theologians have held that sexual difference is built into creation by God as a good, and that to remove the opposite-sex nature of marriage would be to detract from its capacity to be a microcosm of this difference (for more on this, see Roberts 2007).

This type of argument is picked up in the Church of England's *Issues in Human Sexuality*, and is used to argue that heterosexual marriage is legitimate in a way that homosexual relationships are not: 'In heterosexual love … personal bonding and mutual self-giving happen between two people who, because they are of different gender, are not merely physically differentiated but also diverse in their emotional, mental and spiritual lives' (Church of England 1991, p. 37). This seems to rest on the assumption that there are particular patterns of emotional, mental and spiritual life that men and women respectively fall into, and that spouses of the same sex could not similarly bring different qualities into their relationship. But is this really the case?

One of the most theologically sophisticated arguments for same-sex marriage comes from Eugene F. Rogers. Rogers considers marriage redemptive, a stable context in which humans can live out their relationships with each other, with other people and with God. Marriages, and the broader communities built on them, become communities of redemption. 'Given that no human beings exhibit faith, hope and charity on their own, but only in community,' says Rogers, 'it is hard to argue that gay and lesbian people ought to be left out of social arrangements, such as marriage, in which these virtues are trained' (2004, p. 27). Homosexual people entering covenantal relationships, like heterosexual people entering covenantal relationships, commit themselves to discipline and self-denial for the good of the spouse and the broader community. Such covenantal relationships are (as Barth argued) a mixture of similarity and difference; Rogers' departure from Barth is to argue that,

> For the risk of commitment to be worth it and to have the best chance of success, the community must have plenty of time and be made up of the right sort of people. Growth takes a lifetime. The right sort of people are those who will succeed in exposing and healing one another's flaws. For gay and lesbian people, the right sort of otherness is unlikely to be represented by someone of the opposite sex, because only someone of the apposite, not opposite, sex will get deep enough into the relationship to

expose one's vulnerabilities and inspire the trust that healing requires. (2004, p. 28)

Sexual desire prefigures God's entering into humans and being entered into by them (1999, p. 241). If homosexual people are denied marriage, they are denied an arena in which to use their bodily desires most fully for God (p. 230). Furthermore, people who oppose same-sex marriage, says Rogers, are not only denying homosexual couples these communities of redemption, but are shutting *themselves* out as well, since, he argues, stable relationships benefit everyone, not just those directly involved. In short, 'Weddings, gay or straight, build up the eucharistic community both by contributing the institutional stability of marriage, and because weddings represent the trinitarian life' (p. 244).

Along similar lines, David Matzko McCarthy argues,

Marriage ... is an enactment of God's faithfulness and the unity of Christ and the church, and it is a means through which the agency of a particular person's body is taken into redemption ... If homosexual men and women desire to give their bodies over to another and to fulfilment in God's reconciliation, any theological account of same-sex unions ought to identify the way in which the unions are cultivated on the same terrain. (1998, p. 96)

Heterosexual marriage and celibacy have both been acceptable signs in the theological tradition of giving over one's body, just as God gave Godself over to humanity. But homosexual Christians desire to give over their bodies for others, and 'to offer their bodies [as] signs of God's self-giving' (p. 102), just as much as heterosexual Christians do. Where homosexual Christians cannot publicly acknowledge their sexualities or their relationships, they cannot allow their bodies to be 'theologically communicative' of who they are in relation to God and the rest of the community (p. 109).

Some commentators argue that, even if bonding and uniting can take place to an extent within covenantal same-sex relationships, such relationships are still less perfect than heterosexual marriages, and should not be considered ordained by God. Those who argue along these lines point to the Bible, which seems to attest that there is something abominable or illegitimate about sexual relationships between people of the same sex. (These texts are examined in more detail in Chapter 7.) The Roman Catholic document 'Letter to the Bishops of the Catholic Church on the Pastoral Care of Homosexual Persons' says that homosexual orientation is a 'more or less strong tendency ordered toward an intrinsic moral evil; and thus the inclination itself must be seen as an objective disorder' (Congregation for the Doctrine of the Faith 1986).

The Church of England's 2005 statement on civil partnerships restated the 1987 General Synod motion that homosexual genital acts fall short of the ideal, and the 1991 assertion in *Issues in Human Sexuality* that 'heterosexuality and homosexuality are not equally congruous with the observed order of Creation or with the insights of revelation as the Church engages with these in the light of her pastoral ministry' (Church of England 2005; Church of England 1991, p. 40), but that homosexual orientation is not sinful. It also reinforced the 1998 Lambeth Resolution that same-sex unions for clergy and lay people should not be blessed or legitimized. The 2005 statement says, 'It remains the case that in law, as in the eyes of the Church, marriage can be entered into only by a man and a woman. The Government has stated that it has no intention of introducing 'same-sex marriage'. Civil partnerships are not a form of marriage' (Church of England 2005). However, as the bishops go on to point out, there are lots of ways in which civil partnerships are very much like marriages: in England and Wales, civil partners are given the same legal protections as spouses in terms of property, tax, pensions, and so on. The difference is that a civil partnership does not assume any sexual activity. While a marriage is assumed to entail a sexual relationship between the partners (to the extent that, if sexual intercourse does not take place, the marriage can be annulled), there is no such assumption of a civil partnership. It is for this reason that the Church of England does not ultimately forbid its clergy or laity from entering civil partnerships: it distinguishes between homosexual orientation and homosexual activity, with the line that the latter is officially illegitimate but the former is not. By this logic, a civil partnership doesn't necessarily entail sex, so it is legitimate; but, by the same token, it can't be understood as properly covenantal or sacramental, since it is in sexual intercourse that covenant and grace are instantiated and renewed.

In short, it might seem that the Church of England is simultaneously endowing same-sex sexual activity with a lot of significance, and no significance at all. It is significant in the sense that doing it is deemed to transgress the biblical ideal, but it is insignificant in the sense that it is not considered able to mediate grace in the same way that heterosexual married sex does.

Summary

Rogers says that, in debates on homosexuality, what is really interesting is that theologians both for and against it appeal to metaphors of marriage and embodiment (2002c). Questions about sex inside and outside marriage might be understood as echoing questions about the broader earthly and heavenly significance of bodies and how we use them. We turn to the question of homosexuality in the next chapter, but as we do, it would be well to keep in mind Rogers' reminder that, for Christian theologians, talk about the body always happens in the context of talk about the Holy

Spirit, and vice versa (p. xxi). Theologians are concerned about bodily acts because they believe those acts have meanings with cosmic reach and cosmic consequences.

Sex in marriage is sometimes purported to be a microcosm of the marriage relationship itself. Stanley J. Grenz argues that sex repeats and reaffirms the covenant made at marriage (1990, pp. 82–3). He also points to 1 Corinthians 7 to assert that sex in marriage is a mark of the mutual submission that should characterize the marital relationship (p. 88). Importantly, this has implications beyond the marital relationship itself:

> The sex act also becomes a physical embodiment of the meaning of marriage as a spiritual metaphor. Like the relationship to which it is intimately tied, this act is a vivid reminder of the self-giving love of Christ for the church, which is described by analogy to marriage in Ephesians 5.22–23. The sex act ... is an appropriate reminder of the spiritual truth that Jesus has given himself completely for his church. (p. 89)

Conceivably, then, a marriage without sex fails to image God's love for humanity as fully as it could do.

However, Grenz may risk overstating sex, so that it becomes a carrier of *too much* in the way of spiritual symbolic weight. Matzko McCarthy argues that the Roman Catholic account of sex in marriage may similarly try to claim so much for it spiritually that it actually undermines its everyday reality:

> Through any given sexual act, spouses might express love, desire, generosity, frustration, fatigue, or manipulative intent, but they will do so in the semantic context of a day, week, a stage of life, and a series of specific events, and all set within the broader context of a shared life. Any particular sexual encounter need not say anything earth shattering; it need not point to the fullness or full meaning of a sexual relationship ... Most sex within marriage is just ordinary, a minor episode in a larger story ... The true superiority of sexual intercourse in marriage is that it does not have to mean very much. (2004, p. 8)

Indeed, Grenz's account raises questions for the significance of marriages where the spouses are no longer able, because of age or disability, to engage in sexual intercourse; for people who are physically unable to have sexual intercourse at all; and for marriages where the spouses are no longer attracted to one another physically, but nonetheless have a deep committed love for each other. If sex is a part of the good of marriage, it is only a part.

We began this chapter by noting that ideas about what constitutes marriage differ between times and contexts, and that even the Bible does not present a consistent or unchanging picture of marriage. We noted that

Christians who appeal to 'biblical marriage' probably mean only some of the ways in which marriage is presented there. More broadly, we engaged with Witte's suggested five models of marriage in the Western Christian tradition: sacramental, social, covenantal, commonwealth and contract.

We then examined the links between sex and procreation and asked whether these are obvious or self-evident. We focused on the teachings about sex and marriage in two Christian denominations, the Church of England and the Roman Catholic Church. We noted that the purposes of marriage are identified as including procreation of children, unity and comfort for the spouses, and as providing a place where people may have sex without sinning. We saw that the question of whether procreation is understood as the primary purpose of marriage or simply one among others differs according to time and denomination, and that this similarly affects whether the use of contraception is considered legitimate.

Thinking about sex, divorce and remarriage, we considered the cosmic significance of sexual activity, and whether or not sex could only ever have full justice done to it in a context of marriage. Finally, we considered whether same-sex covenants could properly be called marriages, and noted Rogers' argument that homosexual couples need a formal context in which to use their sexualities for God just as much as heterosexual couples do.

In Chapter 6, we move on to considering sexual activity that takes place outside marriage, and how theologians have responded to these forms of sex.

Questions for study and reflection

1 Critically assess the statement that only sex which takes place within marriage can be truly sacramental.

2 Must sexual activity always be open to the possibility of conceiving children in order to be good? Why or why not?

3 'Given that no human beings exhibit faith, hope and charity on their own, but only in community, it is hard to argue that gay and lesbian people ought to be left out of social arrangements, such as marriage, in which these virtues are trained' (Rogers). Do you agree?

Further reading

Cahill, Lisa Sowle, 1996, *Sex, Gender, and Christian Ethics*, Cambridge: Cambridge University Press – especially chapter 6, 'Sex, Marriage, and Family in Christian Tradition'.

Coleman, Peter, 2004, *Christian Attitudes to Marriage: From Ancient Times to the Third Millennium*, London: SCM Press.

Porter, Muriel, 1996, *Sex, Marriage, and the Church: Patterns of Change*, North Blackburn, Victoria: HarperCollinsReligious.

Roberts, Christopher Chenault, 2007, *Creation and Covenant: The Significance of Sexual Difference in the Moral Theology of Marriage*, New York, NY: T&T Clark International.

Thatcher, Adrian, 1999, *Marriage After Modernity: Christian Marriage in Postmodern Times*, Sheffield: Sheffield Academic Press.

6

Sex Outside Marriage

In the previous chapter, we saw that marriage, and sex within marriage, have been understood differently by different theologians, with some giving an almost mystical significance to marital sexual activity.

However, Duncan Dormor suggests that changes over the last half-century, most significantly the widespread availability of reliable contraception, have profoundly changed the terms of the debate about sex outside marriage. Reliable contraception, used well, means that people who have sexual relationships responsibly can now go a long way toward avoiding the conception of children for whom they could not provide emotionally or materially. Has this not, asks Dormor, removed one of the primary reasons for the Christian assertion that sex properly belongs in marriage (2004, pp. 2–3)?

Indeed, the overwhelming majority of people in the West who now marry have lived together and had a sexual relationship beforehand. Many, as Dormor notes, would consider it *less* ethical and *less* responsible to marry without having already lived together (p. 3). However, in the main, the Christian denominations have still tended to see cohabitation as a less optimal situation than marriage and have given little attention to thinking theologically about the significance of sex between unmarried couples (except to say that it is undesirable). More progressive accounts might figure living together as a step *on the way* to getting married (Dormor 2004, p. 1; Board for Social Responsibility 1995, p. 113) – Dormor cites the 1995 Church of England publication *Something to Celebrate* as an example – but marriage is still the 'gold standard'.

Is it possible, then, to consider sex outside marriage in theological terms, without undermining the ways in which marriage has been held to promote theological goods such as stability, commitment, faithfulness and mediating grace? And where do other kinds of sex outside marriage fit into the picture – sex that happens in exchange for money; or committed sexual relationships between more than two people; or masturbation, solo sex by yourself (which a character in Woody Allen's movie *Annie Hall* referred to as 'sex with someone I love')?

'Premarital' versus 'preceremonial' sex

Something to Celebrate affirms that many Christian couples as well as others live together prior to marriage. However, it notes a concern among many Christians that couples who live together are not making a formal, public declaration of commitment to each other in the way that couples who marry do (Board of Social Responsibility 1995, p. 113). Cohabiting couples do not make a covenant to each other, and may not be recognized as couples within their communities. This, the report notes, might be understood as a privatization of sexual relationship, rather than the outward-looking, community-focused marriage relationship. The authors of the report also believe that cohabitation may be less committed than marriage (1995, p. 114), and that couples who live together might be holding something back from fully giving themselves to their partner.

Nonetheless, the report concludes that commitment and public recognition as a couple is more important than the wedding ceremony itself:

> Some forms of cohabitation are marriages already in all but name. Theologically and morally, what makes a marriage is the freely given consent and commitment in public of both partners to live together for life ... In terms of the theology of marriage, cohabitation which involves a mutual, life-long, exclusive commitment may be a legitimate form of marriage. (Board for Social Responsibility 1995, p. 116)

One priest quoted in the report said that he had become aware that the majority of couples marrying in his church had lived together and had sexual relationships beforehand. He said, 'It has made me decide that the kind of marriage preparation I used to give won't do any longer. I need to find a way of honouring their experience of each other, helping them affirm the strengths that their relationship already has and bring all of these into their new commitment' (quoted in Board for Social Responsibility 1995, p. 109).

We saw in Chapter 4 that there is some debate about how to define when sexual intercourse has actually begun to take place, depending on how virginity and intercourse are defined. Adrian Thatcher argues, further, that it's unhelpful to insist that marriage, consummation, and first sexual intercourse must all happen on the same day. He suggests that the real 'consummation' of a marriage doesn't take place suddenly and all at once, but gradually and over a long period, as the spouses' relationship grows and develops (Thatcher 2002, p. 235). He calls for a return to older traditions of betrothal, which recognized and celebrated the reality of relationships, including sexual ones, prior to formal marriages.

Couples have not always had to have a public ceremony in order to be considered married. Postponing sex until after a wedding service is a surprisingly recent trend (Dormor 2004; Gillis 1985; Stone 1977, p. 604). In fact, at certain periods many brides were pregnant or already had a child by the time they got married (Lawler 2002, pp. 170–4; Stone 1977, pp. 607–11). Premarital conception didn't always carry with it connotations of shame or indecency, as it came to do later on. Thatcher suggests that people who believe cohabitation and premarital sex threaten marriage often think of marriage as an unchanging institution, but that this is not the case (1999, p. 129). It hasn't always been the expectation even within 'Christian' marriages that the spouses would not have any physical sexual relationship before the wedding.

Thatcher says that marriage should therefore be understood as a process, happening gradually. The couple grow together, and mediate grace to each other, even during the time of exploring together whether they want to formalize their marriage (2002, p. 217). In other words, a couple's relationship does not begin at the wedding service. Rather, the service is the point at which the couple affirm (and their friends and family witness to) their *existing* relationship. Thatcher suggests that, for this reason, Christians today should reconsider whether sexual intercourse must only ever happen after a wedding service has occurred. He wants to distinguish between *premarital* sex and *preceremonial* sex. The wedding does not begin the relationship, but witnesses to an existing relationship, so Christians should not assume that all preceremonial sex (sex which has taken place before the wedding ceremony) is also premarital (since the 'marriage' might be understood to have begun earlier, and gradually over time rather than all at once). *Something to Celebrate* also recognizes that some couples who live together might be described as living in 'pre-ceremonial' or 'without ceremonial' marriages (Board for Social Responsibility 1995, p. 116).

However, Thatcher takes the argument further. Preceremonial sex might, he says, be understood not only as legitimate, but actually as helpful – strengthening marriage rather than threatening or eroding it. Sexual activity before marriage could be 'an opportunity to learn the values that the maintenance of married life and love requires. Since marriage is not for everyone, the opportunity may instead become the learning that one is not 'called' to marriage at all' (2002, p. 267). Unmarried people might be actively helped to develop their capacity for sexual pleasure and enjoyment (alone or with a partner), and to integrate it into the broader friendship which may become the firm foundation for a permanent relationship.

Despite his affirmation of the goodness of sex even outside marriage, Thatcher believes that marriage is still the best scenario for creating stable families and promoting the welfare of children (since married couples are statistically less likely to break up than cohabiting couples) (see for example Haskey 1999, pp. 18, 20–1). Thatcher also affirms the value of what he calls a 'theology of waiting'. He believes that, while it's natural that a couple will want to express their love more and more physically as their relationship deepens,

[t]here is still value in restraint. If a couple regard their sexual contacts as symbolic of their whole relationship, they may still feel that uninhibited sexual intercourse might be reserved to symbolize a state of permanence, mutual self-giving and commitment that the relationship as a whole has yet to achieve ... St Paul regarded the presence of the Spirit as a foretaste of a more complete future state (Romans 8.14–30) and so taught that the entire Christian life may be viewed as a state of anticipation. It is open to a Christian couple to regard their committed but technically unconsummated relationship in a similar way. (Thatcher 1993, p. 104)

Christian theologians sometimes talk as though the phenomenon of couples living together and having sexual relationships prior to marriage is a recent one which threatens to undermine the stability of marriage. However, as Dormor, Thatcher and others note, marriage always has been a shifting institution. Indeed, says Dormor,

> That Christian ideas about marriage and its formation should develop from their origins within a largely agrarian society ruled by a semi-divine Emperor and ruthless military machine, economically under-girded by slavery and characterized by high death rates, to a post-industrial democracy with equal rights legislation, universal family planning and high levels of life expectancy is inevitable and appropriate. (2004, p. 61)

Indeed, he adds, in one sense the rise in the number of people cohabiting before marriage (from about 5 per cent of couples in the late 1960s to around 80 per cent by the late 1990s – Dormor 2004, p. 3) represents not a decaying or dissolving of the centrality of marriage in society, but a return to a situation more as things were prior to 1753, when public wedding ceremonies first became legally necessary (p. 62).

QUESTION BOX

Is the distinction between 'premarital' and 'preceremonial' sex a useful one? Why or why not?

Jo Ind describes her reasons for delaying having penetrative vaginal sex:

> Because it is the way we make babies, I have never felt able to have vaginal intercourse in relationships in which I felt fear rather than joy at the prospect that the condom might just burst. Through a mixture of choice and circumstance, this meant the only person with whom I have shared vaginal intercourse has been the man that I did eventually marry. I think

> there is a great deal to recommend about this. It meant that through my decades of being single I had no fear of unwanted pregnancies, minimal risk of disease and some glorious woman-centred sex along the way. It also meant that when I did marry I had a way of being with my partner that I had not experienced with anybody else before. I enjoy that. (2003, pp. 87–8)

Dominian, Montefiore, Rogers: the fullness of sex

Many Christian theologians and ethicists assert that sexual intercourse can only have full justice done to it within marriage. Jack Dominian and Hugh Montefiore are among them. What is the basis for this argument? In part, it stems from pragmatic concern (shared with Thatcher) for the children who might be produced from the sexual relationship. However, Dominian and Montefiore also believe that sexual intercourse's emotional life-giving capacity 'is powerless to operate when it is experienced in transient, unreliable and unpredictable circumstances' (1989, p. 32). As a couple's relationship changes over time, the potential of sex for communicating and creating love also changes and develops. This, they suggest, is one of its strengths, and can't be experienced in short-term or casual sexual relationships. Although one-night stands provide some affection and companionship for lonely people, they still don't allow sex to be all that it really is. Drawing on Dominian's work, Peter Coleman says,

> The offence of using a prostitute or having a one-night stand is that we do not take the other person seriously, nor expect them to take us seriously as a person ... We are called by God into sustaining relationships with him through Jesus and with each other by friendship and one-flesh activities. Sex is not a game of tennis. (2004, p. 234)

Eugene F. Rogers also affirms that 'A one-night stand may transform, but growth usually takes more than an instant' (2006, p. 163). For Rogers, however, this means that marriage *cannot* be the only legitimate arena for sexual intimacy – precisely because (in most jurisdictions at the time of writing) marriage is not open to same-sex couples, but same-sex couples need the 'sanctification' of a deep long-term sexual relationship just as much as heterosexual couples do. 'It is evil', says Rogers, 'to attempt to deprive people of the means of their own sanctification' (p. 164).

It is also important to note the argument, made by Rowan Williams, that sexual intercourse should not necessarily be understood as good or legitimate *just* because it happens within marriage, is potentially procreative, and so on (2002). Some marriages are exploitative and violent; being married to someone is no guarantee that one will want to have sex with them at any given moment. Some theologians have appealed to 1 Corinthians 7.5 to suggest that spouses should not refuse each other sex (except, as the verse allows, by mutual agreement), and this has been pushed to its limits by those who argue that therefore it is always the duty of a married person to be sexually available to their spouse (to give them their 'conjugal rights'). However, in recent years there has been a shift to acknowledging that marriage does not constitute once-and-for-all consent to sex, and, since the late twentieth century, most countries have criminalized marital rape.

Masturbation

Masturbation involves solo sexual activity including stimulation of one's genitals using other body parts or sex toys such as vibrators. Almost everyone masturbates at some point, and masturbation occurs in people of all ages, including babies and young children. Masturbation has sometimes been figured as self-indulgent and therefore to be avoided by those who pursue self-control and ascetic purity. Jordan notes that, in the writings of the seventh-century theologian John Climacus, masturbation is figured as problematic particularly for monks, who spend much time alone but who are nonetheless encouraged to control their physical desires in favour of 'higher' spiritual thoughts (2002, p. 99). Jordan notes that masturbation in the medieval era was also linked to the taboo on bodily fluids in the Hebrew Bible's Holiness Code, whereby someone who ejaculates is unclean until evening: '[Medieval] theologians view masturbation mainly as deliberate self-pollution ... Semen outside of its proper place is conceived as polluting: wasted semen, like menstrual blood, is the by-product of failed fertility' (p. 101).

Theological objections to masturbation

Like homosexuality and the use of contraception, masturbation in Roman Catholic teaching is deemed to transgress Natural Law. If the natural use of the genitals is in marital sexual activity which can lead to the conception of a child, masturbation frustrates this 'natural' purpose, since it does not take place with a spouse and cannot lead to conception. It therefore goes against what Thomas Aquinas (1225–74) (and the Roman Catholic teachings which have followed him) considered one of the main imperatives of human nature, reproduction. Some commentators suggest that this rests on an older model of anthropology in which each sperm was believed to be a tiny complete person: ejaculating sperm anywhere other than inside a woman's body where it could safely implant and grow was tantamount to murder, therefore also contravening another of Aquinas' primary precepts, the preservation of life. (Jordan notes that medieval theologians were therefore much less condemnatory of female masturbation, since women were not believed to contribute any material to new human persons, so female masturbation was not a waste of potential life – Jordan 2002, p. 102).

The *Catechism of the Catholic Church* amplifies the assertion in the 1975 declaration *Persona Humana* that 'masturbation is an intrinsically and gravely disordered action', since 'the deliberate use of the sexual faculty, for whatever reason, outside of marriage is essentially contrary to its purpose' (Congregation for the Doctrine of the Faith 1975). The argument runs that, in masturbation, sexual activity takes place outside a context of mutual self-giving, and is therefore inappropriate. Since masturbation takes place alone, it cannot serve the function of mediating grace to a partner: it is essentially selfish. However, the Catechism also acknowledges that masturbators may be more or less morally culpable depending on their levels of maturity, anxiety or psychological circumstances. *Persona Humana* states that, although masturbation is not expressly banned in the Bible,[1] it can be assumed to fall under the category of impurity or unchastity. (As we'll see in Chapter 7, some translators have suggested that the word *malakoi* in 1 Corinthians 6 may mean 'masturbators', but this is debated.) Masturbators, says the declaration, should not be complacent: even if masturbation is a relatively modest sin, those who engage in it should draw on 'the necessary means, both natural and supernatural, which Christian asceticism from its long experience recommends for overcoming the passions and progressing in virtue' (Congregation for the Doctrine of the Faith 1975).

The evangelical theologian Dennis P. Hollinger says of masturbation, 'The crucial moral issue is not so much the act itself with its intense physical excitement and pleasure. Rather, the two primary ethical issues related to masturbation are lust and the solitary nature of this act in contrast to the nature of sex, which is companionship oriented' (Hollinger 2009, p. 140). Hollinger's argument is similar to that of the Roman Catholic position above: sexual activity is designed to unite two people physically, emotionally, and spiritually. If sexual activity occurs outside the context of a two-person relationship, it cannot fulfil its potential. Masturbation does not allow sex to be all it can be.

Theological endorsements of masturbation

Notwithstanding this kind of argument, some people argue that masturbation, even if it is not the fullest expression of sexuality possible, is still

---

1 Some interpreters have suggested that the condemnation of Onan who 'spilled his seed on the ground' in Genesis 38.8–10 is a condemnation of (male) masturbation. For this reason, masturbation has sometimes been called 'Onanism'. However, others have countered that Onan's specific sin was his failure to father a child by his dead brother's wife (according to the custom of Levirate marriage), not the 'spilling of his seed' as such.

preferable either to extramarital sex (if the masturbator is unmarried) or to adultery (if the masturbator does not have their sexual desires met within their marriage). Masturbation has been figured either as a harmless, pleasurable form of self-exploration, or as the 'lesser of two evils'. Masturbation may provide a safe way for people to satiate their sexual urges without engaging in a sexual relationship for which they are not emotionally ready and which exposes them to the risks of sexually transmitted infections and unwanted pregnancies. Masturbation may promote the integration of self-esteem and body-esteem, reinforcing confidence in one's personal identity 'which in the long run can enhance the quality of attachment and commitments' (Louw 2011). Masturbation may also be a healthy way for young people to learn what feels pleasurable to them so that they are later able to communicate this better to a sexual partner – and may be an important way for girls, in particular, to explore their bodies and their sexual anatomies as sites of joy, not shame (Jung 2000, p. 37).

Patricia Beattie Jung, a Roman Catholic ethicist, suggests that masturbation should not be figured as inherently selfish or self-indulgent. Rather, she says, 'Arousal draws us toward others, and ignites their attraction to us; sexual desire helps to sustain relationships. Even the delights of solitary sex can enliven in us our sense of connection to life. Sexual pleasure inclines those who enjoy it not toward a state of selfish isolation but toward the world' (p. 44). Along similar lines, Margaret Farley notes that although masturbation might *seem* contrary to a central tenet of just sexual activity, namely that it promote relationality, in actual fact many women, in particular, may through masturbation learn things about their own bodies' capacity for pleasure which then enrich their sexual relationships with their partners (Farley 2006, p. 236). In other words, masturbation does not inherently or inevitably make people selfish and inward-focused. Rather, sexual pleasure in itself, even outside a relational context, disposes people to seek relationality.

ACTIVITY

Read this passage, extracted from a letter written by the evangelical Christian author C. S. Lewis in 1956. How persuasive is Lewis's argument as an objection to masturbation? What might Jung or Farley say in response?

The stuff about 'wastage of vital fluids' is rubbish. For me the real evil of masturbation would be that it takes an appetite which, in lawful use, leads the individual out of himself to complete (and correct) his own personality in that of another (and finally in children and even grandchildren) and turns it back; sends the man back into the person of himself, there to keep a harem of imaginary brides. And this harem, once admitted, works against his *ever* getting out and really uniting with a real woman. For the harem is always accessible, always subservient, calls for no sacrifices or adjustments, and can be endowed with erotic and psychological attractions which no real woman can rival. Among those shadowy brides he is always adored, always the perfect lover; no demand is made on his unselfishness, no mortification ever imposed on his vanity. In the end, they become merely the medium through which he increasingly adores himself. (Lewis, letter of 6 March 1956, quoted in Purtill 2004, p. 132)

Polyamory

Is polyamory incompatible with Christianity?

Polyamory literally means 'many loves' and refers to romantic or sexual relationships involving more than two people simultaneously with the full knowledge and consent of everyone involved. Each lover may or may not also have additional lovers of their own. Polyamory is not identical with polygamy: unlike the 'sister wives' of polygamous husbands, who never have sexual relationships between themselves, the partners in polyamorous relationships may be sexually active in various configurations. Traditionally, Christianity has opposed polygamy and polyamory, on the grounds that it is only possible to have a covenantal marriage relationship with one person and that sexual activity should only take place in a marital context. In most countries it is not legal to be married to more than one person simultaneously.

Discussing polygamy, Karl Barth (1886–1968) sets out some of the reasons why he believes marriage should only ever involve two partners, never more:

In marriage as such ... they are faced only by the duty and task of full life-partnership in which their choice has to vindicate itself ... They are confronted by this task and duty, and it can be accomplished only by a couple, not by three or four. The two who have chosen each other have to prove themselves in it. There can be no third person alongside them. How can that mutual liberation and freedom in fellowship which is so constitutive of marriage be genuinely attained if at the same time it is also demanded of a second partner and can be to the advantage of this or that third party? And how can there be fellowship in this freedom if the orientation on each other in which alone it can be realized has to be constantly divided between two very different second partners? And how can the order of life-partnership be fulfilled if there are two firsts and two seconds? In every dimension a third party, whether male or female, can only ... disturb and destroy full life-partnership. If marriage as such, under and in virtue of the divine command, is full life-partnership, it is necessarily monogamous. (1961, pp. 196–7)

This discussion comes within the context of Barth's discussions of marriage and of human maleness and femaleness. For Barth, the necessity of there being two and only two partners is that the marital relationship of male and female echoes the relationship of God and humanity. Involving more than two people would, claims Barth, detract from the theological potency of marriage.

However, Kathy Rudy suggests that polyamorous relationships are profoundly challenging to the assumption that the monogamous model is the best and even most Godly way. She argues that polyamorous practices initiate those concerned into a larger community identity into which, in turn, they can invite others, and which can be a source of mentoring and friendship (1996, p. 10). Rudy argues that those who engage in sexual relationships with more than one long-term partner simultaneously might be more open to sharing other aspects of their lives with a broader community than just their partner or immediate biological family. Of course, this polyamorous vision is somewhat idealistic, as Rudy herself acknowledges (p. 92); and as others have noted, it may render sex a less special way of communicating intimacy (Clark 1994, pp. 217–19).

However, some scholars suggest that polyamory might actually find echoes in the Bible. Robert E. Goss makes a particularly interesting reading of the gender codes in Ephesians 5.21–32.[2] He suggests that, if Christ is a 'bridegroom', then he is a bridegroom with multiple 'brides' (both male and female): that is, multiple human beings. Thus, 'Christ is polyamorous in countless couplings and other erotic configurations' (2004, p. 61). God's love is not limited to only one group or tribe. Goss notes the teaching in Matthew 22 that there will be no marrying or giving in marriage in heaven: does this mean that sexuality will also end, or rather that sexual activity will not be limited to only one partner (p. 56)? Elizabeth Stuart, too, asserts that God loves 'promiscuously', even if, as she notes, 'many Jews and Christians ... would prefer their God to be strictly monogamous' (1995,

---

2 Many biblical scholars believe that these verses, and indeed the rest of the book, are unlikely to have been written by Paul himself, because their socially conservative theology seems so different from Paul's more radical teaching about gender relationships in texts such as 1 Corinthians and Galatians. Some scholars suggest that Ephesians was written by a later member of Paul's community, who wrote under Paul's name either in order to honour him or simply in order that people would set more store by what was written. For further discussion, see for example Best 2004, pp. 10–36; Kitchen 1994, pp. 4–7.

p. 190). Laurel C. Schneider also argues that the incarnation symbolizes God's 'promiscuity', and a division of divinity from sexual 'purity' (2010). W. Scott Haldeman explores whether sexual fidelity in Christian theological perspective should be understood as existing in non-traditional forms of relationship. He suggests that while marriage is life-giving for some people, for others it is deadening. Rather than figuring those who cannot live within the bonds of monogamous marriage as somehow lacking, suggests Haldeman,

> What if, instead, we constructed practices and rites that offer challenge and support to absolutely everybody in whatever ways they are discerning to live out their baptized life – honouring and supporting those who find themselves suited to a life of intimate bonding with one other, but also honouring and supporting those who remained less singularly attached. (2010, p. 311)

In this way, Haldeman believes, theology could testify to the fact that endorsing fidelity doesn't necessarily equal an endorsement of patriarchy, control, capitalism and other phenomena sometimes associated with monogamous marriage in its traditional form.

Open fidelity

Anna Sharman suggests that polyamory can still be a site of faithful relationships – they are simply faithful to more than one partner. Indeed, Sharman prefers to use the term 'open fidelity', which she characterizes as 'a more honest way of having loving relationships', where 'partners are open to the possibility of each of them loving other people' (2006, p. 6). She argues that faithfulness is not the same as monogamy: rather, faithfulness is being honest and trustworthy; but this could include being honest and trustworthy within a sexual relationship involving more than one other person (p. 12). For Sharman, open fidelity is deeply ethical: it requires honesty and responsibility, and leads to fewer secret affairs (and the resulting hurt caused), because there is no need to hide the fact that someone is in a relationship with more than one person (p. 10). Sharman says,

> Jesus condemned adultery, but adultery is not the same thing as consensual, honest non-monogamy. Having more than one partner, or being in an open relationship with the full knowledge and consent of everyone involved, isn't mentioned at all in the Bible, so no one can say that the Bible forbids this. (p. 13)

People who practice polyamory often distinguish between committed polyamorous relationships and casual sexual encounters and note that polyamorous lovers usually take great pains to ensure that everyone practices impeccable contraceptive use and undergoes regular testing for sexually transmitted infections in order to safeguard sexual health.

Nonetheless, most Christian theologians reject the idea that a relationship involving more than two partners could be what God intends. Many theologians appeal to marriage's permanency and exclusivity of commitment as goods and believe these are undermined by polyamory. Polyamorous relationships are also more likely to involve children being brought up by adults who are not their biological parents, which some theologians believe undermines the relationship between sex and reproduction as well as possibly having unfavourable results for the children. Furthermore, polyamory may undermine the marital imagery whereby the relationship between two (and only two) human partners is held to echo the relationship between God and humanity, or Christ and the Church. The complete self-giving symbolized in marriage would, in this account, be diluted if the giving of oneself were divided between two or more people.

Prostitution and sex work

'Prostitution' or 'sex work'?

A prostitute is someone who engages in sexual activity with another person in exchange for payment: money, gifts, accommodation, commodities or the promise of protection. Some critics believe that the term 'prostitute' is stigmatizing, and prefer the term 'sex worker'. Others, however, believe that the term 'sex worker' implies that prostitutes are as likely as anyone else to have freely chosen their line of work, which they dispute. In some jurisdictions, it's illegal to work as a prostitute; in others, it's legal to work as a prostitute but not to pay for sex; in others, buying and selling sex is entirely legal. A prostitute can be male or female – though the literature on prostitution mainly focuses on women – and might work alone or with a manager (sometimes called a pimp or madam) who arranges clients for them and may take a cut of the profits, in exchange for a safe place to work or other protection, or commodities such as drugs.

A 2003 report on sex working in nine countries found that, of the 854 female and male sex workers interviewed:

- 71 per cent had been physically assaulted while working as prostitutes;
- 63 per cent had been raped;
- 89 per cent said that they wanted to escape prostitution;
- 75 per cent had been homeless;
- 68 per cent displayed symptoms of post-traumatic stress disorder (Farley et al. 2003, pp. 33–4).

Melissa Farley and her co-researchers claimed that sex workers in countries where prostitution was legalized and regulated also reported similar stories (Farley et al. 2003, p. 61; Farley 2004). The 2003 report characterized prostitution as inherently violent and abusive, causing long-term trauma for sex workers. Some critics suggest that reports like this focus only on extreme cases and do not take account of sex workers who find prostitution safe and satisfying work (see for example Weitzer 2005). However, Esther Reed asks whether sex workers' own right to choose to be involved in prostitution is the only good at stake:

> Should sex-workers not have the right to choose the work they do and the financial control it gives them over their lives? This leads one to ask what, if any, are the reasonable limits that can be imposed upon their right of free sexual expression? To what extent ought their individual rights of sexual expression be restricted in order to achieve some wider social purpose? (1994, p. 71)

Prostitution and the Bible

The biblical tradition represents prostitutes almost exclusively as lascivious, highly sexual, 'whorish' women who entice men with their wiles. Sometimes these are 'symbolic' women whose 'whoredom' represents unfaithfulness to God – for example, Gomer, the wife of the prophet Hosea, who is presented as echoing Israel's dalliances with foreign gods, and the broad symbolic figure of the 'whore of Babylon' in Revelation, who may represent imperial Roman rule. There is little sense in the Bible that someone might be a sex worker because of economic necessity or exploitation. In short, argues Avaren Ipsen (2009), the language of the Bible is strikingly violent and oppressive toward prostitutes. However, the Bible also contains narratives of women who work as prostitutes but are nonetheless honoured. Throughout the Gospels, Jesus is accused of associating with prostitutes, and he himself notes in Matthew 21.31–2 that prostitutes had followed John the Baptist and says that they will enter the Kingdom of God ahead of the chief priests and elders. The fullest biblical account of a prostitute is that of Rahab, who is visited by Israelite spies in Joshua 2 and agrees to hide them from the Canaanite men in return for protection for herself and her family. In Hebrews 11.31, Rahab is presented as an example of someone with great faith. Rahab's canny actions have been understood as subversive and proto-feminist by some scholars (Bird 1989; Ipsen 2009, pp. 85ff), though others see them as a possible betrayal of her own ethnic roots, particularly given that a woman called Rahab also appears in Jesus' Israelite genealogy (Matthew 1.4) (Donaldson 2006; Dube 2000, p. 77; Dube 2006). Rose Wu notes that feminist–liberationist readings of Rahab in particular have sometimes focused on Rahab's sexual freedom and economic independence, and sometimes on her example as an exemplar of faith for other prostitutes (Wu 2001, p. 78; see also Streete 1997 and Guider 1995).

Another woman often figured as a prostitute in the Roman Catholic tradition, although the Bible itself does not describe her as such, is Mary Magdalene, who in Mark's, Matthew's and John's Gospel accounts is the first person to see Jesus alive after his resurrection. It is important to note that Roman Catholics honour Mary Magdalene as a penitent, that is, with the assumption that she ceased working as a prostitute and repented of this activity. Such 'rehabilitation' of Mary Magdalene might lead to the marginalization of other Christian women sex workers (Corley 1989).

Prostitution and the Christian tradition

The Christian tradition has frowned upon prostitution for several reasons:

1 Many Christian theologians have argued that the place of sexual activity is within exclusive marital relationships. Prostitution removes sex from this context. Prostitutes are likely to have multiple sexual partners, therefore undermining the exclusivity of sex.
2 In Christian thought, one of the important purposes of sexual activity is for procreation. People who have sex with prostitutes are unlikely to be open to the possibility of parenting and raising a child with them.
3 Some Christians argue that sexual activity which takes place from solely lustful motivations is wrong. Prostitution, they believe, divorces sex from love.
4 Prostitution commodifies sex, making it into a transaction rather than a gift to be freely given and received by the participants. This erodes the capacity of sexual activity to be sacramental and to mediate grace.
5 Many Christians and others hold that prostitution tends to be exploitative of those who are sex workers, and to reinforce the objectification of women in particular. The **trafficking** of human beings for the purposes of sex work is considered particularly problematic in ethical terms.
6 In the Hebrew Bible tradition, prostitution was often associated with non-Israelite cultic religion, and was therefore deemed illegitimate for the people of God. In the New Testament era, Jewish prostitutes may have been condemned for their association with the ruling Roman authorities.

However, there is also evidence of Christians accepting prostitution for pragmatic reasons. Both Augustine (354–430) and Aquinas (1225–74) seemed to consider prostitution a sad but necessary phenomenon in a lustful world; Augustine suggested that abolishing it would mean there was no outlet for lust, which, if suppressed, might dangerously unsettle society (*De Ordine* 2.4.12). Aquinas, in the *Summa Theologica*, cites and endorses Augustine's argument, suggesting it might be appropriate for those in authority to tolerate a particular evil in order to avoid a greater one (see Dever 1996). For Aquinas, the existence of prostitutes with whom men could satisfy their lusts safeguarded the virtue of other women. In other words, publicly sanctioned prostitution was the lesser of two evils.

Christians who have opposed prostitution as a phenomenon have not necessarily condemned prostitutes themselves. For example, the nineteenth-century social reformer, Josephine Butler (1828–1906), campaigned for the repeal of the Contagious Diseases Act which she felt was demeaning to women. The Act stated that women who were believed to work as prostitutes must submit themselves to regular examinations to ensure that they did not have any sexually transmitted infections which might spread to their clients and thereby weaken the population. In effect, any woman living in areas where prostitution was common (e.g. near sea ports and army barracks) was likely to be forced to undergo an internal examination. Women who refused were imprisoned. Butler believed that this demonized women who worked as prostitutes, removing responsibility from their clients (who were not expected to undergo similar examinations). She felt women were being treated as publicly owned amenities rather than human beings. Butler also campaigned against child prostitution, and was instrumental in the British age of sexual consent for females being raised from 13 to 16.

Wu, Ipsen and Scholl: contemporary theologies of prostitution/sex work

Rose Wu comments that, for Christian theologians, studies of prostitution can't be only about the morality of adultery or sex outside marriage. Wu says, 'We cannot just focus on sex as a personal moral issue; rather, we must examine the unequal power structures and social constructions of gender, sexuality, class and race that create systems that exploit the vulnerable, especially the poor, the young, people of colour, and socially outcast women' (2001, p. 71). In other words, women who work as prostitutes should not be understood as loose women who entice men; rather, prostitution should be interpreted through a lens which examines critically who buys and sells sex and why, and who really has power and control in the transaction. Reflections on power are relevant on a global as well as a local basis: Wu blames the arrival of Western capitalist values in Asia for the rise in sex tourism in countries like Thailand (p. 73). Wu notes that feminists in different contexts, including feminist theologians, have figured sex work differently. White and Western feminists are more likely to figure prostitution as a freely chosen occupation, or to emphasize the subversive or empowering dimensions of making men pay for sex, whereas non-white and non-Western feminists are more likely to stress the financial and social factors which may make some women disproportionately likely to enter prostitution.

Avaren Ipsen, in *Sex Working and the Bible*, draws on narratives from sex workers themselves surrounding biblical texts about prostitution.[3] Ipsen aims to formulate a liberationist reading of the texts that does not exclude prostitutes or marginalize them further by ignoring their perspectives. Many conventional readings of the texts, she suggests, assume that sex is inherently indecent or dangerous, and that prostitution is deviant and the preserve of either licentious or exploited women (2009, pp. 2–3). Ipsen notes that many women who work as prostitutes figure themselves first and foremost as mothers and/or daughters, and engage in sex work mainly in order to be able to provide for their families (p. 99). There are some problems with Ipsen's book: for example, by focusing on and doing Bible readings only with those who are activists in favour of prostitution, or who are still working as prostitutes, the perspectives of those who have come to see prostitution as problematic may be ignored. Nonetheless, her close reading of texts with and alongside sex workers raises important questions about whose interpretations are erased in biblical criticism, and is a reminder that violence toward prostitutes persists both inside and outside the biblical narratives.

Lia Claire Scholl (2012) argues that most Christians' responses to sex work characterize prostitutes either as sinners or victims, with no middle ground. Assuming that all prostitutes are victims, argues Scholl, erodes their agency and leads to fewer rather than more choices for them. Scholl believes that the most effective Christian response to sex work must be to provide viable economic alternatives for prostitutes, such as providing free childcare for those seeking work, or paying for them to attend college. Christian communities should also welcome sex workers non-judgementally, in order to combat their stigma and isolation.

QUESTION BOX

Would it be possible to construct a theological argument in favour of prostitution? What theological resources could you draw upon in constructing such an argument?

---

3 These were the story of Rahab in Joshua 2 and 6; the story of the two prostitutes fighting over a child in 1 Kings 3; the Gospel accounts of the woman who anointed Jesus with ointment; and the texts about the 'whore of Babylon' in Revelation 17–19 (Ipsen 2009, p. 9).

Summary

In this chapter we explored various kinds of sex which take place outside a context of marriage. They are not the only ones: we might also have considered sex after a marriage has ended because of the death of a spouse; or sex with another partner which takes place when one's spouse has dementia (Ellison 2012, p. 41); or a variety of other kinds of activity. You may want to do further reading on these topics yourself.

We examined Thatcher's account of premarital versus preceremonial sex, and his suggestion that sex before marriage should not be dismissed as inherently problematic by Christians. Next, we considered the suggestions that masturbation is self-indulgent, an improper use of the genitals, and a selfish rather than self-giving kind of sexual activity. We noted Jung's suggestion that masturbation might be a useful and healthy means of self-exploration for people who are not yet ready for physical sexual relationships with others. Then, we asked whether polyamorous relationships might be figured as more open and inclusive than monogamous ones, whether polyamory is inherently antithetical to Christianity, and to what extent faithfulness can apply to relationships involving more than two partners. Finally, prostitution and sex work were examined through the lens of the biblical treatment of prostitutes. We asked whether the removal of sex from a context of marriage is always problematic, and whether prostitution always and inherently involves the commodification of sex and the exploitation of those involved. We noted the arguments of scholars like Ipsen and Wu that it is important to speak with and learn from sex workers, not condemn them.

In this chapter, the focus has been on types of sexual activity – and, perhaps, *what* people do more than *why* they do it. But the *why* question is a crucial one for theologians, because it gets to the root of some big issues: what sex is for, and how our sexual relationships fit into a bigger picture of how we conceptualize and treat other people. In some respects, getting hung up on particular activities can be a bit of a red herring. As Margaret Farley (2006) makes clear, and as we'll see in the Conclusion, more important questions than 'Is this activity okay?' might be 'What does my sexual activity say about myself and others?', 'Does my expression of sexuality promote justice?', and 'Is love served?' Any sexuality which does not promote justice, love and relationality, and a deeper respect and regard for others, is likely to remain questionable in Christian theological terms.

In the following chapter, we'll focus in detail on same-sex relationships and the Christian tradition.

Questions for study and reflection

1 Is sexual activity outside marriage ever justifiable in Christian theological terms?

2 Would it ever be permissible for a Christian to work as a prostitute or to pay for sex? Why or why not?

3 What resources are there in the Christian theological tradition, if any, for constructing positive theologies of sex beyond marriage?

Further reading

Dormor, Duncan, 2004, *Just Cohabiting? The Church, Sex and Getting Married*, London: Darton, Longman and Todd.

Ellison, Marvin M., 2012, *Making Love Just: Sexual Ethics for Perplexing Times*, Minneapolis, MN: Fortress Press.

Ipsen, Avaren, 2009, *Sex Working and the Bible*, London: Equinox Press.

Thatcher, Adrian, 2002, *Living Together and Christian Ethics*, Cambridge: Cambridge University Press.

7

Same-Sex Relationships and Christian Theology

It is only in the marital relationship that the use of the sexual faculty can be morally good. A person engaging in homosexual behaviour therefore acts immorally. To choose someone of the same sex for one's sexual activity is to annul the rich symbolism and meaning, not to mention the goals, of the Creator's sexual design. Homosexual activity is not a complementary union, able to transmit life; and so it thwarts the call to a life of that form of self-giving which the Gospel says is the essence of Christian living. This does not mean that homosexual persons are not often generous and giving of themselves; but when they engage in homosexual activity they confirm within themselves a disordered sexual inclination which is essentially self-indulgent. (Congregation for the Doctrine of the Faith 1986)

Homosexuality and 'nature'

Homosexuality and Natural Law

People who oppose homosexual activity often do so on the grounds that homosexuality is 'unnatural' (many appealing to Paul's words in Romans 1). Some assert that homosexuality is just not part of how God intended the world to be (Grenz 1990, pp. 232–3). Homosexual desires must therefore result from sin, good sexual impulses led astray, or the fallen nature of creation (Hollinger 2009, p. 181). Mark D. Jordan suggests that this belief underlies Christian concern to 'shield' impressionable young people from homosexual influences in case their developing sexualities are corrupted in this direction (Jordan 2011).

Some theologians argue that homosexual activity is 'unnatural' based on the Roman Catholic **Natural Law** tradition. Theologies from Natural Law are grounded in the thought of Thomas Aquinas (1225–74), the Catholic philosopher and theologian, who was influenced by Aristotle (384–22 BCE). Aristotle, a Greek philosopher, believed that there were certain goals or goods to which human life was oriented, including courage, justice, wisdom and self-control, and that living according to these would bring about the happiness of the 'good life'. Aquinas picked up on these and added to them the specifically Christian goods of faith, hope and love. Within Aquinas' Natural Law thinking, humans and other creatures have specific purposes for which God has designed them. Failing to fulfil these purposes 'frustrates' God's work. Humans, believed Aquinas, have been given wisdom and reason which reflects God's own wisdom and reason. If our reason is working properly, our own goals for our lives should match those God has ordained. We will be able to discern what is good for us by looking at the good, God-created world around us. However, because of the existence of sin, our reason does *not* always work perfectly: sometimes our judgement is clouded, and we cannot tell what the right course of action is. Sometimes we know what we *should* do, but deliberately sin by choosing to do something else instead.

The idea that we should be able to discern God's will from looking at the world around us seems to be the root of some opposition to homosexual behaviour. Some proponents of Natural Law appeal to evidence from non-human animals, arguing that sex in other animal species seems to be primarily about reproduction rather than pleasure, and doesn't take place between animals of the same sex. However, recent research shows that this is not necessarily the case: scientists have observed same-sex sexual activity in species including dolphins, penguins, toads, flies, snakes, apes, sheep and fish. Nathan W. Bailey and Marlene Zuk acknowledge that it is difficult to call this 'homosexuality' per se: scientists simply note what animals *do*, not what their motivations are (2009, p. 441). Even so, some studies suggest that same-sex sexual behaviour in animals serves a wide range of social purposes including bonding, and isn't limited to 'forced' occasions (in other words, it doesn't take place only when no opposite-sex partner is available) (pp. 441–2). Bonobo apes engage in a variety of reproductive and non–reproductive sexual activity (including genital rubbing and oral sex), and scientists have suggested that bonobo sex, too, is important for forming social bonds. Same-sex activity might therefore be more 'natural' than is often claimed (though some scholars counter that observing how the world *is* does not necessarily tell us how it *ought* to be – Hays 1986, p. 194).

Another problem with applying Natural Law thinking to homosexuality is that Aquinas believed there are primary and secondary moral precepts (or principles). While the primary precepts are, he believed, common across human times and cultures, their outworkings – the secondary precepts – may vary. So while humans might agree on the primary precept that it is good to have and bring up children, there might be some variation in ideas about precisely how this should take place: should all children be brought up by their own biological parents, or are children better cared for in groups or co-operatives by adults who are not their parents? Do all parents need to be married couples of opposite sexes, or can single people, unmarried couples and same-sex couples also be good parents? Are artificial interventions such as IVF legitimate ways to help people have children, or should infertility be accepted as a sad but unchangeable fact of life?

This comes into particularly sharp focus when we think about the inter-relations between having sex and having children. Some theologians argue that since a 'natural' purpose of sex is reproduction, homosexual sex is un-natural, because it can't lead to the birth of biological children. Of course, by the same logic, using artificial contraception to prevent the conception of children by heterosexual couples is also illegitimate – as Roman Catholic teaching does indeed state. We saw in Chapter 5 that there has been debate in the theological tradition about whether having children is the *primary* purpose of sex in marriage or merely *a* purpose among others. If sex is mainly for creating children, and if children are a good that all couples should welcome, same-sex relationships indeed miss what sex is 'for'. But if sex is for *more* than making children, and if people can become parents by non-biological means such as adoption, then the relationship between sex and children is weaker, and it's harder to argue that same-sex relationships are illegitimate or unnatural.

Some theologians go further, and argue that the very nature of the male and female genitalia makes it clear that they are 'made for each other' (Gagnon 2001). The 'anatomical fittedness' of the penis and vagina, and the fact that only penetrative vaginal sex can lead to reproduction, makes it clear that this alone is God's intention for sex, argues Robert Gagnon. But this is problematic for several reasons: first, it makes reproduction the sole or highest purpose of sex, and sex the sole or highest purpose of the genitals. Second, it fails to take into account those people whose genitals make it difficult or impossible for them to participate in sex of this kind (including, for example, many intersex people). Third, it writes moral norms onto bodies in a way that may be unjustified: couldn't I similarly observe that the fact my finger fits so neatly into my nostril means it was 'meant' to be there?

Is 'nature' always and obviously good?

Aquinas believed that the natural world reflected the will of the creator God and therefore pointed humans toward God. But is everything natural also good? What about natural diseases, such as cancer, or natural disasters such as earthquakes and tsunamis? Some Christians might counter that these things were not part of God's original intention for creation, but have come about because creation is fallen and imperfect. However, Christopher Southgate and other theologians have noted that death, predation and loss seem to be built into the very structures of the universe (Southgate, Negus and Robinson 2003; Southgate 2008). Nature can be violent, destructive and oppressive of life.

So there is a bigger question to be considered here, about the extent to which nature coincides with culture. The 'natural' state of humans is to be animals who live outside and do not wear clothes: that is how we existed at an earlier stage of our development. As part of our culture, however, many human societies have developed forms of dress and housing which allow us to live in climates which we could not 'naturally' tolerate, because they would be too cold, hot, or otherwise inhospitable. Are humans behaving 'unnaturally' by wearing clothes and living in air-conditioned or centrally heated buildings? In fact, Aquinas would probably counter that to be rational and intelligent is part of how humans reflect God – and is, therefore, precisely appropriate to humans' nature.

The question, then, is how we discern *which* 'unnatural', 'artificial' technologies are virtuous ones and promote the common good. By analogy, we also need to ask whether things which are sometimes dismissed as being 'unnatural' actually just fail to fit in with a particular *cultural* standard – and how we assess the ways in which nature and culture interact.

Importantly, things considered natural in one time and context aren't necessarily considered natural in every context. Paul writes in 1 Corinthians 11.14 that it's obvious men should have short hair and women long hair because 'nature itself' demonstrates that this should be the case. Loader comments, '*We* might define that as cultural convention ... but ... *Paul* sees natural as proper, the way nature and creation was meant to be' (2010, p. 24). Similarly, phenomena such as slavery, feudalism and racial segregation have been understood in the past (including by those who believed themselves to be devout Christians and faithful readers of the biblical texts) as part of the natural order of things, but have now, by and large, been rejected as unjust outworkings of imperfect social norms. Ideas about what is natural and good change: contrary to what Aquinas believed, faithful and rational people don't all interpret the world in the same way.

Romans 1.26–8 seems to provide a clear condemnation of homosexual activity for both men and women on the grounds that it is 'against nature' (in Greek, the phrase used is *para phusin*). However, it's important to remember that what Paul understood as natural and unnatural was conditioned by his culture. In Paul's context, some scholars remark, 'unnatural' sexual acts might have included *any* sexual acts which can't lead to procreation, whether same-sex or opposite-sex (Loader 2010, p. 18; Hanks 2006, pp. 591–2; Fredrickson 2000), or acts in which men failed to take an appropriately active role and women a passive role as befitted their social standing (Swancutt 2003; Brooten 1998, pp. 260–5; Fredrickson 2000). Paul seems to suspect that Gentiles are especially susceptible to sexual temptations of this kind, and another theory is that Paul wants believers to distance themselves from idolatrous sexual practices (Countryman 2007, pp. 109–15; Loader 2010, pp. 14–15).

Scholars including Eugene F. Rogers have re-read this passage noting that exactly the same phrase, *para phusin*, is used again in Romans 11 to describe God's activity in grafting Gentiles into the tree of salvation (2009, pp. 19–21, 25). The metaphor is agricultural: grafting branches from one species onto a plant growing from the roots of another species is clearly 'unnatural', doing something nature itself has not. It is going *beyond* nature, beyond what is usual (Martin 2006, pp. 54–9). However, it is *not* therefore inherently negative or to be condemned. In fact, suggests Elizabeth Stuart, Christians, too, 'are called to imitate their God in acting *para phusin*, in excess of nature' (2003, p. 106). This might mean rejecting the 'natural' desire for marriage and family in favour of more open forms of community. According to this argument, whether or not something is 'natural' doesn't tell us much about its moral status.

Furthermore, theologians have observed that all human sexuality – whether heterosexual, homosexual, or something else – has been affected by the fact that we live in an imperfect world. Geoffrey Rees, for instance, says Christians shouldn't argue that it's just as legitimate to be homosexual as heterosexual, because that misses the point: even heterosexuality is 'broken'. Being heterosexual can't save us from the fact that we're all affected by sin (2011). In light of Rees's argument, the question then is why so many Christians continue to believe that homosexuality is *more* broken, *more* damaged and *more* imperfect than heterosexuality – and why church statements on sexuality can hold that, while imperfect heterosexuality at least 'gestures toward' God's plan, imperfect homosexuality is 'objectively disordered'.

ACTIVITY

Read the following passage written by Elizabeth Stuart and Adrian Thatcher, who are Roman Catholic and Anglican respectively. What light does their argument shed on the Natural Law objection to homosexuality? How successful is the analogy of the red hat when thinking about the 'natural' purposes of sex?

A year ago a group of people presented one of us with a splendid red hat. Instead of being worn regularly, it was hung above a desk. So the hat which could be worn on the head has become an ornament, a piece of art. The givers of this gift would not, we think, be offended that the hat is rarely worn – we think they would be amused and delighted with the use of their gift. If, however, the hat had been cut up and used as a dish rag or if the cat had been allowed to use the hat as a litter tray they would have justifiably been offended and hurt. Contempt would have been demonstrated for their gift and lack of gratitude. When we apply this insight to the realm of sexual activity it is easy to see that rape and abuse of any sort is a gross and

---

debasing misuse of the gifts God has given us, including the gift of people. We are given people to love, so to fail to love them or to treat them in ways incompatible with love is a clear misuse of a gift. But what about homosexual activity? This activity need not be any more inherently offensive to the giver than the hanging of the hat on the wall, provided it is done in love and leads to gratitude to God. (1997, p. 176)

The ex-gay movement: can people be healed of homosexuality?

Some Christians, particular in conservative evangelical Churches, believe homosexual people can change their sexual orientation through prayer, counselling and therapy, and, in some cases, come to have successful hetero-sexual relationships. The 'ex-gay' movement teaches that homosexuality stems from a lack of adequate socialization into one's gender (Gerber 2008, p. 15): men who know they are 'real men' and have appropriate friendships and role models among other men will have no problem being sexually attracted to women. The movement is controversial, because many critics believe it leads to homosexual people suppressing their true natures, which might itself be deeply psychologically damaging. However, ex-gay people usually claim that their homosexual orientation is *not* natural, but a distor-tion of God's intention for humans.

In her study of a Californian ex-gay programme, New Hope Ministry, Tanya Erzen comments that many involved with the movement acknow-ledge that change is not easy or unproblematic: 'To them, change is a process of conversion and belonging that is uncertain, fraught with relapses and some temporary successes. For many, years after doing a program, change remains simply a leap of faith or a belief that they are doing what God wants for them' (Erzen 2006, p. 218). Erzen notes that some ex-gay people criticize non-Christians for framing sexuality mostly as a question of desire. Ex-gay advocates argue that wholeness and fulfilment depend on obeying God, not the fulfilment of sexual desires (pp. 220–1). Their homosexual desires may feel 'natural' to them, but since according to the Bible they are *un*natural, their desires cannot be trusted (Gerber 2008, p. 19).

Some scholars suggest that ex-gay communities are themselves 'queer' spaces, since they provide a designated place for evangelical Christians who identify as homosexual. Erzen says,

Although the political goals of the ex-gay movement and queer activists are radically distinct, by accepting that a person's behaviour and desire will not necessarily correspond with their new ex-gay identity or religious identity, ex-gay men and women enact a queer concept of sexuality when they undergo queer conversions. Although men and women in ex-gay ministries do not and cannot envision homosexuality as a positive way to be, their lives also exemplify the instability and changeability of their own identities rather than serve as a testament to heterosexuality. (2006, p. 14)

In short, says Mark D. Jordan, 'There is no ex-gay without gay' (Jordan 2011, p. 151). However, comments Kristin Aune,

Yet, in the ex-gay movement ..., queer elements are limited ... by evangelicals' simultaneous adherence to normative models of gender and sexuality. These models claim that heterosexuality and hegemonic notions of masculinity are the ideal that all men should aim for. (2009, p. 49)

Homosexuality and the Bible

Christians who believe that same-sex relationships are illegitimate usually base their objections, in part, on the Bible. Passages in both the Hebrew Bible and the New Testament seem to state that homosexuality is wrong.

ACTIVITY

Look up the following Bible passages. Gather several different translations of the Bible, including some pre-twentieth-century ones if possible. If you have studied Hebrew or Greek, look at an interlinear version. What similarities and differences do you notice between translations? What strikes you about the kinds of behaviour that are condemned?

Genesis 19.1–11
Leviticus 18.22
Leviticus 20.13
Romans 1.18–32
1 Corinthians 6.9–10
1 Timothy 1.9–10

Lost in translation?

You probably noticed that the translations differed in terms of exactly what they seemed to be condemning. Some theologians and biblical scholars suggest that things are not clear-cut when assessing what the Bible says about homosexuality. In fact, they argue, the Hebrew and Greek words usually translated as 'homosexual' in English versions of the Bible actually have different or ambiguous meanings. No contemporary reader who reads the Bible in translation can read the Bible independently of its history of interpretation, since translation from one language to another always involves ideological decisions about precise shades of meaning, especially when the word or phrase being translated is an uncommon or obscure one. The way in which readers interpret texts is known as **hermeneutics**. Different readers have different hermeneutical strategies depending on how they believe it is legitimate to use the Bible or other texts. As Martti Nissinen states,

> Applying the biblical texts to our time ... is always a hermeneutical event, in which the differences between the biblical and the contemporary worlds are in some way smoothed out. In practice, the tradition of biblical interpretation, several thousand years old, serves as the bridge, whether this is acknowledged or not. Internalized reading guided by this tradition is often unconscious to the point that the readers of the Bible do not even notice that they are constantly interpreting what they are reading. (1998, p. 4)

A famous example comes from analysis of the words *arsenokoites* and *malakoi* in 1 Corinthians 6. In the New Revised Standard Version of the Bible, *arsenokoites* is translated 'sodomites' and *malakoi* as 'male prostitutes'. Other versions' translations of *arsenokoites* include 'lecherers' and 'liers with mankind' in older versions, and 'sexual perverts', 'homosexual offenders', 'homosexual perverts' and 'male homosexuals' in newer ones (Martin 2006, p. 38). Other translations for *malakoi* in older translations include 'weaklings' and 'effeminates', with the shift to homosexual perversion coming only in the mid-twentieth century (pp. 43–4). Dale B. Martin believes that the shift in interpretations of these words over time demonstrates that each generation of translators reads its own particular concerns into the text: it is not obvious that a word literally meaning 'soft' should be translated 'homosexual', yet this is what many recent translators have done, because they already assume the text condemns homosexuality.

The question, then, is whether what is condemned by the biblical texts is really the same thing meant by 'homosexuality' today. Martin is doubtful: 'Interpretations of *arsenokoites* and *malakos* as condemning modern homosexuality have been driven more by ideological interests in marginalizing gay and lesbian people than by the general strictures of historical criticism' (pp. 37–8). Daniel A. Helminiak has a similar view. He notes that, until the Reformation, 'the word *malakoi* was thought to mean 'masturbators'. It seems that as prejudices changed, so have translations of the Bible' (1994, p. 86). Helminiak also says,

> The Catholic Church's very recent New American Bible invites the same cynicism. It translated *arsenokoitai* as 'practicing homosexuals.' How

amazing! A first-century text would now seem to teach exactly what Roman Catholicism began teaching only in the mid-1970s: to be homosexual is no fault, but to engage in homogenital acts is wrong. (pp. 86–7)

Martin and Helminiak argue that the biblical texts on homosexuality simply might not mean what they seem to mean, that the words translated 'homosexual' may mean other things, and that the acts being forbidden are actually far more specific acts, like anal rape, or sex between a much older man and a much younger boy, rather than all homosexual activity in all contexts.

Similarly, scholars have argued that the 'sin of Sodom', condemned in the Genesis 19 story and passages such as Zephaniah 2.8–11 and Matthew 10.15, is not homosexual activity at all. For warrant, they turn to Ezekiel 16.49: 'This was the guilt of your sister Sodom: she and her daughters had pride, excess of food, and prosperous ease, but did not aid the poor and needy.' Here, the 'sin of Sodom' sounds like something other than homosexual activity. In fact, many scholars argue that the real sin of Sodom is the inhospitality to outsiders shown by the men of Sodom, not the homosexual activity itself. Some suggest that the story is about sexual violence (both the men of Sodom's attitudes toward the guests, and Lot's willingness to give the men his virgin daughters instead), and should not be understood as outlawing all homosexual activity. Jordan argues that 'sodomy' to mean homosexual anal sex is a 'medieval artifact', of which 'no trace' is found before the eleventh century (Jordan 1997, p. 1). The Church Fathers seem to have understood sodomy to be pride, lust, blasphemy or immodesty, not homosexuality specifically. Jordan suggests the real 'sin of Sodom' is inhospitality, or broad 'sexual irregularity', not simply homosexual activity (1997, p. 32). The biblical scholar Walter Brueggemann suggests that, given the context of the story, even if the Genesis passage *is* condemning a particular kind of sexual behaviour, it must be violence and rape rather than homosexual activity as such (1982, p. 164).

Texts and contexts

Scholars have made similar arguments about the other passages which seem to condemn homosexual activity. Nissinen argues that it is not possible to read biblical texts about homosexuality outside the context of other ancient texts and information about beliefs surrounding sex, gender roles and sexuality in contemporaneous societies. He suggests that the verses in Leviticus which characterize same-sex sexual activity as an 'abomination' must be read in the context of ancient Israelite belief. For the ancient Israelites, it was particularly important to be seen as distinct from their neighbouring tribes. This underlies the 'Holiness Code' of Leviticus 17—26: rules about purity and cleanliness which, if followed, would mark out Israel as distinct. The Hebrew word translated 'abomination', says Nissinen, 'is a general term with strongly negative connotations and which denotes a transgression of a divinely sanctioned boundary ... often used in connection with different, usually not fully defined customs of a mostly cultic nature affiliated with worship of foreign gods' (1998, p. 39). The real problem with homosexual behavior is therefore that it is associated with non-Israelite tribes – and especially with the Canaanites, descendents of Noah's son Ham. It is prohibited because it is linked with idolatry, not because it is wrong in and of itself.

Similarly, scholars have suggested that, at a time when it was particularly important for Israel to be strong in numbers, there might have been compelling reasons to prohibit non-procreative sexual activity – but that this prohibition was contingent on its time, not binding for today. 'Unnatural' relations in passages such as Romans 1.26, often interpreted as outlawing lesbianism, might actually refer to non-procreative (and therefore 'unnatural') anal sex between women and men. Recently, scholars have suggested that the New Testament's condemnation of homosexuality might rest on its links with Roman imperialism and is therefore, again, a question of identity rather than morality as such (Johnson 2010). For fuller accounts of the biblical texts on homosexuality which suggest that they may not in fact condemn all present-day same-sex sexual activity, see Martin 2006, Helminiak 1994, Vasey 1995, Nissinen 1998, and Scroggs 1983.

But what if the biblical texts actually do mean exactly what they seem to mean in many English translations – that all homosexual activity is wrong? In this case, the question is a much broader one: as the bishops of the Church of England say, 'Once we have ascertained what the texts say we still have to ask whether they are binding upon us, and, if they are, how we should apply them today' (House of Bishops 2003, p. 119). In particular, what does it mean to read and interpret the Bible given that it contains texts which seem troubling to modern readers – texts which seem to sanction genocide and murder and to subordinate women to men as well as renouncing homosexuality?

Some readers conclude that, unfortunately, it is not possible for Christians to sanction or justify homosexual activity. Other readers conclude that the Bible does indeed condemn what we now understand as homosexual activity, but that this condemnation was contingent on its time and culture and does not apply today. Contemporary Christian readers eat shellfish, trim their hair and wear mixed-fibre garments, although the Bible explicitly prohibits these behaviours, so contemporary Christian interpreters might also justify homosexual activity on the grounds that what is appropriate in one society might not be appropriate in another. In this account, the Bible is still an important text for Christians, but the 'big picture' of love and justice throughout the Bible should take precedence, not a few scattered texts about homosexual activity.

Other scholars counter that it is simply not possible to explain away the anti-homosexual texts. Reading the Bible therefore involves dealing with these texts. This might entail lamenting the fact that they are there at all, challenging their authority, railing against them, or simply accepting with regret that they exist; Michael Carden says of the Sodom story, for instance, 'Genesis comes from an ancient and alien culture and if there are aspects of that culture that shock and dismay today then so be it' (2006, p. 25).

Gene Robinson argues that it is crucial to take account of the ways in which broad worldviews have changed since the time the biblical texts were produced:

> The ancient Hebrews' understanding of the science of reproduction and sexual activity was different from ours today. Male sperm was thought to contain all of nascent life; the only contribution made by women in the reproductive process was providing a place for the foetus to incubate. So any 'spilling' of male seed was considered tantamount to murder. Ancient Hebrews were a small minority, living in a hostile, heathen environment, struggling to reproduce, build up their population, and survive, so any waste of male sperm was antithetical to that survival and synonymous not only with murder, but a betrayal of the national interest ... Today, we understand that both sexes contribute to the process of human reproduction, and our day's problem is over-population rather than under-population. We believe sexuality to have purposes far beyond reproduction. Yet these few verses of scripture are quoted as if nothing has changed in our understanding since biblical times. (2008, p. 21)

'Gay-friendly' texts?

Some interpreters explicitly argue that not only does the Bible *not* condemn homosexual relationships, it actually endorses them.

ACTIVITY

Read 1 Samuel 18, 19, 20 and 23, and 2 Samuel 1, which chart the story of David and Jonathan's close friendship. What features, if any, might suggest that this friendship has something in common with present-day homosexual relationships? What features, if any, might suggest that this friendship is different from present-day homosexual relationships? What problems might there be in calling David and Jonathan's relationship 'homosexual'? What advantages might there be in calling David and Jonathan's relationship 'homosexual'? Why have some lesbian and gay interpreters, in particular, been so keen to read David and Jonathan's relationship as a proto-homosexual one?

What did you make of this story? You probably noticed that David and Jonathan both have relationships with women: David, in particular, has several wives and concubines with whom he has children. However, the two men are also described as kissing each other, and weeping passionately when they have to part; 2 Samuel 1.25–6 portrays David lamenting Jonathan after his death, saying, 'Greatly beloved were you to me; your love to me was wonderful, passing the love of women.' Some interpreters read this as a suggestion that David's love for Jonathan was similar to his love for women (i.e. also sexual), but stronger; others believe David considered his friendship with Jonathan more powerful than simply sexual love could be.

It is important to remember that, in many parts of the ancient world, women were not considered rational or spiritual agents to the same extent as men. For this reason, a man would not necessarily have expected to be able to have a close intellectual and spiritual friendship with his wife or another woman: deep, passionate friendships were considered only to take place between men, who had the capacity for them. Although the language of David and Jonathan's friendship might sound sexual or romantic to our modern ears, we should be wary of anachronism. Even today, behaviour understood as sexual or romantically significant in one society might be read differently in another. In many Western countries, for example, it's common for couples of opposite sexes to hold hands in the cinema or when they walk along the road. As a result, if two men or two women are seen to be holding hands in a similar situation, the assumption is that they, too, are probably involved in a romantic relationship. However, in some other cultures, holding hands is considered a sign of friendship between people of the same sex and, while many male friends walk along holding hands, it isn't something habitually done by a husband and wife or a boyfriend and girlfriend. Ken Stone remarks that it would be anachronistic to assume that, in the social world of the Hebrew Bible, the persons with whom one experienced the greatest closeness and intimacy were the same persons with whom one engaged in sexual activity. He says,

> It is quite possible that David's lament over Jonathan actually testifies to a world in which the lives of most people were characterized by, on the one hand, ongoing sexual relations with persons of the opposite sex; and, on the other hand, affectionate and emotionally intimate relations and companionship with persons of the same sex which, however, did not necessarily entail sexual intercourse. (Stone 2006, p. 208)

In other words, calling their relationship 'homosexual' might lead us to think it has more in common with a modern homosexual relationship than we can really be sure about. The word 'homosexuality' has only existed since the nineteenth century; the idea of *a* homosexual – that is, someone whose homosexual activity comes to characterize their identity – is very recent.

The idea that someone might have sex *only* with men or *only* with women is modern. This is not to say that we can be sure there was *no* sexual activity between David and Jonathan. However, it does mean that any sexual activity between them cannot be understood to characterize their entire identity. Both had sexual relationships with women: if they also had a sexual relationship with each other, this did not render them entirely different from the norms and expectations for Jewish men of their time, which were that men should marry women and have children. However, Stone also comments that, although 'love' in the ancient context could mean a political or intellectual relationship, not just a sexual one, 'the specific comparison that David makes between Jonathan's "love" and "the love of women" ... is somewhat unusual even within the framework of those ancient Near Eastern political "love" relations' (2006, p. 206). Thus 'some readers of the Bible argue that a more intimate, and possibly even sexual, understanding of Jonathan's love for David is less forced than the political meaning' (p. 206). Stone concludes that, while it is not possible to arrive at any definitive answer about the exact nature of David and Jonathan's relationship, the very fact that it has multiple interpretations can be read as 'queer' and as pointing to diversity and ambiguity in the Bible (p. 208).

Even if it would be anachronistic to characterize them as 'homosexual' as such, then, the story of their relationship can still help modern readers to explore whether the assumption that same-sex relationships are entirely alien to the biblical texts is a reasonable one. The David and Jonathan narrative might be identified as 'gay friendly', and has therefore become an important focus for some lesbian and gay Christians who have felt alienated from some other parts of the Bible because of the way it has been used to vilify them.

Similarly, lesbian and gay readers have identified other biblical stories, narratives, characters and themes which they consider particularly precious to queer and LGBT people. These include the close relationship between Ruth and Naomi; Ruth's words of promise to Naomi in Ruth 1.16 have been used in some services of blessing for same-sex partnerships. Indeed, the fact that they have also been used in heterosexual marriage services is a cause of anger and sadness to the lesbian minister Nancy Wilson, who says, 'Heterosexuals have ripped off our love stories for too long!' (Wilson 1995, p. 156). Furthermore, Wilson explicitly argues that figures such as the businesswoman Lydia in Acts 16, and the centurion with a deep affection for his ill slave in Matthew 8 and Luke 7, are lesbian or gay. Indeed, she says, 'I believe that it is essential for gay men, lesbians, and bisexuals to take back the Bible. If we are not included among the stories and characters of the Bible, then it cannot be our book' (Wilson 1995, p. 164).

QUESTION BOX

Do you agree with Wilson that lesbian and gay people today need to be able to see lesbian and gay figures in the Bible in order to feel it is part of their own tradition rather than something alienating and dangerous to them?

Church teachings on homosexuality

Church of England

In 2003, Jeffrey John, at the time a Church of England vicar in the diocese of Southwark, was nominated for the post of Bishop of Reading. John, an openly homosexual priest, had a long-term same-sex partner. The fact that a homosexual person had been nominated to such a high-profile role in the Church of England caused consternation among conservative Anglicans who believed homosexuality was illegitimate. The heated disagreement threatened to split the Anglican Communion and, at the request of the then Archbishop of Canterbury Rowan Williams, John stepped back from accepting the appointment. Afterwards, Williams requested that no member congregations of the Anglican Communion should appoint openly gay bishops, since the unity of the Communion took precedence. However, in 2009, the Episcopal Church in the USA elected the lesbian priest Mary Glasspool as a bishop in Los Angeles. Williams expressed regret at the appointment, suggesting that it would shatter the 'period of gracious restraint in respect to actions which are contrary to the mind of the Communion' (http://www.archbishopofcanterbury.org/2650). Much frustration was expressed at Williams' apparent stepping-back from his formerly open liberal views on homosexuality in order to preserve the unity of the Anglican Communion. What, then, is the official Church of England standpoint on homosexuality, both for clergy and for lay people?

In the late 1980s, the issue of homosexuality was under close discussion in the **General Synod**. Tony Higton, a priest in Essex, brought a motion to the 1987 General Synod asserting that the Church of England should affirm that 'homosexual acts are sinful in all circumstances'. However, the Synod softened the wording, and the motion eventually passed stated that 'homosexual genital acts fall short of [the] ideal and are to be met by a call to repentance and the exercise of compassion'. This language of 'falling short' reappeared four years later in the 1991 document *Issues in Human Sexuality*. The document states that, because clergy are in a position of being public representatives of the Church, they should not do anything which could lead people to lack confidence in them, and that 'There can be no doubt that an ordained person living in an active homophile relationship does for a significant number of people at this time present such a difficulty' (House of Bishops 1991, p. 44). As a result, 'in our considered judgement the clergy cannot claim the liberty to enter into sexually active homophile relationships' (1991, p. 45).

Notice the distinction between *identifying as homosexual* and *being sexually active*. The document doesn't state that homosexual clergy should renounce their orientation, but rather that their call is ideally to celibacy.[1] The bishops make clear that the standard for clergy is more rigorous than for lay people, because the clergy are figureheads and pastors for whole communities. Nonetheless, Jeffrey John himself believes this argument is weak, since married people, celibate people, and partnered homosexual people should *all* be able to look to the clergy as examples of how to live faithfully (John 2003, pp. 55–6). More cynically, Elizabeth Stuart and Adrian Thatcher suggest that the bishops' focus on clerical relationships is 'not ... because the issue of homosexuality among the laity has been re-solved, but because church authorities implicitly recognize that their control over the laity is limited, whereas they have much more power over the lives of ordained ministers' (Stuart and Thatcher 1997, p. 168).

Many people were disappointed that the 1991 document seemed so conservative, given the more liberal nature of a booklet produced by the General Synod's Board for Social Responsibility, *Homosexual Relationships: A Contribution to Discussion*, sometimes called the 'Gloucester Report', which asserted,

> We have not brushed aside what the Bible has to say about sexuality: we have indeed taken great pains to interpret it rightly. On the other hand we have not felt bound simply to repeat its every utterance ... We have at the same time laid claim ... to a liberty of discerning what God is saying to us here and now, whether it be something old or something new. (Central Board of Finance 1979, p. 4)

The Gloucester Report argued that there were some individuals for whom heterosexual attraction seemed deeply unnatural, who would be unlikely to be fulfilled by heterosexual marriage but were also not called to celibacy (1979, p. 51). As a result, 'We do not think it possible to deny that there are circumstances in which individuals may justifiably choose to enter into a homosexual relationship with the hope of enjoying a companionship and physical expression of sexual love similar to that which is to be found in marriage' (p. 52). The report still did not consider homosexual relationships

---

1 This distinction is one reason why Rowan Williams' request that Jeffrey John should step back from his appointment as Bishop of Reading caused such anger among many Christians, given that John and his partner had indeed had a celibate relationship.

'as the moral or social equivalent of marriage' (p. 52), but this was, nonetheless, a major step.

A decade later, in 1989, a document known as the 'Osborne Report' was produced. This was the result of a working party set up to advise the Church of England bishops on the pastoral issues surrounding homosexuality, and, importantly, involved close consultation with homosexual people. The report stated that not all homosexual activity was morally identical, and that 'even those Christians who believe that objectively speaking, all genital sexual intercourse outside heterosexual marriage is wrong' should acknowledge that 'homosexual promiscuity and lustful self-indulgence is one thing; homosexual activity in a young person's exploration on the way to maturity is another; deliberately chosen physical expression in a mature and long-standing relationship is yet a third' (Board for Social Responsibility Working Party 1989, p. 53). The authors affirmed that there was still something distinctive about male–female relationships, but admitted that they had struggled to voice what or why (p. 62). They noted that Anglicanism had a history of respecting personal moral choice even when this conflicted with the official line, so that 'if homosexual Christians ... do not find the formal statements of the Church about their lives at all helpful the Church needs both to behave in a way which recognizes their liberty of conscience and provides space to test the matter out in pastoral and theological discussion' (p. 83). Jane Shaw and others have suggested that the 'listening process' so central to the Osborne Report, drawing on the experiences and stories of homosexual people and insisting the bishops remember that they were first and foremost dealing with *people*, failed to occur in subsequent reflections on the topic (Shaw 2012, p. 14). Perhaps because of the climate in the General Synod following the Higton motion, the Osborne Report was not officially published or endorsed,[2] and, instead, the bishops released *Issues in Human Sexuality* in 1991 (Shaw 2012, p. 14).

In 2003, the House of Bishops published a longer follow-up document, *Some Issues in Human Sexuality: A Guide to the Debate* (House of Bishops 2003). This reinforced the earlier teaching that homosexual activity could not be endorsed as an equally valid moral choice as married heterosexual activity. However, the bishops also remarked,

> The Anglican tradition ... has sought to combine long-held principles with a response to changes in society in a mature and responsible pastoral manner. On some issues, for example the need for faithfulness within and abstinence outside marriage, its beliefs have not changed. On others, for example contraception and divorce, the Church of England, in a relatively short space of time, accepted what had previously been regarded as morally unacceptable ... We have to accept that the Church of England

2 The Osborne Report had been leaked in 1990, but was not made publicly available until January 2012, via the website of the *Church Times*.

could in principle change its current approach in the case of the particular issues under consideration in this report [including homosexuality] providing that (a) it had sufficient theological grounds for so doing and (b) that such a change did not entail a change to its core ethical beliefs. Much of the current debate, for example on homosexuality, turns on whether (a) and (b) apply. (p. 35)

Roman Catholic Church

The Catechism of the Catholic Church states,

> Homosexuality ... has taken a great variety of forms through the centuries and in different cultures. Its psychological genesis remains largely unexplained. Basing itself on Sacred Scripture, which presents homosexual acts as acts of grave depravity, tradition has always declared that 'homosexual acts are intrinsically disordered.' They are contrary to the natural law. They close the sexual act to the gift of life. They do not proceed from a genuine affective and sexual complementarity. Under no circumstances can they be approved. The number of men and women who have deep-seated homosexual tendencies is not negligible. This inclination, which is objectively disordered, constitutes for most of them a trial. They must be accepted with respect, compassion, and sensitivity. Every sign of unjust discrimination in their regard should be avoided. These persons are called to fulfill God's will in their lives and, if they are Christians, to unite to the sacrifice of the Lord's Cross the difficulties they may encounter from their condition. Homosexual persons are called to chastity. (from the Catechism of the Catholic Church, 3.2.2; online at http://www.vatican.va/archive/ccc_css/archive/catechism/p3s2c2a6.htm)

Although homosexual people are not blamed for their orientation, and are to be treated with respect and compassion, *both* homosexual acts *and* the inclination to homosexuality itself are characterized as 'disordered'. Homosexual people are called to chastity, which the Catechism defines as 'the integration of sexuality within the person', which 'includes an apprenticeship in self-mastery' (ibid.). Homosexual activity cannot be deemed valid, because marriage between a man and a woman is deemed the only legitimate arena for sexual activity.

As we saw in the opening quotation in this chapter, the Roman Catholic Church also figures homosexual activity as 'self-indulgent', because people of the same sex who have sexual intercourse are, by definition, not open to the possibility of creating new biological life, and are therefore – according to the logic of the Roman Catholic Church – limiting their self-giving.

The Roman Catholic account has been criticized from several angles: it caricatures homosexual people; it pathologizes their 'condition'; it fails to allow them to integrate their sexuality within themselves; it makes them objects of pity, which some might resent; it characterizes their sexuality as somehow more fallen than anyone else's sexuality. Stuart and Thatcher argue that, if it is indeed true that most homosexual people find their homosexuality a trial, this 'is not likely to be the consequence of homosexuality itself but of reactions to it' (Stuart and Thatcher 1997, p. 178).

Gareth Moore, a Dominican friar, believes that given the inconclusiveness of the biblical evidence on homosexuality, there are not grounds on the strength of the Bible alone for affirming that homosexuality is anything other than good. For this reason, he believes, the official Roman Catholic position on homosexuality is untenable: 'It is irrational for serious, reflective Christians ... to accept church teachings on homosexuality. The only rational course at the moment for such Christians is to continue to believe in the possible goodness of homosexual relationships' (2003, p. 282). Criticizing the Vatican 'Letter to the Bishops of the Catholic Church on the Pastoral Care of Homosexual Persons', Moore rejects its teaching that fidelity to Christ demands suffering on the part of homosexuals (since they do not have any legitimate genital outlet for their sexual desires) (p. 17). He notes that many Catholics find Catholic teaching on homosexuality abhorrent, and argues that questioning it is legitimate: just as children's questioning of their parents and teachers does not mean they reject all their parents' and teachers' authority, so questioning the Catholic hierarchy about its position on homosexuality does not necessitate rejecting Catholicism outright (p. 21). Tradition and truth are not necessarily identical (p. 25).

Similarly, another Catholic, James Alison, asks,

Is the teaching of the Vatican Congregations ... compatible with the Gospel ...? I'll quote it for you again: 'the homosexual inclination, though not itself a sin, constitutes a tendency towards behaviour that is intrinsically evil, and therefore must be considered objectively disordered'. To me at least it is clear. This teaching is interposing itself between the regard of Christ and our own sense of being in a way which tends to pervert the simple regard of one who loves us as we are, and as loved we will find ourselves becoming someone different. It is teaching us instead that God will only love us if we start from somewhere else ... It is because I think that the teaching is incompatible with the Gospel at this very fundamental level that I also think that, despite the protestations of the current office-holders in the Roman Curia, it cannot in fact be the teaching of the Church. (2003, p. 106)

Queer theologies

Reclaiming and reframing

Some theologians and biblical interpreters have argued that most human societies are biased in favour of heterosexual people and against homosexual people. This bias is sometimes called heterosexism. Heterosexism is also linked with **heteronormativity**, the idea that not only is it normal and right to be heterosexual, but that people who do not fit this model are deviant. Heterosexism is sometimes expressed as homophobia, prejudice or violence against homosexual people. Some critics suggest that the Bible privileges heterosexual sexuality and family structures; others suggest that the Bible is actually quite ambivalent about heterosexuality, marriage and family, but that homophobic interpreters have projected their own agenda onto the Bible and made it seem much more anti-homosexual than it actually is.

Since the early 1980s, some scholars have been engaged in queer theology and queer biblical interpretation. The term 'queer' has been 'reclaimed', having in the past been used as a derogatory insult for LGBT people. Many queer theologians and biblical scholars are themselves lesbian, gay, bisexual or transgender, although queer theology has a broader remit than simply LGBT concerns. Queer theology builds on queer theory, a critical discourse which examines the reasons why homosexuality is considered abnormal or perverse in many societies, and seeks to uncover or demystify the ways in which heterosexuality is made normative.

In the early days of queer theology and biblical criticism, some scholars sought to do the kinds of 'reframing' and 'reclaiming' work outlined above. This included reinterpreting the biblical texts which seemed to condemn homosexuality, and seeking queer 'ancestors' – figures such as David and Jonathan, Ruth and Naomi, and the eunuchs – in the texts. Some writers, like John J. McNeill and Troy Perry (who founded the gay-friendly Metropolitan Community Church), strongly asserted that they had been born gay, and that this was how God had created them and meant them to be, not a sinful route they had chosen (McNeill 1976, Perry 1972). Other early queer theological writers, like Robert E. Goss, were particularly interested in embodiment, arguing that bodily experiences were legitimate ways of encountering God, and that homosexual bodily experiences could be just as revelatory of God's goodness and love as heterosexual ones (Goss 1993).

However, other queer theologians follow queer critical theorists like Judith Butler who argue that there is no such thing as a 'natural' sexuality, whether heterosexual or homosexual. Gender and sexuality are, suggests Butler, *constructed* and *performed* (Butler 1990). In this account, asking whether there is a 'gay gene', or whether God made people homosexual, misses the point (Schneider 2000, p. 4). There is no such thing as 'natural' sexuality. The real question is therefore why society (and especially religious society) endorses some constructions of sexuality more than others, and why calling a despised sexuality 'unnatural' remains such a potent marker of rejection.

Extending the boundaries of queer theology

More recently, queer theologians and biblical scholars have expanded the kinds of work they do. Although queer theology and biblical studies are particularly invested in questioning why heterosexuality is considered superior to homosexuality in many societies and religious traditions, queer interpretation is not exclusively concerned with sexuality. Queer readers also call into question why particular races, classes, genders and bodies have often been considered more perfect or legitimate than others in religious terms. Queer interpreters have worked closely with black, feminist, **womanist**, liberationist, and **postcolonial** theologians. They are interested in power, and how one group comes to have power over another. Whose ideas become the influential, accepted ones in any given society? What are the processes by which this happens? If the powerful voices in a religious community, the 'gatekeepers' of a community's activity and doctrine, are also the voices privileged by society in general – which might mean white, male, heterosexual, educated, economically stable voices in particular – then to what extent can religious traditions be sources of hope for those whose perspectives are not considered normative? Rachel Muers characterizes queer theology simply as 'a critical and constructive rereading of established categories of sex and gender from a Christian theological perspective' (2007, p. 200). On this reading, queer theology is not only or exclusively to be concerned with or done by homosexual people.

Some queer theologians assert that the Christian tradition is actually very positive about queer and LGBT people, and that the anti-homosexual emphasis of much contemporary Christianity distorts Christianity's true message. Others conclude that the Christian tradition does indeed seem either negative or at least ambivalent about homosexuality – in which case the question is whether Christianity can ever be a 'healthy' tradition for queer people to be involved with, or whether they should simply walk away from it.

Queer theologians also ask what it would mean if the Christian theological tradition were read queerly. For example, what might a queer portrayal of Jesus look like? Such a reading does not necessarily mean asserting that Jesus was homosexual (though some writers have done so). Thomas Bohache says that a queer Christology 'will not try to argue for or against the gayness of Jesus, but will seek rather to determine what his Christ-ness says to marginalized peoples of all generations, including today's queer community' (2003, p. 19). In this account, it is possible to call Jesus 'queer' regardless of what one believes about his sexual orientation, for his queerness is to do with his critique of power structures. Lewis Reay, for example, claims that Jesus queers gender by overturning normative patriarchal social structures (2009, p. 157). In other words, by behaving in ways that transgressed the expected gender norms of his time – associating with women, speaking to them in public, not marrying – and by questioning established patterns of family, Jesus resists the idea that the heterosexual family, led by a male, is the most desirable social pattern.

The contributors to a collection called *Take Back The Word* (Goss and West 2000) seek to reframe the way the *whole* Bible is read, rather than trying to find homosexual 'ancestors' or specific 'gay-friendly' texts. They suggest that, while such strategies might be of comfort or empowerment for some people, a radical reframing of the whole Bible will go further in developing the way queer Christians understand themselves, and how readers deal with and live with texts which represent danger as well as opportunity for them. Queer readings often suggest that there is no such thing as the 'true', 'original' meaning of a text (and, therefore, that arguments about the 'real meanings' of words such as *arsenokoites* and *malakos* are futile). Rather, queer interpreters often argue that texts always have multiple, differing interpretations that exist alongside one another – and that this is part of the fullness of interpretation and the mystery of the text, not something to be avoided. However, for this reason, notes Mary Ann Tolbert, the Bible is also always likely to remain dangerous for queer people in some respects, because its open-endedness means that it will always be used against them by certain people (2000, p. ix). In this account, it is no more possible to say unambiguously that the Bible does *not* condemn homosexuality than that it *does* condemn homosexuality.

Queer theology and Christian history

Queer theologies have also encompassed parts of the Christian tradition beyond the Bible itself. Some commentators, for example, have looked back to the writings of the Church Fathers and have suggested that they are radical, subversive and queer. Michael Nausner and Virginia Burrus suggest that the writings of Gregory of Nyssa (c.335–c.395) contain strands subversive of fixed gender norms (Nausner 2002; Burrus 2007). Other scholars suggest that figures like Mary Magdalene and Mary the mother of Christ, revered by Roman Catholic women in particular, might be read as queer and revolutionary, given their non-typical sexualities (Althaus-Reid 2000; Córdova Quero 2006). The question is whether calling Gregory and other figures 'queer' or 'gender-bending' is simply anachronistic, or whether these kinds of creative re-readings are a way of disturbing the unquestioned heteronormativity of the tradition.

Queer theologians also suggest that, not only are homosexual people not condemned by God, but that aspects of their lives and faith actually make them prophetic figures, showing heterosexual people how they themselves should live. Kathy Rudy suggests that lesbian and gay patterns of relationship and friendship may mean that homosexual people can more readily form the kinds of community envisaged by Jesus, grounded in friendship and loyalty to many members of a community, not just one's partner and biological children (1996). Similarly, Elizabeth Stuart believes that heterosexual marriages have often repeated unhelpful patriarchal and authoritarian patterns that are an overhang from times when wives were counted as part of their husbands' property. She does not believe that homosexual people should campaign to be allowed to marry, because marriage itself has usually been an oppressive institution, and homosexuals' broader patterns of family and community, rooted in friendship rather than legality, are more equal (1995, p. 43). She suggests that homosexual people may have particularly strong and welcoming friendship networks precisely because they are less likely than heterosexual people to be split up into nuclear family units (p. 49).

John Boswell, a Roman Catholic historian, argued that the Christian tradition had not been as anti-homosexual as is often assumed. In *Christianity, Social Tolerance and Homosexuality* (1980), he argued that concern about stamping out same-sex activity had not really arisen in the Church until about the twelfth century. In *The Marriage of Likeness: Same-Sex Unions in Pre-Modern Europe* (1994), he argued that at certain points in its history, the Christian Church had not only accepted but actually celebrated same-sex partnerships. Boswell appealed to liturgies in Christian prayer books which he believed were designed to consecrate same-sex personal relationships in a similar way to heterosexual marriages – though other scholars have argued that these rites were more like rites of adoptive brotherhood than of sexual or romantic partnership. Although some critics argue that Boswell too unproblematically drew parallels between ancient and modern forms of same-sex relationship (though he himself acknowledged that it would be anachronistic to term those who took part in the ancient rites 'homosexual' since this concept was a nineteenth-century invention), his work remains a valuable reminder that the Christian tradition has not necessarily always treated close same-sex relationships with suspicion.

QUESTION BOX

1 What do you make of Stuart's account of homosexual friendship? Do you agree that heterosexual marriages tend to repeat oppressive patterns? Is this inevitable? Do you agree that homosexual people can more easily form open and welcoming communities than heterosexual married people can?

> 2 What difference might it make to contemporary theologies of sexuality if Boswell were correct in his belief that Christianity had consecrated same-sex relationships at some earlier points in its history?

Is Christianity 'healthy' for queer people?

Some queer Christians have decided that, in all good conscience, they can no longer remain affiliated with the Christian tradition. For many such people, it's simply not possible to divide what Christianity *could* be from what it *has* been, or escape the fact that it has oppressed and rejected so many homosexual people. However, others suggest that, despite their struggles with aspects of Christianity, it is still their tradition, and that to walk away from it would actually make it less likely, rather than more likely, to be open to homosexual people in the future (Sweasey 1997, p. 79). Moreover, Alison Webster notes that many people do hold together identities which seem contradictory, and that this is simply part of the complexity of being human. Discussing what it means to be both a lesbian and a Christian, Webster says,

> It does not make sense that, as a lesbian, I enjoy romantic Hollywood heterosexual feel-good movies. But I do. Likewise, it does not make sense that I feel attracted to Christianity – enmeshed in and by religion, when intellectually I have decided that at many levels it is rubbish, and damaging rubbish at that. The truth is that I cannot leave it alone, intellectually or personally, and that is what I have to make sense of. (1998, p. 31)

Similarly, says Grace M. Jantzen,

> For many who have had the straight rule of christendom applied in hurtful and destructive ways, the answer is to slam the book shut altogether and have nothing more to do with this story. For some people that is surely a healthy response, not just 'understandable' in a condescending way, but a very good conclusion to the particular script they have been required to read. But for me that will not do. Part of the reason is that christendom has not only been the worst of my personal past but also the best of it; and the need to deal with the former requires a reappropriation and transformation of the latter. I will not become a more flourishing person by cutting off my roots. (2001, pp. 276–7)

Bisexuality

Not everyone is attracted only to people of the same sex as themselves, or only to people of the 'opposite' sex. In fact, some researchers, most famously Alfred Kinsey, have argued that most people fall somewhere along a scale of bisexuality. However, there has been little Christian theological reflection on bisexuality. This may be for several reasons:

1 Christian theologies which legitimize only heterosexual sexuality will not endorse same-sex attraction, even if only as part of a range of attraction.
2 It is often assumed that bisexual attraction leads to unfaithfulness, and most Christian theologies have focused on the goods of monogamy and loyalty to a single partner.
3 It is sometimes argued that bisexuals simply have not yet worked out whether they are homosexual or heterosexual. Bisexual people are sometimes characterized as closeted homosexuals, and treated with suspicion by both homosexual and heterosexual people. Even some LGBT and queer theologies have not given space for reflection on the experiences of bisexual people of faith (Bernhardt-House 2012).
4 Although some bisexual people participate in polyamorous relationships with more than one partner at a time, most bisexual people have only one partner at a time: bisexuals with same-sex partners are often assumed to be homosexual, and bisexuals with opposite-sex partners to be heterosexual. This means bisexuality can be 'invisible'.

Phillip Bernhardt-House believes that even queer and LGBT-accepting interpretations of biblical texts on homosexuality may prove 'unfriendly' to bisexual people, since they often focus on the category of nature and assume that everyone is 'naturally' either homosexual or heterosexual, thereby leaving bisexuals out in the cold (2012, pp. 26–8).

Stephen Lingwood criticizes the Church of England for its account of bisexuality in the 2003 report *Some Issues in Human Sexuality* (2012). The bishops state,

> We recognize that there are those whose sexual orientation is ambiguous, and who can find themselves attracted to partners of either sex. Nevertheless it is clear that bisexual activity must always be wrong for this reason, if for no other, that it inevitably involves being unfaithful. The Church's guidance to bisexual Christians is that if they are capable of heterophile relationships and of satisfaction within them, they should follow the way of holiness in either celibacy or abstinence or heterosexual marriage. In the situation of the bisexual it can be that counselling will help the person concerned to discover the truth of their personality and to discover a degree of inner healing. (House of Bishops 2003, p. 215)

Lingwood counters that to figure bisexuality as an absence of a clear orientation, rather than an orientation in its own right, is dehumanizing. He also notes the misconception that bisexuality inevitably equals unfaithfulness (2012, p. 35): *attraction* to people of more than one sex does not necessarily entail simultaneous sexual *relationships* with more than one partner, of whatever sex. Lingwood also engages with the theology of Marcella Althaus-Reid, who believed that bisexuality, like queerness, could disrupt mainstream theology's over-association with heterosexual norms and narrow certainties. Lingwood argues, however, that bisexuality should not in fact be understood as alien to Christianity. First, he notes, even God might be understood as somehow bisexual: 'The bisexual person, whose sexual love is not limited by gender boundaries, is more open to an understanding that God's love is not limited to any one group. Indeed, to the extent that God's love extends to men and women, God can be called bisexual' (p. 40). Second, he argues, 'Bisexuality ... displays a strong parallel with a major theme in the Judeo-Christian story: namely love that transgresses boundaries' (p. 43). Homosexual people who have been liberated from having to hide their sexuality should not in turn oppress bisexual people. Likewise, bisexual people should realize that God frees them not just for self-expression but in order to help others (p. 42).

In a sociological study of bisexual Christians in Britain, Alex Toft notes that most of the respondents were wary about discussing their bisexuality openly in a religious context, and most did not feel able to talk to other members of the congregation about being bisexual. Indeed, some were 'out' as bisexual to everyone *except* at their churches (2009, p. 76). For this reason, Toft claims that many bisexual Christians have had to 'privatize' their spiritualities, having necessarily 'adjusted what Christianity means to them and re-located their beliefs into a self-constructed belief system' (p. 79) in order to survive.

Summary

The majority of Christian denominations which officially consider homosexuality a 'fallen', distorted or less perfect version of sexuality than heterosexuality nonetheless counsel that homophobia and prejudice against homosexual people are completely unacceptable. They urge compassion and love toward homosexual people. Nonetheless, an increasing number of critics are asking whether it is really possible simultaneously to love and accept a homosexual person *and* to tell them that their sexuality is 'objectively disordered' (Williams 1997a, p. 17). Given that the Bible records nothing said explicitly by Jesus about homosexuality, argue some Christians, it can't be as big an issue as all that; Jesus said far more about poverty and injustice, so perhaps that's where people of faith should be turning their attention. Other Christians counter that the argument from silence is not compelling: Jesus didn't mention climate change, drugs, IVF or pornography, either, because they didn't exist as issues in his time in the way they do in ours, but that doesn't mean that Christians today shouldn't try to formulate responses to them informed by broader theological principles.

It's important to remember that Christian theological objections to homosexuality and same-sex relationships are grounded in the assumption that human beings only have two sexes, male and female. However, we saw in Chapter 3 that the existence of intersex makes very clear that human sex is more complex than that. Whether they base their objections to homosexuality on biblical passages which seem to oppose it, on Natural Law-type grounds concerning reproduction, or on a belief that heterosexual relationships are part of the orders of creation set out by God, then, theologians opposed to same-sex relationships will need to think very carefully about exactly how sex is defined.

We started this chapter by examining the Natural Law objection to homosexuality, and asked to what extent nature is still a useful category for theologians by which to assess whether or not an activity is legitimate. We noted different treatments of the biblical texts on homosexuality, and observed that some scholars believe they do not refer to homosexuality at all but to other kinds of sins, perhaps rape or being inhospitable. We asked whether, even if the Bible does prohibit what we understand as homosexual activity today, this should be binding on readers in the twenty-first century.

We noted that some readers believe the Bible is actually positive about homosexuality, containing explicitly 'gay-friendly' texts and figures, while other readers believe that, regrettably, the Bible does indeed express hostility to homosexuality.

We explored teachings from the Church of England and Roman Catholic Church on homosexual orientation and activity. Next, we engaged with queer theologies, which re-examine the Bible and the Christian theological tradition in light of the experience of non-heterosexual readers. Finally, we noted that many people identify not as homosexual or heterosexual but as bisexual, and that bisexuality has received very little attention in Christian theologies to date.

In the Conclusion, I'll go on to suggest that all Christian thinking about sex and sexuality must happen in the context of the broader Christian story, and especially the conviction that a new and just age is coming and has already begun.

Questions for study and reflection

1 What are some of the problems and potentials of using the category of 'nature' when assessing what kinds of sexual activity are proper for Christians?

2 Some Christians maintain that *attraction* to someone of the same sex is morally neutral, but that homosexual *activity* is sinful. Do you find this a convincing position, or do you see difficulties with it?

3 Does the Bible condemn homosexuality? What does your answer mean for Christians today?

Further reading

Cheng, Patrick S., 2011, *Radical Love: An Introduction to Queer Theology*, New York, NY: Seabury Books.

Cornwall, Susannah, 2011, *Controversies in Queer Theology*, London: SCM Press.

Jordan, Mark D. (ed.), 2006, *Authorizing Marriage? Canon, Tradition, and Critique in the Blessing of Same-Sex Unions*, Princeton, NJ: Princeton University Press.

Loader, William, 2010, *Sexuality in the New Testament: Understanding the Key Texts*, London: SPCK.

Martin, Dale B., 2006, *Sex and the Single Savior: Gender and Sexuality in Biblical Interpretation*, Louisville, KY: Westminster John Knox Press.

Conclusion

Sexchatological Tensions: Sex in Light of the Last Things

Sex changes

Although our journey in this book through some approaches to sexuality in the Christian tradition hasn't been a chronological one, we've nonetheless seen that Christian attitudes toward sex, gender and sexuality have been impacted by contemporaneous norms and changes in culture and society. Gareth Moore suggests that there has, in the twentieth and twenty-first centuries, been a particularly significant shift in the relationship between theological teachings and social-cultural norms. He notes that Christian teachings on adultery, masturbation, homosexuality and certain other sexual behaviours used to paint them as objectively sinful because of their apparent transgression of Natural Law goods. Of course, people did these things anyway – but their transgression of Christian teaching was considered 'a sign of the power of sin rather than of the weakness of the teaching' (1998, p. 223). More recently, however, the wisdom and authority of the teaching itself has been challenged by social shifts.

What changed? There is not one simple answer to this. Moore suggests that factors include the influence of Freud and other psychologists in the nineteenth century, who argued that sexuality was an element of personality and that repression of one's sexuality could lead to problems in terms of maturity and mental well-being. This in itself built on an increasing emphasis, since the eighteenth century, on individualism and personal freedom, goods sometimes in tension with the institutional norms of organized religion. Moore also notes the important, growing influence of the feminist and lesbian and gay movements in the twentieth century, which challenged traditional attitudes in a variety of areas: in their light, notes Moore, what had been 'established truths' began to look more and more like 'merely the views of socially dominant heterosexual males' (1998, p. 225). Duncan Dormor adds that changes in the middle of the twentieth century 'brought about a fundamental shift in the relationship between individuals and traditional forms of authority, whether they were political, religious or legal' (2004,

p. 72). In addition, Moore notes the impacts of multiculturalism and global-ization: increasing awareness of other societies and how they functioned made clear that Christian responses to sexuality and other ethical issues existed alongside a range of other sophisticated ethical and belief systems, and could not necessarily be understood as unproblematically self-evident (1998, p. 225).

Christianity, sexual abuse and sexual violence

In the course of this book, we've considered Christian accounts of sexuality which have portrayed it as sacred, beautiful, sacramental, pointing humans toward God, and something which communicates the deepest and most pro-found truths about who we are as human beings. But there's another side to sexuality, one which can tend toward violence and exploitation. Although Christian theologians have often opposed prostitution, pornography and exploitative sex, sadly, Christianity has, at times, itself been accused of being complicit in violent and abusive sexual practices. Sometimes, church structures or inadequate safeguarding procedures have been blamed for making it difficult to bring people in positions of authority to account. Even worse, both abusers and abused people sometimes understand the abuse to be explicitly sanctioned by the Bible or the Christian tradition.

Marjorie Procter-Smith, who has explored some links between Christian-ity and domestic violence, says,

> People who work with battered women note the frequency with which abused women interpret their abuse as divinely ordained, and cite scrip-tural support for their interpretation. One woman said, 'God punished women more,' and cited Gen. 3.16. Another, who complained to her hus-band that she had sustained injuries after one of his attacks, was told by him: 'your bones are my bones – just like it says in the Bible.' Another, regularly beaten and raped by her husband, interpreted this abuse as God's correction of her tendency to rebel against her husband's author-ity. In general, battered women who were strongly religious tended to interpret their experiences of abuse according to the Genesis stories of creation and the fall; the New Testament 'household code' admonitions to wives to be subject to their husbands; the saying of Jesus about divorce; and assorted other Gospel texts which urge meekness, self-abnegation, suffering, and sacrifice as marks of the Christian life. (1995, p. 431)

Of course, the vast majority of people who believe that Christianity advo-cates leadership for men and submission for women would be aghast at the idea that sexual and domestic abuse could be justified by appeals to Chris-tian gender complementarity. Furthermore, it's clearly not the case that all sexual and domestic abuse is perpetrated by men on women: some women abuse their male partners, and sexual abuse and violence also occur in same-sex relationships, as well as between adults and children. However, claims Andy Smith in her discussion of sexual violence in evangelical communities, complementarian accounts of gender might be especially vulnerable to *distortion in the direction of* violence because, she argues, they contain an inherently unbalanced account of power:

> The issue of consent is further complicated in an evangelical context because of the power differential between *all* Christian men and women. Not only do ministers have the authority of God behind them, but so do all evangelical men ... When women are taught that they must obey and follow men, it is not surprising if they are not sure they have the right to refuse sexual contact when it is forced upon them. (1995, p. 343)

Lesley Macdonald, in her discussion of Christianity and sexual violence, adds, 'It is not difference *per se*, but the way that difference is used to systematize subordination, which has normalized the possibility of violence and abuse in gender relations' (1997, p. 52).

Eva Lundgren, a feminist sociologist of religion, conducted interviews with ten committed Christian couples in Norway over a period of several years. In each case, the man in the relationship had been repeatedly sexually violent and abusive toward the woman, and justified this behaviour as part of a process of reinforcing appropriate Christian gender roles. Excerpts from Lundgren's interviews with some of these men make harrowing reading:

> I have never been so angry that I've lost control, far from it. But I do get frightfully angry, I get so upset when she goes off on her mad outings. And then I do hit her, of course I do, of course. Well, I've got to set limits. I've taken courses in Christian **pedagogy**, they've been extremely useful, because at those courses you learn about setting limits. (Dagfinn, quoted in Lundgren 1994:, pp. 34–5; bolding added by me)

> I've never been the type to beat for the beating's sake. I've always had God with me. I thought it was right. I knew what was right to do when she got too loose and wanted to deprive me of what it meant to be a man, see to it that everything was in order. And, of course, I was responsible for my woman, that's perfectly clear, the Bible says that the man is to care for and honour his woman. And I cared for her. The times I had to beat her, well, I bandaged her up afterwards, and I never left her. (Hans, quoted in Lundgren 1994, p. 36)

> Rebellious and stubborn, that's what she is. And I believe firmly in the Bible. So I have the means ... even hitting ... You cannot stand the order

of creation on its head. Only the man is the Lord of Creation, and he cannot allow himself to be dominated by womenfolk. So hitting has been my way of marking – that I'm a man, a masculine man. (Anders, quoted in Lundgren 1994, p. 37)

The men interviewed by Lundgren frequently raped their wives. Two of the men say:

Yes, that's what it is ... strength ... and like really feeling your strength, it's the same feeling you get standing in front of a congregation, you know, having them in the palm of your hand ... first with some resist-ance, and then suddenly you have them, and they're caught. And it's sort of the same thing sexually ... you somehow conquer the resistance, that's the fantastic thing, it's like a victory, you get the upper hand, you have the power to conquer that which has been closed to you ... It is not for nothing that we men were made in God's image. (Unnamed man, quoted in Lundgren 1994 pp. 38–9)

I was created man, and I have the pleasure and the ability to celebrate the Lord in my sex life. He can be with me in it in a way that is impos-sible for a woman; I am the Lord ... and my sexual organ is a wondrous image of Christ and the church, this very, if I may say so, tool God has endowed me with ... We are talking about two units that were made for each other. There is earth and there is heaven above it, there is woman and there is man above her, there's church and there is Christ above it, all these images are in accord, and are symbolized by sexuality itself. This is fundamental Christian dogma. (Kjell, quoted in Lundgren 1994, p. 42)

Accounts like this point to a clear distortion of loving and just sex-gender relationships, justified by misguided appeals to male and female roles which the abusers understood to be biblical. Sadly, however, Christian churches haven't always done enough to protect those who have been abused. Beth R. Crisp has described the difficulties faced by many survivors of sexual abuse in continuing their spiritual lives, particularly if the abuse was carried out by a minister, priest or other church leader. In some cases, those who had been abused were told that they, and not their abusers, should leave the Church in order to avoid a scandal (Crisp 2009, pp. 66–7; Crisp 2010). In cases involving the sexual abuse of children by Roman Catholic priests, it's been claimed that the priests concerned were sometimes not removed from contact with children even when abuse had been reported over a period of years, and that the church hierarchy 'closed ranks' to protect abusers (see for example Plante and Daniels 2004, p. 388; Isely 1997, pp. 279, 283; Frawley-O'Dea 2007, p. 219).

It's important to remember that other faiths and institutions also contain stories of sexual abuse and violence in which damaged and vulnerable people have been inadequately protected. Sexual violence and abuses of power aren't unique to the Christian Church. Furthermore, it's clear that (as we've seen throughout this book) Christianity also affirms embodied sexuality as good, a site for the outworking of right and just relationships and physical joys. How, then, might Christians and others ensure that people aren't sexually abused and wronged in the name of Christianity, and that it is good, just and life-giving theologies of sexuality which persist into the future?

Bound for the last things

Serene Jones, a feminist theologian, says this of human sexuality in theological terms:

> Theologically speaking, sexuality is both less and more interesting than we are usually led to think. This is because it is both a very ordinary and a quite extraordinary feature of human existence. To say sex is 'very ordinary' is to affirm that having strong sexual and erotic desires for others is part and parcel of being a person. Taking pleasure in satisfying those yearnings, in all their diversity, is very, very normal. That's the way God's creation works. We are creatures with creaturely desires. Our bodies want and we desire. To say sex is 'quite extraordinary' is to affirm that with intimate erotic relationships, there is a range of experiences that stretches beyond our normal cache of social rules and expectations. Erotic intimacy can push the limits of our normal, enfleshed, bounded existence and let us experience the power of being both earthbound animals and skybound lovers. (2010, p. 301)

There's a play on words in her argument which bears broader consideration. Jones talks of humans as being both earthbound animals and skybound lovers. As this makes clear, *bound* simultaneously means two things. Being bound *by* or *to* something can mean being limited: users of mobility aids sometimes used to be described as 'wheelchair-bound'. At the same time, however, being bound *for* something means being destined, directed or headed toward it.

What does this mean for theological talk about sexuality? Christian theologians might want to affirm that their tradition simultaneously *binds* them – by limiting what's endorsed in terms of sexual behaviours and orientations – and renders them *bound for* – directed to – something beyond the tradition itself. To operate as Christian theologians in the context of this tradition means acknowledging that any Christian pronouncement on sexuality takes place with a legacy, for better or for worse, of the ways in which Christians have understood sexuality throughout history – in light of what musician Jon Curtis has called 'the tricky back catalogue of our faith' (2012). Christians who want to reject what they consider the more oppressive, violent and harmful parts of the tradition's accounts of sexuality (such as exclusionary or exploitative attitudes to women or to homosexual people) nonetheless still usually want to appeal to other aspects of the tradition (such as its endorsement of incarnation and the material world, and its focus on love) in constructing and reclaiming their theologies.

For some Christians, the Bible remains the ultimate and most important arbiter of what is and isn't legitimate sexual behaviour. As we've seen, however, there's disagreement about how certain biblical words and phrases should be interpreted, and how Christian hermeneutics deals with drawing contemporary theological and ethical principles from an ancient and, in many ways, remote set of texts. Faithful readers of the Bible can read exactly the same texts and draw very different conclusions. Furthermore, if we're interested in passages in the writings of Jesus and Paul which deal clearly and explicitly with questions of sexuality: well, there simply aren't very many. Rowan Williams comments,

> There are meditations and recommendations to do with marriage, and there are some stark observations about celibacy; there are a few scattered remarks about vaguely defined 'impurity' or 'uncleanness' of behaviour, *porneia*, which seems to refer to anything from adultery to prostitution; there are, in the writings ascribed to St Paul, three disparaging references to sexual activity between men. Jesus is recorded as following a strict line on the admissibility of a man deciding to dissolve his marriage (not exactly a discussion of divorce in the modern sense), and refers in passing to *porneia* as one of the evils that come from the inner core of the self. And that's about it. The overall impression is certainly that sexual activity is an area of moral risk, and that nothing outside marriage is to be commended. But it is, when you look at the texts, surprisingly difficult to find this spelled out in any detail, explored or defended. (Williams 1997b, p. 23)

For Williams, part of the answer is that the Bible is not all that Christians have to go on. Christian theologians can also employ their powers of *reason* as they reflect on the Bible and their own experiences, and they can look to the history of the Christian *tradition*.

To be 'bound into' a tradition, then, isn't negative. For Christian theologians, to be bound by their history is also to be bound for something beyond it, toward a God who exceeds what human beings have been able to say about God. Indeed, all Christian theology can and must take place in a context of eschatology. The word **eschatology** comes from the Greek phrase *ta eschata*, meaning 'the last' or 'the last things', used by some of the New Testament writers. Eschatology is the area of Christian theology and doctrine which deals with beliefs about the end of the world and the afterlife. Eschatology is sometimes characterized with a sense of 'already, but not yet', and theologians sometimes talk about an 'eschatological tension'. This refers to the idea that Christians live 'between the times': after the time of Jesus, when a new kind of living came into existence, but before the end of the world, when this new kind of living will be fully in place. Many theologians, however, affirm that eschatology isn't just to do with the future, because, in and through Christ and the Holy Spirit, the new creation is already coming into being. Christians can and must help to bring about the new creation in its fullness. Elizabeth Stuart says, 'The last things are also the first things for Christians, the defining movements of their characters and lives' (2004, p. 63). Eschatological theology therefore necessitates a simultaneous acknowledgement that there's a new, just order which hasn't yet fully come into being, and a conviction that it's possible for Christians to live this new world into existence.

But what does all this have to do with sexuality?

Sexchatological hopes

True desire, desire for the other, is eschatological. (Ward 1998, p. 54)

Christianity affirms belief in a bodily resurrection: it asserts that humans aren't just disembodied spirits who 'rise above' their embodiment. We saw earlier that this was a way it distinguished itself from some other ancient belief systems such as Manichaeism. The centrality of incarnation, a celebration of materiality and **immanence**, makes clear that, for the Christian tradition, bodies are good. The things that bodies do – eat, sleep, excrete, feel, move, work, desire, give birth, make love – are also good. It's not always clear in theological accounts of resurrection how bodies as we currently experience them will carry forward into the new creation – but, in the Gospel accounts, Jesus ate grilled fish on the beach with his friends after he had risen from the dead, and carried the scars of his crucifixion in his hands and feet and side (even if he could also walk through walls and wasn't immediately recognizable to people who'd known him before his death – see Luke 24.15–16 and John 20.14–20).

In Luke's Gospel, Jesus says, 'Those who belong to this age marry and are given in marriage; but those who are considered worthy of a place in that age and in the resurrection from the dead neither marry nor are given in marriage. Indeed they cannot die any more, because they are like angels and are children of God, being children of the resurrection' (Luke 20.34–6). Richard Price remarks that this seems difficult to some readers, especially, perhaps, those who have been widowed and do hope to be reunited with a beloved partner after their death. Price suggests that Jesus asserted there would be no marriage in heaven *not* because he thought that sexual desire would cease to exist in the new creation, or because the deep love and intimacy between spouses would fade away, but because one of the most universal understandings of marriage is as a location for children to be born and brought up. Price suggests that humans have children because it is a 'reply to mortality and death, it is the way in which we seek to prolong human existence and to imitate the everlastingness of God; this is why Christ in this saying gives the disappearance of death in the life to come as the reason for the disappearance of marriage as well' (2006, p. 127). However, Price goes on, true immortality is rooted in something else, 'a higher level and new intensity of life ... the spiritual horizon of the new life in Christ' (p. 127). This doesn't disparage children, reproduction, or the earthly uses of sexuality, but simply insists that they must be understood as part of something bigger, something divine and eternal. Sexuality in the age to come doesn't need to be or do all the things it is and does on earth.

This means that there must be both continuity and discontinuity between earthly and heavenly sexuality. If there were complete continuity, then there'd be no hope of transformation for the ways in which human sexuality becomes distorted and distorting, damaged and damaging through violence, oppression and sin. On the other hand, if there were complete *dis*continuity, this would undermine the capacity of human sexuality, as it's experienced now, to be good, life-giving and sacred. Resurrected bodily life would have nothing in common with life as we know it (Jordan 2002, p. 159). Theologians who have engaged with disability have argued that the idea that everything we currently know and do in our bodies will be erased in the new creation can be a dangerous one, since it means that bodies on earth can be 'ranked' as more and less perfect, and that the kinds of relationships we have here and now in our specific, various bodies can be accounted as somehow unreal.

Sexuality isn't the only or most interesting thing about us as human beings, and – as many celibate people testify – physical sexual activity isn't the site of ultimate human fulfilment or wholeness. Nonetheless, when sexuality is understood as our energy, our way of relating with other living things, it colours all our interactions with the world. As Margaret Kamitsuka (2010b) notes, some feminist and queer theologians in recent years have argued that just sexuality and gender relations on earth should anticipate the just relationships which humans will enjoy in heaven or the new creation. There is debate over whether or not humans will be gendered or sexed in our resurrection bodies as we're gendered and sexed now, but for some theologians it's very important that there's continuity between our embodied relationships on earth and those of the age to come. For Kamitsuka herself, 'eschatological eros' means carrying over our bodily identities, memories and desires into the new creation (2010b, p. 263).

Elizabeth Stuart also asks what sexual theology done from an eschato-logical perspective might look like (1997b, p. 196). She points to a vision, in the new creation, in which

> The sexualized person is regarded as having ultimate value, to be human is to be sexual, but the performances or categories of sexuality are dis-pensable, historical and social constructions that restrict rather than empower our loving. Human beings are created sexual and relational. These are gifts of grace that have yet to be brought to fulfilment. (p. 199)

For Stuart, there will be no marriage in heaven for the reason that mar-riage on earth has excluded some people, including lesbian and gay people, who haven't been allowed to marry, and people who have found themselves lonely and alienated, because they themselves haven't found a marriage partner. Stuart suggests that, in heaven, 'there is certainly sex, sexuality, relationship, embodiment, but not marriage, no nuclear family, no enforced coupledom' (p. 201).

For Gerard Loughlin, human bodies after death must still be understood as 'sexuate' – as having a sex – because if heaven is figured as somewhere where sex has been erased, it's too easy to deny sexed differences on earth as good. Loughlin fears that this leads to the male sex being privileged as the perfect or default sex, which disparages femaleness (and, we might add, intersex variations). Loughlin says 'heavenly bodies' should be understood as having their sexes 'preserved and enhanced' (1997, p. 218), so that 'the church may even now begin to allow this future body to inform its present practice, just insofar as the church is that community which shapes bodies fit for heavenly fulfilment' (p. 218). Difference and diversity in embodiment stretches both backwards and forwards. This is deeply eschatological, but not in the sense of being postponed until some future time. Rather, it seeks to integrate the next, just order into the current vocation of Christian living: it's a *realized* eschatology, literally an eschatology made real.

Mark D. Jordan suggests that Christian theology contains resources with-in its tradition for a remade moral theology of sexuality in which the key is 'the drawing of all created goods toward Christ' (2002, p. 172). Some read-ers might be suspicious of Jordan's description of 'the transfigurative union in Christ of apparent opposites' (p. 172), since, as we've seen, the erasure of difference often means an erasure of weaker or less privileged identities – which in the realm of sexuality has often meant non-male, non-normative, non-heterosexual identities. However, Jordan continues, the theology he en-visages 'would describe, not the sinful fixity of sex-identities, but the graced capacity for learning, transformation, even exchange' (p. 172). Crucially, this would take place in a context of Christian narratives about creation, redemption, revelation and hope, with a characteristically Christian under-pinning. Key to this would be doing theology in light of 'alternate identities in which the capacity for erotic pleasure was integrated rather than re-jected' (p. 170). This would occur not in separation from other aspects of Christian life and practice, but perfectly integrated with them. For instance, Jordan gives the example of prayer: he suggests that Christians can learn lessons from their sexual lives which they may then apply to their prayer lives (p. 166). As with a sexual relationship, a prayer regimen may fluctu-ate, feeling more and less intimate and immediate at different times. Each takes discipline and practice; each teaches something about being vulnerable and open in the presence of another without grasping or assimilating them to oneself. Jordan's point is that prayer and sexuality shouldn't be con-sidered alien to each other, or understood as existing on entirely different planes: 'In the Christian records of private prayer, we see a striking variety of erotic responses to intimacy with God ... Our intimate encounters with God through prayer are erotic because they are the pleasurable intimacies of creatures with bodies. So the Christian teaching about prayer is already ... the Christian discourse of the erotic' (p. 168).

In light of these and other accounts of theology and sexuality lived and thought out in conjunction, I propose a term and a mode of doing theol-ogy: 'sexchatology'. This means affirming two things simultaneously: first, that all Christian thought and theologizing about sexuality takes place in the context of a present and future hope for a new creation; and second, that this new creation is to be understood not as one in which sexuality has been erased or transcended, but one in which it's become so fully and right-ly integrated into human being that it's no longer a site of pain, tragedy, violence, jealousy, doubt, shame and self-loathing as it sometimes is in the present world. Sexchatological hope means that these just and right patterns of sexuality might be understood as already possible, already being lived out wherever sexuality equals solidarity, justice and love in relationship. Rita Nakashima Brock says,

> *Another Christianity is possible.* It begins when we understand that para-dise is already present. Paradise is not withheld, closed, or removed from us ... Assuredly, we are in a world in which the struggle continues. How-ever, it is also true that we already live on holy ground, in the presence of God ... We recommit ourselves to this world as holy ground when we remember the fullness of life that is possible through our communities, our life-affirming rituals, and our love of beauty, of truth, of goodness. Thus immersed in the flow of desiring, we find ourselves more responsive to and responsible for life in this world. (2011, p. 72)

Brock makes clear that the ethical dimension to this sexchatology, this sexu-ality lived eschatologically, has broader implications than just human ones. When sexuality, sexual desire, functions as 'life-affirming', it serves not to alienate humans from the rest of the created world, but to root them even more deeply within it. As humans we interact physically with a physical, material world. When as humans we use our sexualities unwisely, selfishly and sinfully, we'll find ourselves harming or cutting ourselves off from the rest of creation. Our sexual energy must operate with an awareness that we're creatures among other creatures, and that appropriate use of our bodies and energies also necessitates respect for other creatures than our own species.

Sexchatology requires that those who have sexual relationships, physical or otherwise, take the 'long view' of their significance. This doesn't mean that sexual relationships should be understood as worthless or illegitimate if they don't turn out to be lifelong ones. However, it means that the participants must take account of the implications of their sexual encounters beyond the immediate ones, and reflect on how the way they behave sexually fits with the way they behave generally. Sex is about pleasure and self-fulfilment, but not to the extent that it dismisses the needs of the other or others involved. A society in which there were no long-term, committed sexual relationships would be a spiritually poorer society as a result. Those who have sex with no regard for the wellbeing, flourishing or overall good of their partners are likely to undermine the wellbeing, flourishing and goodness of others in general.

As we've seen throughout this book, Christian theologians of many different backgrounds and persuasions have insisted, in various ways, that sex isn't simply a private matter. The ways in which people behave sexually have implications for their families and communities. Similarly, bodies are never just bodies: we're integrated physical and spiritual creatures, whose bodily acts affect our mental, emotional and spiritual selves. A 'long view' of sex, a view of sex in light of the last things, is one in which questions of safety, consent, emotional and physical justice are voiced and integrated, not dismissed as inconvenient, unsexy distractions. It is responsible, mature, and concerned with morality in the broadest sense.

Marvin Ellison says,

Fidelity means honoring our commitments, working together to maintain trust, and renegotiating with one's partner as needs, desires, and conditions unfold. Fidelity is dependent on mutual openness and honesty. It is violated by dishonesty, but also by an unwillingness to grow and change as the relationship develops. The precise requirements for fidelity cannot be prescribed in advance or in a legalistic, static fashion, but should be assessed in terms of what best honors the needs of both parties and the integrity of the relationship itself ... Special controls on sexuality are not necessary, nor do we need fear-based strategies to restrain erotic power. A mature sexual ethic focuses not on what must be prohibited or kept under control, but rather on the quality of relationship, the pattern of respect and care, and how power is distributed and expressed ... We need an erotic ethic that appreciates how the personal and sociocultural are intertwined, but that also knows how justice makes love more pleasurable and therefore more desirable in all aspects of our lives. (1996, pp. 82–3)

For Ellison, therefore, 'a mature Christian ethic does not restrict sexual activity to marriage alone. Nor does it bless all sex within marriage as morally acceptable' (1996, p. 83).

But is it realistic to assume that people can operate with a mature sexual ethic of the kind Ellison describes? Isn't it the case that many people are morally *im*mature and require guidelines and rules of the sort Ellison might consider legalistic? What about young people who are embarking on sexual and romantic relationships for the first time: wouldn't it be better if there were clear expectations in place about what sexual behaviour was and wasn't appropriate? The key is that, as Adrian Thatcher has suggested, it may be that different sexual ethics are appropriate for different stages of life. The novelist Jeanette Winterson contends that love means existing in a context of relationships, with role models committed to relationships that last: 'Teenagers need to go crazy over each other, to experiment, to come and go without fear, but they also need to see that love can change and deepen. And young people benefit from seeing adults who know how to love their friends, and for whom life is more than work or money' (2012). Faithful communities will therefore be those in which different kinds of relationships are affirmed as positive when they promote love, when they're safe, fulfilling, and committed to the good of all those involved or impacted. This means that any kind of selfish or exploitative sexual activity will be very difficult to integrate into the sexchatological vision. It also means that people who are further on in their sexual lives have a responsibility to model healthy, faithful, mutual sexual relationships, precisely so that less experienced people can come to understand their own sexual lives as something which takes place in the context of, and has implications for, whole communities. In this way, 'An ethic of erotic justice ... *does not lower but raises moral expectations*' (Ellison 1996, p. 90).

Principles for just sexual activity

Like Ellison, Margaret Farley argues that a Christian model of sexuality cannot help but to be profoundly concerned with justice. This might include gender justice (that is, questioning inequalities between men and women), a non-instrumentalist understanding of human beings (that is, refusing to use people as means to an end), and a particular consideration of locations and sites of sexuality which seem to repeat exploitative and unequal patterns of power. In Farley's account, because our sexual behaviour as humans is understood as communicating something fundamental about ourselves, the way we conduct ourselves sexually symbolizes how we understand inter-personal relationships and ethical behaviour in general. Farley suggests that a just Christian sexual ethic should take into account the following seven principles:

1 *Do no unjust harm.* Sexual activity makes people vulnerable to one an-other; we should not abuse this vulnerability by deliberately betraying or deceiving those with whom we have sexual relationships (2006, p. 217).

2 *Free consent.* Humans should not be violent or coercive in their sexual relationships, but should be truthful and keep their promises so that their partners are fully aware of exactly what they are consenting to (p. 219). We might add to Farley's point that sexual activity should therefore not take place with those who are unable to consent to sex – because they are too young and therefore not considered able to understand the implications of consenting, because they do not have the mental capac-ity to consent to sex, or for some other reason. Issues of agency might come to the fore here, as well as questions about the extent to which any of us is really free to choose to exercise our sexuality justly in a society saturated with coercive and objectifying images of sex.

3 *Mutuality.* Sex should be understood as an activity in which both part-ners take active roles, rather than being something which is done *by* one person *to* another. In just sex, both partners should give to and receive from the other (p. 222).

4 *Equality.* In contexts where the partners in a sexual relationship are dras-tically unequal in terms of power, perhaps because of their respective genders, financial statuses, or professional roles, this will grossly impede the capacity of the relationship to be just or for free consent to take place (p. 223). For example, imagine a situation in which an employee is coerced into having a sexual relationship with their boss: even if the employee verbally agrees to the relationship, has this consent really been 'freely' given if the employee knows that refusing to take part will result in them losing their job?

5 *Commitment.* Farley believes that brief or fleeting sexual encounters cannot provide the same capacity for nurturing free consent and mutu-ality as committed sexual relationships do. This commitment need not necessarily be as permanent as a commitment to marriage: however, a commitment to the ideals of equality, mutuality and so on will go a long way to ensure just sexual relationships (p. 226).

6 *Fruitfulness.* This is not just to do with the procreation of biological children, but also with an understanding that loving, relational interac-tions have social consequences and should not exclude everyone but the participants. Rather, just, loving sexual relationships should encourage the participants to look outwards, and to seek to be loving of others too (p. 228).

7 *Social justice.* This ideal holds within it all the others, and necessitates a commitment to treat other people as ends in themselves, and to take responsibility for the consequences of the sexual choices we make and the sexual behaviour in which we engage (p. 229).

Farley's ideals are grounded in **virtue ethics**, and the notion that, rather than trying to follow a list of rules outlining certain approved and proscribed behaviours, it is more important to attend to becoming a virtuous person for whom just behaviour will become second nature. For Christians, becoming virtuous will entail integrating sexual activity into love for God (pp. 243–4).

Jo Ind suggests that healthy, ethical, just sexuality is sexuality that is lived well. She says that this means sexuality which increases self-esteem, does not cause physical or emotional harm to ourselves or others, does not lead to compulsive or abusive sex, draws us closer to others and promotes emotional intimacy, is good sexuality (2003, pp. 104–5). For Ind, consent is a crucial marker of just sexual activity. She insists that consent must be given and received moment to moment, not once and for all: getting married is not consenting to have sex with one's spouse at absolutely any time thereafter. Consenting to kiss and cuddle someone is not consenting to have penetrative sex with them; consenting to penetrative sex once is not consenting to it again; 'consenting to having sex with a lot of different men is not consenting to having sex with any and every man' (p. 119).

Holding consent as a central principle also reinforces the necessity to reject sex with those who are not capable of consenting. Ind suspects that many women involved in pornography, for instance, have not had the opportunity to refuse. She emphasizes that sex with children is also always non-consensual:

> When we are children our sexualities are very much in process. We do not have sufficient autonomy in our sexualities to be capable of consent … 'Interfere' is a good word to describe what happens when an adult touches a child for his or her sexual gratification. When an adult touches a child sexually, it gets right in there to the place of the child's becoming and interferes with the delicate and mysterious process through which he or she is developing. The adult walks away having had ten minutes of sexual thrill. The child experiences the disturbance of a process which can have consequences for the rest of his or her life. (pp. 124–5)

However, consent is probably not a perfect gauge for determining the rightness or wrongness of particular sexual activity. Some critics argue that if a given sexual activity is wrong, then it is wrong whether or not someone has freely consented to take part in it. Furthermore, theologians have raised questions about the extent to which *any* consent can be really 'free' in a sinful world and a society which operates with a distorted picture of sexuality. Sara Maitland adds,

The problem with consent in the arena of sexuality is that it is nearly impossible to know what you are consenting to and whom you are consenting to – not only before you consent but during and after the acts to which you have consented ...The point about sex, surely, is that it is done at risk. In our society ... sex is constructed as liminal space, we go there chancily, perilously – with curiosity at the very least – even when we do not consent to that. Sex, like prayer, is a place where it is impossible to get the good bits if you go into it demanding the right to know what they will be. (2004, p. 117)

Maitland believes that Ind's picture of consensual sex is problematic, because there is something inherently dark and mysterious about sex. It involves dreams, instincts and drives which are, at least on some level, unconscious (p. 116). Maitland also asks *whose* consent must be taken into account: citing the example of a man in Germany who had been charged with murder after cooking and eating another man with whom he had made contact on the internet, Maitland says,

The partner knew exactly what he was being asked to consent to and he consented, explicitly. Suppose that it was indeed for him an ecstatic, glorious orgasmic moment; an adventure, a passage through a dark place, a consummation. Must I consent to that consent[?] ... If I do not consent then were they having consensual sex? Is it, should it be, any of my business? If it should then what do I do about all the people out there who might not consent to my sexual practices? (p. 117)

The question of consent is a thorny one, but at its root is a conviction that sexual acts and sexual encounters take place not on paper but in real life, between real people with real, broader life stories.

QUESTION BOX

1 Are there some types of sexual relationships which can never be truly consensual and must always be prohibited? What types of sexual relationship might you include in such a list?
2 To what extent is the category of consent a helpful one in theological considerations of sexual ethics?

Complex sex

A question of continuing importance to Christian theologians and ethicists, then, is whether there are some types of sexual activity or relationship which must be ruled out as *always* inappropriate for Christians in pursuit of sexualities integrated with a vision of justice. Violent, brutal and non-consensual forms of sex – such as rape, or sex with those who can't consent, be they children, animals or people with severe intellectual disabilities – are indefensible. But in many respects, these are the easy cases. Much trickier are types of sexual encounter which many Christians believe are absolutely abhorrent and alien to Christianity, and yet which other Christians have defended and promoted as prophetic, life-giving, or subversive of unjust social structures. These include polyamorous relationships, paid sex work, casual or semi-anonymous sexual encounters, BDSM practices, and even committed homosexual relationships between permanent, exclusive partners.

This book hasn't set out to give definitive answers to questions about whether these expressions of sexuality are right or wrong. Rather, it's set out to give readers an overview of some of the different responses to sexuality from the Christian tradition, and to equip readers with critical questions to pose to the tradition itself about the broader goods against which particular sexual phenomena are to be assessed. Nonetheless, a central thread running through Christianity from its earliest days is its high view of love, and its conviction that love (which comes from God) is a great and precious good. This, argues Gareth Moore, means that the fundamental question which should be posed to all sexual acts is 'Is love served?' He says, 'When thinking about the morality of a particular interpersonal sexual act, the central question should not be whether the act is allowed or not, but whether it contributes to the couple's relationship ... [and] to the partners' relationships with others' (1998, p. 229).

Of course, this doesn't solve the problem entirely. The gauge of love is still an uncertain one. Is it always loving to allow people to self-define and to decide for themselves whether a particular kind of sexual behaviour is loving and life-affirming? Or might it sometimes be more loving to intervene, and to say, 'It's my belief that the way you're behaving sexually, even though *you* believe it to be good and life-affirming, is actually damaging to yourself and to other people'? Moore asserts that thinking rationally in the area of sexuality – that is, acknowledging that part of what it is to be human is to use the powers of reason given us by God – means continuing to ask questions about *what it is* that truly promotes human happiness, flourishing and love – and then doing that. This can't be individualistic, but must concern whole communities, since one person's happiness can't be won at the expense of another's (p. 237).

It's for this reason that, although Moore believes the goodness and meaning of any sexual activity must be assessed in light of its context, there's still a sense in which any sex which doesn't promote love simply can't be understood as good sex in Christian terms. Since sexual activity is, he suggests, '*apt* to express love' (p. 241), using it differently erodes its capacity to carry this particular meaning. He suggests it's a bit like using swearwords: they're not necessarily bad in themselves, or always inappropriate, but if you use them all the time, they can stop being effective, and lose their capacity to be powerful when you really are angry, upset or in pain. Likewise, he suggests, 'Those who partake in sexual activities outside a context of love, if they have sex with people regardless of how, or whether, they feel about them, evacuate their sexual gestures of sense; they can no longer use sex to express love' (p. 241). What Moore insists, though, is that *what counts as loving* still isn't necessarily as clear as we might like. For some people, being loving in sexual activity necessitates marriage and, perhaps, an openness to the conception of a child. On the other hand, 'There are a number of things which might make [sex] expressive of love, such as the desire to engage in a mutually pleasurable activity' (p. 244). Sex and people are complex things. Christians have a responsibility to walk alongside even those whose expressions of sexuality they cannot accept, journeying together as they continue to challenge one another on what it is that promotes life, love and justice in sexuality as in other areas.

Strange as it might seem at the end of a book about theological accounts of sexuality, then, it might be – as Moore concludes – that Christian theology now and in the future, theology in light of the last things, should resolve to say *less* than it has done in the past about sex (p. 245). This is not to say that Christian theologians are no longer bound by or to their tradition, but rather to acknowledge that the tradition itself contains many voices and strands – not all of which have been given their due in mainstream accounts of theology and sexuality – and that a theological ethic in which sex is the only concern is an ethic which misses the point. Saying less about sex might free up more time and energy for saying and doing more about poverty, injustice, exploitation, violence, war, oppression, abuse, the powers, and the future of the earth.

Dorothy L. Sayers, the journalist and writer, wrote in the 1940s,

Suppose, during the last century, the Churches had devoted to ... [tackling] intellectual corruption one quarter of the energy they spent on nosing out fornication – or denounced legalized cheating with one quarter of the vehemence with which they denounced legalized adultery. But the one was easy and the other was not ... Therefore [the Church] will acquiesce in a definition of morality so one-sided that it has deformed the very meaning of the word by restricting it to sexual offences. And yet, if every man living were to sleep in his neighbour's bed, it could not bring the world so near shipwreck as that pride, that avarice, and that intellectual sloth which the Church has forgotten to write in the tale of capital Sins. (Sayers 1942)

Do you agree with Sayers that the Christian Church has sometimes over-emphasized sexual immorality at the expense of other kinds of sin? If so, why might this be the case? Would Sayers' accusations hold water if levelled at the Church today?

Ends and beginnings

Rowan Williams (2002) suggests that really understanding what it is to give and receive grace in and through our bodies and our sexualities means we have to have a concept of what grace is in the first place. While sexual encounters can certainly be part of what helps us understand as humans that we are joyous and delightful, it will be difficult for us to understand the power of giving and receiving in our human relationships, suggests Williams, if we don't contextualize this within a greater truth about what it is to be known and loved as joyous and delightful by God.

Christian theology affirms that we're whole people, not separate bodies, minds and spirits which have nothing much to do with one another. And that means that Christian theologies of sexuality always have to be about all three of those things: body, mind and spirit. We can't treat our bodies and bodily desires as unimportant, insignificant or an embarrassment to be transcended; on the other hand, nor can we make our bodies and their desires the be-all and end-all, to be indulged regardless of what that means emotionally, mentally and spiritually for ourselves and others.

Sex in light of the last things, and in light of questions about what it is that we're really supposed to do and be as human beings – that is, sex in light of what we might call *ends* – is also, always and simultaneously, sex in light of new beginnings. For Christian theologians, one of the greatest and most enduring elements of the Christian faith is the idea, as summed up in Romans 8.38–9, that nothing whatsoever has the power to separate humans from the love of God as communicated in Jesus. That doesn't mean that our choices and actions are insignificant, or that they don't have consequences for ourselves and others, but it does mean that, in Christian thought, humans aren't condemned to keep walking any one path on which we've started out. Each of us has probably done things we'd rather we hadn't, in our sex lives or elsewhere; each of us has undoubtedly hurt other people, deliberately or otherwise. We're also people coloured by our own histories: people who've experienced abusive or exploitative forms of sex often find it very difficult to experience sex as a loving, safe and positive thing.

The Christian tradition affirms that that isn't the end of the story. Nothing we've done or not done, and nothing which has ever happened to us, can separate us from the love of God, says Paul; it isn't the case that we have to keep on making the same mistakes, or projecting the same image of ourselves that other people might have come to expect of us. New beginnings are always possible, because Christians believe in a new creation which is still coming into existence.

Glossary

agape	Greek term for the deep, sacrificial, self-giving love between friends. In the New Testament it is used to refer to the love of God for humans.
Apocrypha	A collection of ancient books printed, in some Bibles, between the Hebrew Bible (Old Testament) and the New Testament. Roman Catholic and Orthodox Christians accept the Apocryphal books as scriptural, but most Protestant Christians do not.
apotheosis	Glorifying a person, thing or idea so much that it takes on a divine or almost divine status.
asceticism	Refraining from physical pleasures. In Christianity, a belief that austerity and the denial of physical pleasures can lead to a heightened spiritual state or the more faithful living of a religious life.
BDSM	Bondage, domination, sadism and masochism. A set of sexual practices involving the stylized acting out of domination and submission, often involving accessories such as handcuffs, gags, chains, and leather clothing. See individual entries on sadism and masochism.
Canon Law	The internal body of law of a Christian Church, such as the Roman Catholic Church or the Anglican Communion.
cisgender	Non-transgender, that is, someone living in the gender that 'matches' their biological sex. The word comes from the Latin *cis*, meaning 'to the near side' (as opposed to *trans*, 'crossing to the other side').
concupiscence	The human tendency to desire satisfaction of bodily appetites, especially for sex and food; a tendency to sin leading from such desires.
constructivism	The belief that human sexual orientations and gender roles are influenced by social norms and structures, and, in some cases, that gender identity is not necessarily contingent on any particular biological sex.

consummation	The time at which a marriage is deemed to have become fully created and legally binding, usually at the moment of the first penetrative sexual intercourse between the spouses.
encyclical letter	A letter written by the Pope and sent out to Roman Catholic bishops, designed to guide them in their ministry.
eschatology	In Christianity, doctrines concerning the 'last things' or 'end times' – usually the end of the world and/or the afterlife. The word comes from the Greek phrase *ta eschata* (the last things).
essentialism	The belief that human sexual orientations and gender identities are inborn, and, in some cases, that gender identity is, or should be, contingent on a particular biological sex.
eros	Greek term for intimate, passionate, sexual or romantic love.
eunuch	A male who has been castrated (that is, had his testes removed). In the ancient world, eunuchs often worked as government officials or servants who guarded women. Eunuchs were sometimes understood to exist outside typical gender norms.
Fall	In Christian theology, humans' fall into sinfulness, often associated with the story of Adam and Eve eating the fruit of the tree of the knowledge of good and evil in Genesis 3. Many Christian theologians believe that all humans are sinful because of this first sin. The existence of natural disasters and other suffering not directly caused by humans is also sometimes attributed to the effect of the Fall on the whole of creation.
fetish	An object believed to have supernatural powers. Within discourses of sexuality, a fetish is an object or type of behaviour not normally considered sexual which becomes a focus of sexual arousal for a particular individual or group.
General Synod	The governing body of a Church: in this case, that of the Church of England, made up of representatives from bishops, clergy, and lay people.
genitality	An understanding of sexuality which is just to do with genital activity rather than the whole person.
Gnosticism	An ancient set of beliefs based on the assertion that it is possible to escape the material world via special intuition or secret knowledge (in Greek, *gnosis*) of the spiritual realm.

hermeneutics	The way in which texts are read and interpreted; this might include beliefs about whether a text's true meaning lies within itself, in the intentions of its authors, or in the meanings brought to it by readers.
heteronormativity	The belief that heterosexuality is the norm and only desirable state for the whole of society. It usually assumes that sexes, genders and sexualities are stable and self-evident.
incarnation	Embodiment. In Christianity, belief in the incarnation is belief that God became human in the person of Jesus Christ. More broadly, this underlies the Christian affirmation of embodiment and the material world as good.
immanence	In Christianity and more broadly in philosophy, the idea that God or the divine is present in the material world.
Lambeth Conference	A meeting of all the bishops of the Anglican Communion, which takes place once every ten years led by the presiding Archbishop of Canterbury.
LGBT	Lesbian, gay, bisexual and transgender.
Manichaeism	An ancient Persian religion based on a dualistic cosmology in which spirit is good and matter, including the body, is bad.
masochism	The enjoyment of experiencing physical and/or emotional pain. Within discourses of sexuality, masochism specifically refers to sexual arousal caused by being on the receiving end of domination, humiliation or physical pain.
mystic	A person who experiences God or a supreme reality on a level beyond normal human experience, or who believes they can encounter the divine directly via intuition.
Natural Law	In theology, the idea that all created things are directed toward God and have natural ends, and that God's will can be discerned through observation of the natural world.
original sin	The Christian belief that all humans are born into a sinful state, regardless of whether they have committed personal sin. Augustine of Hippo believed that original sin was transmitted via sexual intercourse.
patriarchy	A social and/or religious system in which men are the primary agents and have authority over, and responsibility for, women, children and property. The word comes from the Greek words *pater* (father or ancestor) and *arche* (origin, rule or leader).
paedophilia	A psychological state, and behaviour stemming from it, in which the main sexual desires of adults are directed

toward pre-pubescent children rather than toward other adults. The word comes from the Greek words *pais* (child) and *philia* (love or friendship).

pedagogy An approach to teaching, training or instructing other people. The word comes from the Greek words *pais* (child) and *ago* (lead, guide or direct).

perichoresis The mutual indwelling and interaction between the Persons of the Trinity. Sometimes more broadly used to mean the mutual indwelling of God and humanity. The word comes from the Greek words *peri* (around) and *chorein* (contain).

postcolonialism A set of critical discourses based on analysis of societies in light of the cultural legacy of the colonial era. In theology and biblical studies, this includes hermeneutical strategies grounded in the experiences of people in formerly colonized nations.

queer A set of critical discourses and theories grounded in resistance to normativities of various kinds, especially heteronormativity. Also associated with work by and for lesbian, gay, bisexual and transgender (LGBT) people.

Reformation The sixteenth-century European uprising against the Roman Catholic Church which led to the founding of the Protestant churches.

repression (Freud) The attempt to suppress socially unacceptable desires or impulses (often of a violent or sexual nature) that arise within one's own psyche.

sacrament A ritual practice or outward sign which signifies the presence or inner activity of God; a means of mediating grace. Christian sacraments include baptism and Eucharist (also called Mass or Holy Communion).

sadism The enjoyment of inflicting physical and/or emotional pain on other people. Within discourses of sexuality, sadism specifically refers to sexual arousal caused by inflicting domination, humiliation or physical pain on others.

Second Vatican Council (Vatican II) A meeting of Roman Catholic bishops in the 1960s that considered the Roman Catholic Church's relationship to the modern world, and led to changes such as the revision of the liturgy and the celebration of the Mass in local languages as well as Latin.

sexual orientation Romantic or sexual attraction directed toward a particular group of people, usually people of a specific gender.

Stoicism A philosophy popular in Greece and the Roman Empire in the third century BC to the sixth century AD. The Stoics

believed that extreme emotions were rash and dangerous and that moral people should remain impassive.

trafficking
The illegal transportation of goods or people across
borders. Human trafficking involves the coercion, abuse
or deception of those being trafficked, who are sometimes forced into prostitution or slave labour by their
traffickers.

transgender
A state in which someone's physical sex does not
'match' their gender identity (for example a biological
female who identifies as a man). A transgender person
may transition to living in a different gender, and may
undergo surgery or hormone therapy to change their
body and make it more in line with their gender identity.

virtue ethics
A system of ethics based on cultivating a good moral
character rather than on following a particular set of
rules or working toward a particular set of outcomes.

womanism
A literary and theological discourse based on the experiences of black women. It suggests that white feminists
have too unproblematically universalized female experience, and have continued to perpetuate the oppression
of non-white women.

Works cited

Adams, Marilyn McCord (2002), 'Trinitarian Friendship: Same-Gender Models of Godly Love in Richard of St Victor and Aelred of Rievaulx', in Rogers, Eugene F. (ed.), 2002, *Theology and Sexuality: Classic and Contemporary Readings*, Oxford: Blackwell, pp. 322–40.

Ahlgren, Gillian T. W., 2005, 'Julian of Norwich's Theology of *Eros*', *Spiritus: A Journal of Christian Spirituality* 5.1 (Spring 2005), pp. 37–53.

Alison, James, 2003, *On Being Liked*, London: Darton, Longman and Todd.

Allen, John L., 2003, 'The Word from Rome', *National Catholic Reporter*, 5 September 2003, online at www.nationalcatholicreporter.org/word/word090503.htm.

Althaus-Reid, Marcella, 2000, *Indecent Theology*, London and New York: Routledge.

Althaus-Reid, Marcella, 2003, *The Queer God*, London and New York: Routledge.

Althaus-Reid, Marcella, 2004, 'Queer I Stand: Lifting the Skirts of God', in Althaus-Reid, Marcella and Lisa Isherwood (eds), 2004, *The Sexual Theologian: Essays on Sex, God and Politics*, London and New York: T&T Clark, pp. 99–109.

Althaus-Reid, Marcella, 2006, 'Mark', in Guest, Deryn, Robert E. Goss, Mona West and Thomas Bohache (eds), 2006, *The Queer Bible Commentary*, London: SCM Press, pp. 517–25.

Althaus-Reid, Marcella and Lisa Isherwood (eds), 2009, *Trans/Formations*, Controversies in Contextual Theology, London: SCM Press.

Aune, Kristin, 2002, *Single Women: Challenge to the Church?*, Carlisle: Paternoster Press.

Aune, Kristin, 2009, 'Between Subordination and Sympathy: Evangelical Christians, Masculinity and Gay Sexuality', in Hunt, Stephen (ed.), 2009, *Contemporary Christianity and LGBT Sexualities*, Farnham: Ashgate, pp. 39–49.

Bailey, Nathan W. and Marlene Zuk, 2009, 'Same-Sex Sexual Behavior and Evolution', *Trends in Ecology and Evolution* 24.8, pp. 439–46.

Barth, Karl, 1958, *Church Dogmatics III/1: The Doctrine of Creation*, trans. Thomson, G. T. et al., Edinburgh: T&T Clark.

Barth, Karl, 1961, *Church Dogmatics III/4: The Doctrine of Creation*, trans. Mackay, A.T. et al., Edinburgh: T&T Clark.

Beardsley, Christina, 2005, 'Taking Issue: The Transsexual Hiatus in Some Issues in Human Sexuality', *Theology* 58.845, pp. 338–46.

Bearman, Peter and Hannah Brückner, 2005, 'After the Promise: The STD Consequences of Adolescent Virginity Pledges', *Journal of Adolescent Health* 36.4, pp. 271–8.

Benedict XVI (Pope), 2005, *Deus Caritas Est*, online at http://www.vatican.va/

holy_father/benedict_xvi/encyclicals/documents/hf_ben-xvi_enc_20051225_deus-caritas-est_en.html.

Bennett Moore, Zoë, 2002, *Introducing Feminist Perspectives on Pastoral Theology*, Sheffield: Sheffield Academic Press.

Bernhardt-House, Phillip, 2012, 'Reinforcing Binaries, Downgrading Passions: Bisexual Invisibility in Mainstream Queer Christian Theology', in Hutchins, Loraine and H. Sharif Williams (eds), 2012, *Sexuality, Religion and the Sacred: Bisexual, Pansexual and Polysexual Perspectives*, London: Routledge, pp. 22–31.

Bersamin, Melina M., Deborah A. Fisher, Samantha Walker, Douglas L. Hill and Joel W. Grube, 2007, 'Defining Virginity and Abstinence: Adolescents' Interpretations of Sexual Behaviors', *Journal of Adolescent Health* 41, pp. 182–8.

Best, Ernest, 2004, *Ephesians*, International Critical Commentary, London: T&T Clark.

Bird, Phyllis, 1989, 'The Harlot as Heroine', *Semeia* 46, pp. 119–39.

Blevins, John, 2005, 'Broadening the Family of God: Debating Same-Sex Marriage and Queer Families in America', *Theology and Sexuality* 12.1, pp. 63–80.

Board for Social Responsibility Working Party, 1989, 'Report to the House of Bishops on Homosexuality' (the 'Osborne Report'), unpublished document, online at http://www.churchtimes.co.uk/uploads/documents/osborne_report.pdf.

Board for Social Responsibility, 1995, *Something to Celebrate: Valuing Families in Church and Society*, London: Church House Publishing.

Bohache, Thomas, 2003, 'Embodiment as Incarnation: An Incipient Queer Christology', *Theology and Sexuality* 10.1, pp. 9–29.

Bonhoeffer, Dietrich, 2001, *Letters and Papers from Prison: An Abridged Edition*, London: SCM Press.

Boswell, John, 1980, *Christianity, Social Tolerance, and Homosexuality: Gay People in Western Europe from the Beginning of the Christian Era to the Fourteenth Century*, Chicago, IL: University of Chicago Press.

Boswell, John, 1994, *The Marriage of Likeness: Same-Sex Unions in Pre-Modern Europe*, New York, NY: Villard Books.

Brock, Rita Nakashima, 2011, 'Paradise and Desire: Deconstructing the Eros of Suffering', in Shults, F. LeRon and Jan-Olav Henriksen (eds), 2011, *Saving Desire: The Seduction of Christian Theology*, Grand Rapids, MI: Eerdmans, pp. 55–72.

Brock, Rita Nakashima and Susan Brooks Thistlethwaite, 1996, *Casting Stones: Prostitution and Liberation in Asia and the United States*, Minneapolis, MN: Augsburg Fortress.

Brooten, Bernadette J., 1998, *Love Between Women: Early Christian Responses to Female Homoeroticism*, Chicago, IL: University of Chicago Press.

Brown, Peter, 1988, *The Body and Society: Men, Women, and Sexual Renunciation in Early Christianity*, New York: Columbia University Press.

Browning, Melissa D., 2010, 'Acting Out Abstinence, Acting Out Gender: Adolescent Moral Agency and Abstinence Education', *Theology and Sexuality* 16.2, pp. 143–61.

Brueggemann, Walter, 1982, *Genesis*, Louisville, KY: John Knox Press.

Burrus, Virginia, 2006, 'Introduction: Theology and Eros After Nygren', in Burrus, Virginia and Catherine Keller (eds), 2006, *Toward a Theology of Eros: Transfiguring Passion at the Limits of Discipline*, New York, NY: Fordham University Press, pp. xiii–xxi.

Burrus, Virginia, 2007, 'Queer Father: Gregory of Nyssa and the Subversion of Identity', in Loughlin, Gerard (ed.), 2007, *Queer Theology: Rethinking the Western Body*, Oxford: Blackwell, pp. 147–62.

Burrus, Virginia and Catherine Keller (eds), 2006, *Toward a Theology of Eros: Transfiguring Passion at the Limits of Discipline*, New York, NY: Fordham University Press.

Butler, Judith, 1990, *Gender Trouble: Feminism and the Subversion of Identity*, New York and London: Routledge.

Cahill, Lisa Sowle, 1996, *Sex, Gender, and Christian Ethics*, Cambridge: Cambridge University Press.

Calvin, John, 1849, *Commentaries on the Twelve Minor Prophets, Volume Fifth: Zechariah and Malachi*, trans. Owen, John, Edinburgh: Calvin Translation Society.

Carden, Michael, 2006, 'Genesis / Bereshit', in Guest, Deryn, Robert E. Goss, Mona West and Thomas Bohache (eds), 2006, *The Queer Bible Commentary*, London: SCM Press, pp. 21–60.

Carter, Angela, 1979, *The Sadeian Woman*, London: Virago.

Castelli, Elizabeth A., 2008, 'Virginity and its Meaning for Women's Sexuality in Early Christianity', in Levine, Amy-Jill with Maria Mayo Robbins (eds), 2008, *A Feminist Companion to Patristic Literature*, London and New York: T&T Clark, pp. 72–100.

Central Board of Finance of the Church of England, 1979, *Homosexual Relationships: A Contribution to Discussion*, London: Church Information Office.

Chambers, Aidan, 1987, *Now I Know: A Novel*, London: The Bodley Head.

Chau, P.-L. and Jonathan Herring, 2002, 'Defining, Assigning and Designing Sex', *International Journal of Law, Policy and the Family* 16, pp. 327–67.

Cheng, Patrick S., 2011, *Radical Love: An Introduction to Queer Theology*, New York, NY: Seabury Books.

Clark, Elizabeth A., 1983, *Women in the Early Church*, Collegeville, MN: The Liturgical Press.

Clark, J. Michael, 1994, 'Men's Studies, Feminist Theology, and Gay Male Spirituality', in Nelson, James B. and Sandra P. Longfellow (eds), 1994, *Sexuality and the Sacred: Sources for Theological Reflection*, Louisville, KY: Westminster/John Knox Press, pp. 216–29.

Coakley, Sarah, 1995, '"Batter My Heart ...?" On Sexuality, Spirituality, and the Christian Doctrine of the Trinity', *Graven Images* 2, pp. 74–83.

Coleman, Peter, 2004, *Christian Attitudes to Marriage: From Ancient Times to the Third Millennium*, London: SCM Press.

Congregation for the Doctrine of the Faith, 1975, 'Persona Humana: Declaration on Certain Questions Concerning Sexual Ethics', online at http://www.vatican.va/roman_curia/congregations/cfaith/documents/rc_con_cfaith_doc_19751229_persona-humana_en.html.

Congregation for the Doctrine of the Faith, 1986, 'Letter to the Bishops of the Catholic Church on the Pastoral Care of Homosexual Persons', online at http://www.va/roman_curia/congregations/cfaith/documents/rc_con_cfaith_doc_19861001_homosexual-persons_en.html.

Córdova Quero, Martín Hugo, 2004, 'Friendship with Benefits: A Queer Reading of Aelred of Rievaulx and his Theology of Friendship', in Althaus-Reid, Marcella and Lisa Isherwood (eds), 2004, *The Sexual Theologian: Essays on Sex, God and Politics*, London and New York: T&T Clark, pp. 26–46.

Córdova Quero, Martín Hugo, 2006, 'The Prostitutes Also Go Into the Kingdom of God: A Queer Reading of Mary of Magdala', in Althaus-Reid, Marcella (ed.), 2006, *Liberation Theology and Sexuality*, Aldershot: Ashgate, pp. 81–110.

Corley, Kathleen E., 1989, 'Were the Women Around Jesus Really Prostitutes? Women in the Context of Greco-Roman Meals', in Lull, Davis J. (ed.), 1989, *Society of Biblical Literature 1989 Seminar Papers*, Atlanta, GA: Society of Biblical Literature.

Cornwall, Susannah, 2009, "State of Mind' versus 'Concrete Set of Facts': The Contrasting of Transgender and Intersex in Church Documents on Sexuality', *Theology and Sexuality* 15.1, pp. 7–28.

Cornwall, Susannah, 2010, *Sex and Uncertainty in the Body of Christ: Intersex Conditions and Christian Theology*, London: Equinox.

Cornwall, Susannah, 2011, *Controversies in Queer Theology*, London: SCM Press.

Countryman, L. William, 1989, *Dirt, Greed and Sex: Sexual Ethics in the New Testament and their Implications for Today*, Philadelphia, PA: Fortress Press.

Countryman, L. William, 2007, *Dirt, Greed and Sex: Sexual Ethics in the New Testament and their Implications for* Today, second edition, Minneapolis, MN: Fortress Press.

Crisp, Beth R., 2009, 'Beyond Crucifixion: Remaining Christian After Sexual Abuse', *Theology and Sexuality* 15.1, pp. 65–76.

Crisp, Beth R., 2010, *Beyond Crucifixion: Meditations on Surviving Sexual Abuse*, London: Darton, Longman and Todd.

Curtis, Jon, 2012, 'My Greenbelt Five: Jon Curtis', online at http://alturl.com/b6dc5.

Dacanáy, Adolfo N., 2000, *Canon Law on Marriage: Introductory Notes and Comments*, Quezon City: Ateneo de Manila University Press.

DeFranza, Megan, 2011, 'Intersex and *Imago*: Sex, Gender, and Sexuality in Postmodern Theological Anthropology', PhD thesis, Milwaukee, WI: Marquette University.

Dever, Vincent M., 1996, 'Aquinas on the Practice of Prostitution', *Essays in Medieval Studies* 13, pp. 39–50.

Dever, William G., 2005, *Did God Have a Wife? Archaeology and Folk Religion in Ancient Israel*, Grand Rapids, MI: Eerdmans.

Diamant, Louis, 1995, 'Sexual Orientation: Some Historical Perspective', in Diamant, Louis and Richard D. McAnulty (eds), 1995, *The Psychology of Sexual Orientation, Behavior, and Identity: A Handbook*, Westport, CT: Greenwood Press, pp. 3–18.

Dominian, Jack and Hugh Montefiore, 1989, *God, Sex and Love: An Exercise in Ecumenical Ethics*, London: SCM Press.

Donaldson, Laura E., 2006, 'The Sign of Orpah: Reading Ruth Through Native Eyes', in Sugirtharajah, R.S. (ed.), 2006, *The Postcolonial Biblical Reader*, Oxford: Blackwell, pp. 159–70.

Dormor, Duncan, 2004, *Just Cohabiting? The Church, Sex and Getting Married*, London: Darton, Longman and Todd.

Dreger, Alice Domurat, 1998, *Hermaphrodites and the Medical Invention of Sex*, Boston, MA: Harvard University Press.

Dreger, Alice Domurat (ed.), 1999, *Intersex in the Age of Ethics*, Hagerstown, MD: University Publishing Group.

Dube, Musa W., 2000, *Postcolonial Feminist Interpretation of the Bible*, St Louis, MO: Chalice Press.

Dube, Musa W., 2006, 'Rahab Says Hello to Judith: A Decolonizing Feminist Reading', in Sugirtharajah, R.S. (ed.), 2006, *The Postcolonial Biblical Reader*, Oxford: Blackwell, pp. 142–58.

Dunn, James D.G., 1996, *The Epistles to the Colossians and to Philemon: A Commentary on the Greek Text*, Grand Rapids, MI: Eerdmans.

Elliott, Dyan, 1993, *Spiritual Marriage: Sexual Abstinence in Medieval Wedlock*, Princeton, NJ: Princeton University Press.

Ellison, Marvin M., 1996, *Erotic Justice: A Liberating Ethic of Sexuality*, Louisville, KY: Westminster John Knox Press.

Ellison, Marvin M., 2012, *Making Love Just: Sexual Ethics for Perplexing Times*, Minneapolis, MN: Fortress Press.

Ellison, Marvin M. and Kelly Brown Douglas (eds), 2010, *Sexuality and the Sacred: Sources for Theological Reflection*, second edition, Louisville, KY: Westminster John Knox Press.

Elm, Susanna, 1994, *Virgins of God: The Making of Asceticism in Late Antiquity*, Oxford: Clarendon Press.

Engler, Barbara, 2009, *Personality Theories: An Introduction*, eighth edition, Boston, MA: Houghton Mifflin Harcourt.

Erzen, Tanya, 2006, *Straight to Jesus: Sexual and Christian Conversions in the Ex-Gay Movement*, Berkeley, CA: University of California Press.

Evangelical Alliance Policy Commission, 2000, *Transsexuality*, London: Evangelical Alliance.

Evans, Roger Steven, 2003, *Sex and Salvation: Virginity as a Soteriological Paradigm in Early Christianity*, Lanham, MD: University Press of America.

Farley, Margaret A., 2006, *Just Love: A Framework for Christian Sexual Ethics*, New York, NY: Continuum.

Farley, Melissa, Ann Cotton, Jacqueline Lynne, Sybille Zumbeck, Frida Spiwak, Maria E. Reyes, Dinorah Alvarez and Ufuk Sezgin, 2003, 'Prostitution and Trafficking in Nine Countries: An Update on Violence and Posttraumatic Stress Disorder', *Journal of Trauma Practice* 2.3/4, pp. 33–74.

Farley, Melissa, 2004, '"Bad for the Body, Bad for the Heart": Prostitution Harms Women even if Legalized or Decriminalized', *Violence Against Women* 10.10, pp. 1087–1125.

Fiddes, Paul S., 1990, 'The Status of Woman in the Thought of Karl Barth', in Soskice, Janet Martin (ed.), 1990, *After Eve: Women, Theology and the Christian Tradition*, London: Marshall Pickering, pp. 138–55.

Forrester, David, 2012, personal communication to the author, received 2 February 2012.

Foskett, Mary F., 2002, *A Virgin Conceived: Mary and Classical Representations of Virginity*, Bloomington, IN: Indiana University Press.

Foucault, Michel, 1990, *The History of Sexuality: Volume 1: An Introduction*, trans. Hurley, Robert, London: Penguin.

Frawley-O'Dea, Mary Gail, 2007, *Perversion of Power: Sexual Abuse in the Catholic Church*, Nashville, TN: Vanderbilt University Press.

Fredrickson, David E., 2000, 'Natural and Unnatural Use in Romans 1:24–27: Paul and the Philosophic Critique of Eros', in Balch, David L. (ed.), 2000, *Homosexu-*

ality, Science, and the 'Plain Sense' of Scripture, Grand Rapids, MI: Eerdmans, pp. 197–222.

Gagnon, Robert A. J., 2001, *The Bible and Homosexual Practice: Texts and Hermeneutics*, Nashville, TN: Abingdon Press.

Gavanas, Anna, 2004, *Fatherhood Politics in the United States: Masculinity, Sexuality, Race, and Marriage*, Urbana, IL: University of Illinois Press.

Genovesi, Vincent J., 1996, *In Pursuit of Love: Catholic Morality and Human Sexuality*, second edition, Collegeville, MN: The Liturgical Press.

Gerber, Lynne, 2008, 'The Opposite of Gay: Nature, Creation, and Queerish Ex-Gay Experiments', *Nova Religio* 11.4, pp. 8–30.

Gillis, John R., 1985, *For Better, For Worse: British Marriages, 1600 to the Present*, Oxford: Oxford University Press.

Goergen, Donald, 1974, *The Sexual Celibate*, New York, NY: The Seabury Press.

Gorringe, T. J., 2001, *The Education of Desire: Toward a Theology of the Senses*, London: SCM Press.

Goss, Robert E., 1993, *Jesus Acted Up: A Gay and Lesbian Manifesto*, San Francisco, CA: HarperSanFrancisco.

Goss, Robert E., 2004, 'Proleptic Sexual Love: God's Promiscuity Reflected in Christian Polyamory', *Theology and Sexuality* 11.1, pp. 52–63.

Goss, Robert E. and Mona West (eds), 2000, *Take Back the Word*, Cleveland, OH: Pilgrim Press.

Grau, Marion, 2004, *Of Divine Economy: Refinancing Redemption*, New York, NY: T&T Clark.

Gray, Janette, 1997, 'Celibacy These Days', in Davies, Jon and Gerard Loughlin (eds), 1997, *Sex These Days: Essays on Theology, Sexuality, and Society*, Sheffield: Sheffield Academic Press, pp. 141–59.

Grenz, Stanley J., 1990, *Sexual Ethics: An Evangelical Perspective*, Louisville, KY: Westminster John Knox Press.

Grenz, Stanley J., 1998, 'Is God Sexual? Human Embodiment and the Christian Conception of God', *Christian Scholar's Review* 28.1, pp. 24–41.

Grenz, Stanley J., 2001, *The Social God and the Relational Self: A Trinitarian Theology of the Imago Dei*, Louisville, KY: Westminster John Knox Press.

Gross, Sally, 1999, 'Intersexuality and Scripture', *Theology and Sexuality* 11, pp. 65–74.

Guider, Margaret Eletta, 1995, *Daughters of Rahab: Prostitution and the Church of Liberation in Brazil*, Minneapolis, MN: Fortress Press.

Hadley, Judith M., 2000, *The Cult of Asherah in Ancient Israel and Judah: Evidence for a Hebrew Goddess*, Cambridge: Cambridge University Press.

Haldeman, W. Scott, 2010, 'A Queer Fidelity: Reinventing Christian Marriage,' in Ellison, Marvin M. and Kelly Brown Douglas (eds), 2010, *Sexuality and the Sacred: Sources for Theological Reflection*, second edition, Louisville, KY: Westminster John Knox Press, pp. 304–16.

Hanks, Thomas, 2006, 'Romans', in Guest, Deryn, Robert E. Goss, Mona West and Thomas Bohache (eds), 2006, *The Queer Bible Commentary*, London: SCM Press, pp. 582–605.

Haskey, John, 1999, 'Cohabitational and Marital Histories of Adults in Great Britain', *Population Trends* 96, pp. 13–24.

Hays, Richard B., 1986, 'Relations Natural and Unnatural: A Response to John Boswell's Exegesis of Romans 1', *Journal of Religious Ethics* 14.1, pp. 184–215.

Helminiak, Daniel A., 1994, *What the Bible Really Says About Homosexuality*, San Francisco, CA: Alamo Square Press.

Hester, J. David, 2005, 'Eunuchs and the Postgender Jesus: Matthew 19.12 and Transgressive Sexualities', *Journal for the Study of the New Testament* 28.1, pp. 13–40.

Hicks, Joe and Grahame Allen, 1999, 'A Century of Change: Trends in UK Statistics Since 1900', House of Commons Library Research Paper 99/111, online at http://www.parliament.uk/documents/commons/lib/research/rp99/rp99-111.pdf.

Higton, Mike, 2008, *SCM Core Text: Christian Doctrine*, London: SCM Press.

Hite, Shere, 1976, *The Hite Report: A Nationwide Study of Female Sexuality*, New York, NY: Macmillan.

Hite, Shere, 1981, *The Hite Report on Male Sexuality*, New York, NY: Ballantine Books.

Holder, Rodney, 1998a, 'The Ethics of Transsexualism, Part 1: The Transsexual Condition and the Biblical Background to an Ethical Response', *Crucible* 37, pp. 89–99.

Holder, Rodney, 1998b, 'The Ethics of Transsexualism, Part 2: A Christian Response to the Issues Raised', *Crucible* 37, pp. 125–36.

Hollinger, Dennis P., 2009, *The Meaning of Sex: Christian Ethics and the Moral Life*, Grand Rapids, MI: Baker Academic.

Hopko, Thomas, 1997, *The Orthodox Faith: An Elementary Handbook on the Orthodox Church, Volume II: Worship*, New York, NY: Orthodox Church in America, online at http://oca.org/orthodoxy/the-orthodox-faith/worship/the-sacraments/marriage.

Horrell, David G., 2006, *An Introduction to the Study of Paul*, second edition, London: T&T Clark.

House of Bishops, 1991, *Issues in Human Sexuality*, London: Church House Publishing.

House of Bishops, 1999, *Marriage: A Teaching Document from the House of Bishops of the Church of England*, London: Church House Publishing, online at http://www.churchofengland.org/media/45645/marriage.pdf.

House of Bishops, 2003, *Some Issues in Human Sexuality: A Guide to the Debate*, London: Church House Publishing.

House of Bishops, 2005, 'Civil Partnerships – A Pastoral Statement from the House of Bishops of the Church of England', online at http://www.churchofengland.org/media-centre/news/2005/07/pr5605.aspx.

Howard, Kristy, 2008, 'Keeping the Happy in Your Everafter', *Above Rubies* 74, pp. 14–15.

Hutchins, Loraine and H. Sharif Williams (eds), 2012, *Sexuality, Religion and the Sacred: Bisexual, Pansexual and Polysexual Perspectives*, London: Routledge.

Ind, Jo, 2003, *Memories of Bliss: God, Sex and Us*, London: SCM Press.

Ipsen, Avaren, 2009, *Sex Working and the Bible*, London: Equinox Press.

Isely, Paul J., 1997, 'Child Sexual Abuse and the Catholic Church: An Historical and Contemporary Review', *Pastoral Psychology* 45.4, pp. 277–99.

Isherwood, Lisa and Elizabeth Stuart, 1998, *Introducing Body Theology*, Sheffield: Sheffield Academic Press.

Jantzen, Grace M., 2001, 'Contours of a Queer Theology', *Literature and Theology* 15.3, pp. 276–85.

Jensen, David H., 2010, 'The Bible and Sex', in Kamitsuka, Margaret D. (ed.), 2010a, *The Embrace of Eros: Bodies, Desires, and Sexuality in Christianity*, Minneapolis, MN: Fortress Press, pp. 15–32.

John, Jeffrey, 2003, 'Christian Same-Sex Partnerships', in Bradshaw, Timothy (ed.), 2003, *The Way Forward? Christian Voices on Homosexuality and the Church*, second edition, London: SCM Press, pp. 44–59.

John Paul II (Pope), 1979–84, 'General Audiences: Theology of the Body', online at http://www.ewtn.com/library/papaldoc/jp2tbind.htm.

Johnson, William Stacy, 2010, 'The New Testament, Empire, and Homoeroticism', in Kamitsuka, Margaret D. (ed.), 2010, *The Embrace of Eros: Bodies, Desires, and Sexuality in Christianity*, Minneapolis, MN: Fortress Press, pp. 51–66.

Jones, Serene, 2010, 'Afterword', in Kamitsuka, Margaret D. (ed.), 2010, *The Embrace of Eros: Bodies, Desires, and Sexuality in Christianity*, Minneapolis, MN: Fortress Press, pp. 297–302.

Jordan, Mark D., 1997, *The Invention of Sodomy in Christian Theology*, Chicago, IL: University of Chicago Press.

Jordan, Mark D., 2002, *The Ethics of Sex*, Malden, MA: Blackwell.

Jordan, Mark D. (ed.), 2006, *Authorizing Marriage? Canon, Tradition, and Critique in the Blessing of Same-Sex Unions*, Princeton, NJ: Princeton University Press.

Jordan, Mark D., 2011, *Recruiting Young Love: How Christians Talk About Homosexuality*, Chicago, IL: University of Chicago Press.

Joyce, Kathryn, 2009, *Quiverfull: Inside the Christian Patriarchy Movement*, Boston, MA: Beacon Press.

Jung, Patricia Beattie, 2000, 'Sexual Pleasure: A Roman Catholic Perspective on Women's Delight', *Theology and Sexuality* 12, pp. 26–47.

Jung, Patricia Beattie, 2006, 'Christianity and Human Sexual Polymorphism: Are They Compatible?', in Sytsma, Sharon E. (ed.), 2006, *Ethics and Intersex*, Dordrecht: Springer, pp. 293–309.

Kamitsuka, Margaret D. (ed.), 2010a, *The Embrace of Eros: Bodies, Desires, and Sexuality in Christianity*, Minneapolis, MN: Fortress Press.

Kamitsuka, Margaret, 2010b, 'Sex in Heaven? Eschatological Eros and the Resurrection of the Body', in Kamitsuka, Margaret D. (ed.), 2010, *The Embrace of Eros: Bodies, Desires, and Sexuality in Christianity*, Minneapolis, MN: Fortress Press, pp. 261–76.

Karkazis, Katrina, 2008, *Fixing Sex: Intersex, Medical Authority, and Lived Experience*, Durham, NC: Duke University Press.

Kelly, Kevin T., 1997, *Divorce and Second Marriage: Facing the Challenge*, new and expanded edition, Kansas City, MO: Sheed & Ward.

Kinsey, Alfred C., Wardell B. Pomeroy and Clyde E. Martin, 1948, *Sexual Behavior in the Human Male*, Philadelphia, PA: W. B. Saunders.

Kinsey, Alfred C., Wardell B. Pomeroy, Clyde E. Martin and Paul H. Gebhard, 1953, *Sexual Behavior in the Human Female*, Philadelphia, PA: W.B. Saunders.

Kitchen, Martin, 1994, *Ephesians (New Testament Readings)*, London: Routledge.

Kolakowski, Victoria S., 1997, 'Toward a Christian Ethical Response to Transsexual Persons', *Theology and Sexuality* 6, pp. 10–31.

Köstenberger, Andreas and David W. Jones, 2010, *God, Marriage and Family: Rebuilding the Biblical Foundation*, second edition, Wheaton, IL: Crossway Books.

Laqueur, Thomas, 1990, *Making Sex: Body and Gender from the Greeks to Freud*, Cambridge, MA: Harvard University Press.

Lawler, Michael G., 2002, *Marriage and the Catholic Church: Disputed Questions*, Collegeville, MN: The Liturgical Press.

Liao, Lih-Mei and Sarah Creighton, 2007, 'Requests for Cosmetic Genitoplasty: How Should Healthcare Providers Respond?', *BMJ* 334, pp. 1090–2.

Lingwood, Stephen, 2012, 'Bi Christian Unitarian: A Theology of Transgression', in Hutchins, Loraine and H. Sharif Williams (eds), 2012, *Sexuality, Religion and the Sacred: Bisexual, Pansexual and Polysexual Perspectives*, London: Routledge, pp. 32–44.

Loader, William, 2010, *Sexuality in the New Testament: Understanding the Key Texts*, London: SPCK.

Long, Ron, 2002, 'A Place for Porn in a Gay Spiritual Economy', *Theology and Sexuality* 16, pp. 21–31.

Looy, Heather, 2002, 'Male and Female God Created Them: The Challenge of Intersexuality', *Journal of Psychology and Christianity* 21.1, pp. 10–20.

Loughlin, Gerard, 1997, 'Ending Sex', in Davies, Jon and Gerard Loughlin (eds), 1997, *Sex These Days: Essays on Theology, Sexuality, and Society*, Sheffield: Sheffield Academic Press, pp. 205–18.

Loughlin, Gerard, 2004a, *Alien Sex: The Body and Desire in Cinema and Theology*, Oxford: Blackwell.

Loughlin, Gerard, 2004b, 'Sex After Natural Law', in Althaus-Reid, Marcella and Lisa Isherwood (eds), 2004, *The Sexual Theologian: Essays on Sex, God and Politics*, London: T&T Clark, pp. 86–98.

Loughlin, Gerard, 2007, 'Introduction: The End of Sex', in Loughlin, Gerard (ed.), 2007, *Queer Theology: Rethinking the Western Body*, Oxford: Blackwell, pp. 1–34.

Louw, Daniël J., 2011, 'The Beauty (Aesthetics) of Human Sexuality Within the HIV and AIDS Discourse: The Quest for Human Dignity Within the Realm of Promiscuity', unpublished paper given at Pan-African Christian AIDS Network (PACANet) Conference, Addis Ababa, 1–2 December 2011.

Lundgren, Eva, 1994, '"I am Endowed with All the Power in Heaven and on Earth": When Men Become Men Through "Christian" Abuse', *Studia Theologica – Nordic Journal of Theology* 48:1, pp. 33–47.

Macdonald, Lesley, 1997, 'Nightmares in the Garden: Christianity and Sexual Violence', in Galloway, Kathy (ed.), 1997, *Dreaming of Eden: Reflections on Christianity and Sexuality*, Glasgow: Wild Goose Publications, pp. 47–56.

MacDonald, Margaret Y., 2008, *Colossians and Ephesians*, Collegeville, MN: The Liturgical Press.

Maitland, Sara, 2004, 'Review of Ind, Jo, *Memories of Bliss: God, Sex and Us*', *Theology and Sexuality* 10.2, pp. 116–7

Marshall, I. H., 1999, *The Pastoral Epistles*, International Critical Commentary, London: T&T Clark.

Martin, Dale B., 2006, *Sex and the Single Savior: Gender and Sexuality in Biblical Interpretation*, Louisville, KY: Westminster John Knox Press.

Masters, William H. and Virginia E. Johnson, 1966, *Human Sexual Response*, Boston, MA: Little, Brown.

Masters, William H. and Virginia E. Johnson, 1970, *Human Sexual Inadequacy*, Boston, MA: Little, Brown.

Matzko McCarthy, David, 2004, *Sex and Love in the Home: A Theology of the Household*, London: SCM Press.

McCarthy Matzko, David, 1998, 'The Relationship of Bodies: A Nuptial Hermeneutics of Same-Sex Unions', *Theology and Sexuality* 8, pp. 96–112.

McFague, Sallie, 1987, *Models of God: Theology for an Ecological, Nuclear Age*, Minneapolis, MN: Fortress Press.

McGrath, Alister, 2007, *Christian Theology: An Introduction*, fourth edition, Oxford: Blackwell.

McNeill, John J., 1976, *The Church and the Homosexual*, Boston, MA: Beacon Press.

Methodist Conference, 1990, *Report of the Conference Commission on Human Sexuality*, online at http://www.methodist.org.uk/downloads/ne_confcommon humsexuality1990_0305.rtf.

Methodist Conference, 2005, *Pilgrimage of Faith*, online at http://www.methodist. org.uk/static/conf2005/co_17_pilgrimageoffaith_0805.doc.

Meyer, Marvin, 1992, *The Gospel of Thomas: The Hidden Sayings of Jesus*, San Francisco, CA: HarperSanFrancisco.

Miles, Margaret, 2005, *The Word Made Flesh: A History of Christian Thought*, Oxford: Blackwell.

Mollenkott, Virginia Ramey, 2007, *Omnigender: A Trans-Religious Approach*, revised and expanded edition, Cleveland, OH: Pilgrim Press.

Mollenkott, Virginia Ramey, 2009, 'We Come Bearing Gifts: Seven Lessons Religious Congregations can Learn from Transpeople', in Althaus-Reid, Marcella and Lisa Isherwood (eds), 2009, *Trans/Formations*, Controversies in Contextual Theology, London: SCM Press, pp. 46–58.

Moltmann, Jürgen, 1981, *The Trinity and the Kingdom of God*, London: SCM Press.

Montague, George T., 2008, *First and Second Timothy, Titus*, Catholic Commentary on Sacred Scripture, Grand Rapids, MI: Baker Academic.

Moore, Gareth, 1998, 'Sex, Sexuality and Relationships', in Hoose, Bernard (ed.), 1998, *Christian Ethics: An Introduction*, London: Continuum, pp. 223–47.

Moore, Gareth, 2003, *A Question of Truth: Christianity and Homosexuality*, London: Continuum.

Muers, Rachel, 1999, 'A Question of Two Answers: Difference and Determination in Barth and von Balthasar', *Heythrop Journal* 40.3, pp. 265–79.

Muers, Rachel, 2007, 'A Queer Theology: Hans Urs von Balthasar', in Loughlin, Gerard (ed.), 2007, *Queer Theology: Rethinking the Western Body*, Oxford: Blackwell, pp. 200–11.

Myers, Benjamin, 2011, 'The Icon of the Holy Cross: 15 Glances', online at http://www.faith-theology.com/2011/11/icon-of-holy-cross-15-glances.html (blog post for 12 November 2011).

Nausner, Michael, 2002, 'Toward Community Beyond Gender Binaries: Gregory of Nyssa's Transgendering as Part of his Transformative Eschatology', *Theology and Sexuality* 16, pp. 55–65.

Nelson, James B., 1988, *The Intimate Connection: Male Sexuality, Masculine Spirituality*, Philadelphia, PA: The Westminster Press.

Nelson, James B., 1992, *Body Theology*, Louisville, KY: Westminster John Knox Press.

Nissinen, Martti, 1998, *Homoeroticism in the Biblical World: A Historical Perspective*, trans. Stjerna, Kirsi, Minneapolis, MN: Augsburg Fortress.

Nygren, Anders, 1953, *Agape and Eros*, trans. Watson, Philip S., Philadelphia, PA: Westminster Press.

O'Donovan, Oliver, 1982, *Transsexualism and Christian Marriage*, Nottingham: Grove Books.

Oosterhuis, Harry, 2000, *Stepchildren of Nature: Krafft-Ebing, Psychiatry, and the Making of Sexual Identity*, Chicago, IL: University of Chicago Press.

Paul VI (Pope), 1968, *Humanae Vitae*, online at http://www.vatican.va/holy_father/paul_vi/encyclicals/documents/hf_p-vi_enc_25071968_humanae-vitae_en.html.

Perry, Troy, 1972, *The Lord is my Shepherd and He Knows I'm Gay: The Autobiography of the Rev. Troy D. Perry*, with Lucas, Charles L., Los Angeles, CA: Nash Publishing.

Pierce, Ronald W. and Rebecca Merrill Groothuis (eds), 2004, *Discovering Biblical Equality: Complementarity Without Hierarchy*, Downers Grove, IL: Inter-Varsity Press.

Piper, John, 2006, 'A Vision of Biblical Complementarity: Manhood and Womanhood Defined According to the Bible', in Piper, John and Wayne Grudem (eds), 2006, *Recovering Biblical Manhood and Womanhood: A Response to Evangelical Feminism*, Wheaton, IL: Crossway Books, pp. 31–59.

Piper, John and Wayne Grudem (eds), 2006, *Recovering Biblical Manhood and Womanhood: A Response to Evangelical Feminism*, Wheaton, IL: Crossway Books.

Plante, Thomas G. and Courtney Daniels, 2004, 'The Sexual Abuse Crisis in the Roman Catholic Church: What Psychologists and Counselors Should Know', *Pastoral Psychology* 52.5, pp. 381–93.

Porter, Jean, 2005, 'Chastity as a Virtue', *Scottish Journal of Theology* 58.3, pp. 285–301.

Porter, Muriel, 1996, *Sex, Marriage, and the Church: Patterns of Change*, North Blackburn, Victoria: HarperCollinsReligious.

Preves, Sharon E., 2003, *Intersex and Identity: The Contested Self*, New Brunswick, NJ: Rutgers University Press.

Price, Richard M., 2006, 'Celibacy and Free Love in Early Christianity', *Theology and Sexuality* 12.2, pp. 121–42.

Procter-Smith, Marjorie, 1995, '"Reorganizing Victimization": The Intersection Between Liturgy and Domestic Violence', in Adams, Carol J. and Marie M. Fortune (eds), 1995, *Violence Against Women and Children: A Christian Theological Sourcebook*, New York, NY: Continuum, pp. 428–43.

Purtill, Richard L., 2004, *C. S. Lewis' Case for the Christian Faith*, new edition, San Francisco, CA: Ignatius Press.

Reay, Lewis, 2009, 'Towards a Transgender Theology: Que(e)rying the Eunuchs', in Althaus-Reid, Marcella and Lisa Isherwood (eds), 2009, *Trans/Formations*, Controversies in Contextual Theology, London: SCM Press, pp. 148–67.

Reed, Esther D., 1994, 'Pornography and the End of Morality?', *Studies in Christian Ethics* 7.2, pp. 65–93.

Rees, Geoffrey, 2002, '"In the Sight of God": Gender Complementarity and the

Male Homosocial Signification of Male–Female Marriage', *Theology and Sexuality* 9.1, pp. 19–47.

Rees, Geoffrey, 2011, *The Romance of Innocent Sexuality*, Eugene, OR: Cascade Books.

Reis, Elizabeth, 2009, *Bodies in Doubt: An American History of Intersex*, Baltimore, MD: Johns Hopkins University Press.

Roberts, Christopher Chenault, 2007, *Creation and Covenant: The Significance of Sexual Difference in the Moral Theology of Marriage*, New York, NY: T&T Clark International.

Robinson, V. Gene, 2008, *In the Eye of the Storm*, Norwich: Canterbury Press.

Rogers, Eugene F., 1999, *Sexuality and the Christian Body: Their Way Into the Triune God*, Oxford: Blackwell.

Rogers, Eugene F. (ed.), 2002a, *Theology and Sexuality: Classic and Contemporary Readings*, Oxford: Blackwell.

Rogers, Eugene F., 2002b, 'Sanctification, Homosexuality, and God's Triune Life', in Rogers, Eugene F. (ed.), 2002, *Theology and Sexuality: Classic and Contemporary Readings*, Oxford: Blackwell, pp. 217–45.

Rogers, Eugene F., 2002c, 'Introduction', in Rogers, Eugene F. (ed.), 2002, *Theology and Sexuality: Classic and Contemporary Readings*, Oxford: Blackwell, pp. xviii–xxii.

Rogers, Eugene F., 2004, 'An Argument for Gay Marriage', *The Christian Century*, 15 June 2004, pp. 26–9.

Rogers, Eugene F., 2006, 'Trinity, Marriage, and Homosexuality', in Jordan, Mark D. (ed.), 2006, *Authorizing Marriage? Canon, Tradition, and Critique in the Blessing of Same-Sex Unions*, Princeton, NJ: Princeton University Press, pp. 151–64.

Rogers, Eugene F., 2009, 'Paul on Exceeding Nature: Queer Gentiles and the Giddy Gardener', in Roden, Frederick S. (ed.), 2009, *Jewish/Christian/Queer: Crossroads and Identities*, Aldershot: Ashgate, pp. 19–33.

Rosenbaum, Janet Elise, 2009, 'Patient Teenagers? A Comparison of the Sexual Behavior of Virginity Pledgers and Matched Nonpledgers,' *Pediatrics* 123, pp. 110–20.

Rudy, Kathy, 1996, '"Where Two or More are Gathered": Using Gay Communities as a Model for Christian Sexual Ethics', *Theology and Sexuality* 2.4, pp. 81–99.

Ruether, Rosemary Radford, 1983, *Sexism and God-Talk: Toward a Feminist Theology*, Boston, MA: Beacon Press.

Salih, Sarah, 2001, *Versions of Virginity in Late Medieval England*, Cambridge: D. S. Brewer.

Sayers, Dorothy L., 1942, 'The Church's Responsibility', in anon, *Malvern, 1941: The Life of the Church and the Order of Society: Being the Proceedings of the Archbishop of York's Conference*, London: Longmans, Green and Co., pp. 57–78.

Schaff, Philip and Henry Wallace (eds), 2007 [1896], *Nicene and Post-Nicene Fathers: Second Series Volume X – Ambrose Select Works and Letters*, New York, NY: Cosimo Books.

Schindler, D. C., 2006, 'The Redemption of *Eros*: Philosophical Reflections on Benedict XVI's First Encyclical', *Communio* 33, pp. 375–99.

Schneider, Laurel C., 2000, 'Homosexuality, Queer Theory, and Christian Theology', *Religious Studies Review* 26.1, pp. 3–12.

Schneider, Laurel C., 2010, 'Promiscuous Incarnation', in Kamitsuka, Margaret D.

(ed.), 2010, *The Embrace of Eros: Bodies, Desires, and Sexuality in Christianity*, Minneapolis, MN: Fortress Press, pp. 231–46.

Scholl, Lia Claire, 2012, *I Heart Sex Workers: A Christian Response to People in the Sex Trade*, St Louis, MO: Chalice Press.

Scroggs, Robin, 1983, *Homosexuality in the New Testament: Contextual Background for Contemporary Debate*, Philadelphia, PA: Fortress Press.

Sharman, Anna, 2006, *Open Fidelity: An A–Z Guide*, London: Purple Sofa Publications.

Shaw, Jane, 2007, 'Reformed and Enlightened Church', in Loughlin, Gerard (ed.), 2007, *Queer Theology: Rethinking the Western Body*, Oxford: Blackwell, pp. 215–29.

Shaw, Jane, 2012, 'When the C of E Wanted to Talk', *Church Times* 7766, 20 January 2012, p. 14.

Shaw, Teresa M., 1997, 'Creation, Virginity and Diet in Fourth-Century Christianity: Basil of Ancyra's *On the True Purity of Virginity*', *Gender and History* 9.3, pp. 579–96.

Sheffield, Tricia, 2008, 'Performing Jesus: A Queer Counternarrative of Embodied Transgression', *Theology and Sexuality* 14.3, pp. 233–58.

Sherrard, Philip, 1976, *Christianity and Eros: Essays on the Theme of Sexual Love*, London: SPCK.

Shults, F. LeRon and Jan-Olav Henriksen (eds), 2011, *Saving Desire: The Seduction of Christian Theology*, Grand Rapids, MI: Eerdmans.

Smith, Andy, 1995, 'Born Again, Free From Sin? Sexual Violence in Evangelical Communities', in Adams, Carol J. and Marie M. Fortune (eds), 1995, *Violence Against Women and Children: A Christian Theological Sourcebook*, New York, NY: Continuum, pp. 339–50.

Smith, Mark S., 2002, *The Early History of God: Yahweh and the Other Deities in Ancient Israel*, second edition, Grand Rapids, MI: Eerdmans.

Sonderegger, Katherine, 2000, 'Barth and Feminism', in Webster, John (ed.), 2000, *The Cambridge Companion to Karl Barth*, Cambridge: Cambridge University Press, pp. 258–73.

Southgate, Christopher, 2008, *The Groaning of Creation: God, Evolution, and the Problem of Evil*, Louisville, KY: Westminster John Knox Press.

Southgate, Christopher, Michael Robert Negus and Andrew Robinson, 2003, 'Theology and Evolutionary Biology', in Southgate, Christopher (ed.), 2003, *God, Humanity and the Cosmos*, second edition, London: T&T Clark, pp. 154–92.

Stone, Lawrence, 1977, *The Family, Sex and Marriage in England 1500–1800*, London: Weidenfeld and Nicolson.

Stone, Ken, 2006, '1 and 2 Samuel', in Guest, Deryn, Robert E. Goss, Mona West and Thomas Bohache (eds), 2006, *The Queer Bible Commentary*, London: SCM Press, pp. 195–221.

Streete, Gail Corrington, 1997, *The Strange Woman: Power and Sex in the Bible*, Louisville, KY: Westminster John Knox Press.

Stuart, Elizabeth, 1995, *Just Good Friends: Towards a Lesbian and Gay Theology of Relationships*, London: Mowbray.

Stuart, Elizabeth, 1997a, *Religion is a Queer Thing: A Guide to the Christian Faith for Lesbian, Gay, Bisexual and Transgendered People*, London: Cassell.

Stuart, Elizabeth, 1997b, 'Sex in Heaven: The Queering of Theological Discourse on Sexuality', in Davies, Jon and Gerard Loughlin (eds), 1997, *Sex These Days: Essays on Theology, Sexuality, and Society*, Sheffield: Sheffield Academic Press, pp. 184–204.

Stuart, Elizabeth, 1999, 'Sexuality: The View from the Font (The Body and the Ecclesial Self)', *Theology and Sexuality* 6.11, pp. 9–20.

Stuart, Elizabeth, 2000, 'Disruptive Bodies: Disability, Embodiment and Sexuality', in Isherwood, Lisa (ed.), 2000, *The Good News of the Body: Sexual Theology and Feminism*, Sheffield: Sheffield Academic Press, pp. 166–84.

Stuart, Elizabeth, 2003, *Gay and Lesbian Theologies: Repetitions with Critical Difference*, Aldershot: Ashgate.

Stuart, Elizabeth, 2004, 'Queering Death', in Althaus-Reid, Marcella and Lisa Isherwood (eds), 2004, *The Sexual Theologian: Essays on Sex, God and Politics*, London and New York: T&T Clark, pp. 58–70.

Stuart, Elizabeth and Adrian Thatcher, 1997, *People of Passion: What the Churches Teach About Sex*, London: Mowbray.

Swancutt, Diana M., 2003, '"The Disease of Effemination": The Charge of Effeminacy and the Verdict of God (Romans 1:18–2:16)', in Moore, Stephen D. and Janice Capel Anderson (eds), 2003, *New Testament Masculinities*, Atlanta, GA: Society of Biblical Literature, pp. 193–234.

Sweasey, Peter, 1997, *From Queer to Eternity: Spirituality in the Lives of Lesbian, Gay and Bisexual People*, London and Washington: Cassell.

Sytsma, Sharon E. (ed.), 2006, *Ethics and Intersex*, Dordrecht: Springer.

Tanis, Justin, 2003, *Trans-Gendered: Theology, Ministry, and Communities of Faith*, Cleveland, OH: Pilgrim Press.

Taylor, Jenny, 2004, 'A Wild Constraint', *Third Way* 27.6, pp. 12–13.

Thatcher, Adrian, 1993, *Liberating Sex: A Christian Sexual Theology*, London: SPCK.

Thatcher, Adrian, 1999, *Marriage After Modernity: Christian Marriage in Postmodern Times*, Sheffield: Sheffield Academic Press.

Thatcher, Adrian, 2002, *Living Together and Christian Ethics*, Cambridge: Cambridge University Press.

Thatcher, Adrian, 2005, 'Some Issues with "Some Issues in Human Sexuality"', *Theology and Sexuality* 11.3, pp. 9–30.

Thatcher, Adrian, 2011, *God, Sex, and Gender: An Introduction*, Malden, MA: Wiley-Blackwell.

Thistlethwaite, Susan Brooks, 1985, 'Every Two Minutes: Battered Women and Feminist Interpretation', in Russell, Letty M. (ed.), 1985, *Feminist Interpretation of the Bible*, Philadelphia, PA: The Westminster Press, pp. 96–109.

Thomas, J., 2009, 'Virginity Pledgers are Just as Likely as Matched Nonpledgers to Report Premarital Intercourse', *Perspectives on Sexual and Reproductive Health* 41.1, p. 63.

Toft, Alex, 2009, 'Bisexual Christians: The Life-Stories of a Marginalised Community', in Hunt, Stephen (ed.), 2009, *Contemporary Christianity and LGBT Sexualities*, Farnham: Ashgate, pp. 67–86.

Tolbert, Mary Ann, 2000, 'Foreword: What Word Shall We Take Back?', in Goss, Robert E. and Mona West (eds), 2000, *Take Back the Word*, Cleveland, OH: Pilgrim Press, pp. vii–xii.

Towner, Philip H., 2006, *The Letters to Timothy and Titus*, The New International Commentary on the New Testament, Grand Rapids, MI: Eerdmans.

Valantasis, Richard, 1997, *The Gospel of Thomas*, London and New York: Routledge.

Valenti, Jessica, 2009, *The Purity Myth: How America's Obsession with Virginity is Hurting Young Women*, Berkeley, CA: Seal Press.

Van Huyssteen, Wessel (producer/director), 2003, *The 3rd Sex*, broadcast SABC (South Africa), November 2003.

Vasey, Michael, 1995, *Strangers and Friends: A New Exploration of Homosexuality and the Bible*, London: Hodder and Stoughton.

Von Ruhland, Catherine, 2004, 'An Unchosen Chastity', *Third Way* 27.5, pp. 12–15.

Ward, Graham, 1998, 'The Erotics of Redemption – After Karl Barth', *Theology and Sexuality* 8, pp. 52–72.

Ward, Graham, 2004, 'On the Politics of Embodiment and the Mystery of All Flesh', in Althaus-Reid, Marcella and Lisa Isherwood (eds), 2004, *The Sexual Theologian: Essays on Sex, God and Politics*, London and New York: T&T Clark, pp. 71–85.

Warnke, Georgia, 2001, 'Intersexuality and the Categories of Sex', *Hypatia* 16.3, pp. 126–37.

Watts, Fraser, 2002, 'Transsexualism and the Church', *Theology and Sexuality* 9.1, pp. 63–85.

Webster, Alison, 1998, 'Queer to be Religious: Lesbian Adventures Beyond the Christian/Post-Christian Dichotomy', *Theology and Sexuality* 8, pp. 27–39.

Wehr, Kathryn, 2011, 'Virginity, Singleness and Celibacy: Late Fourth-Century and Recent Evangelical Visions of Unmarried Christians', *Theology and Sexuality* 17.1, pp. 75–99.

Weitzer, Ronald, 2005, 'Flawed Theory and Method in Studies of Prostitution', *Violence Against Women* 11.7, pp. 934–49.

Williams, Rowan, 1997a, 'Knowing Myself in Christ', in Bradshaw, Timothy (ed.), 1997, *The Way Forward? Christian Voices on Homosexuality and the Church*, London: Hodder and Stoughton, pp. 12–19.

Williams, Rowan, 1997b, 'Forbidden Fruit', in Percy, Martyn (ed.), 1997, *Intimate Affairs: Sexuality and Spirituality in Perspective*, London: Darton, Longman and Todd, pp. 21–31.

Williams, Rowan, 2002, 'The Body's Grace', in Rogers, Eugene F. (ed.), 2002, *Theology and Sexuality: Classic and Contemporary Readings*, Oxford: Blackwell, pp. 309–21.

Wilson, Nancy, 1995, *Our Tribe: Queer Folks, God, Jesus, and the Bible*, San Francisco, CA: HarperSanFrancisco.

Winterson, Jeanette, 2012, 'The Money Has Gone, So Make Love Our Alternative Currency', *The Guardian*, 14 February 2012, online at http://www.guardian. co.uk/lifeandstyle/2012/feb/14/money-gone-love-alternative-currency.

Witte, John Jr., 1997, *From Sacrament to Contract: Marriage, Religion, and Law in the Western Tradition*, Louisville, KY: Westminster John Knox Press.

Woodhead, Linda, 1997, 'Sex in a Wider Context', in Davies, Jon and Gerard Loughlin (eds), 1997, *Sex These Days: Essays on Theology, Sexuality and Society*, Sheffield: Sheffield Academic Press, pp. 98–120.

Wu, Rose, 2001, 'Women on the Boundary: Prostitution, Contemporary and in the Bible', *Feminist Theology* 28, pp. 69–81.

Index of Biblical References

Index of Names and Subjects

9 780334 045304